AILEEN MILLER'S DESTINY

AILEEN D. MILLER

authorHOUSE®

AuthorHouse™
1663 Liberty Drive
Bloomington, IN 47403
www.authorhouse.com
Phone: 1 (800) 839-8640

Published by AuthorHouse 08/09/2018

ISBN: 978-1-5246-5291-3 (sc)
ISBN: 978-1-5246-5292-0 (hc)
ISBN: 978-1-5246-5290-6 (e)

Print information available on the last page.

This book is printed on acid-free paper.

ABOUT THE AUTHOR

Aileen broke tradition, as she knew it, growing up on a farm, and, since 1945 became a woman Pioneer Doctor of Chiropractic in a male dominated society, a Massage Therapist, a Pioneer Acupuncturist in the United States, an Ordained Minister and a world traveler. She was active in Professional Organizations, holding office in several of them, and received two Humanitarian Awards.

Aileen wore all of those hats, yet lived a happy life with her husband, and raised three children. The Reverend Doctor Miller's efforts paved the way for the rest of the women, who wanted to become professionals, in a male dominated world.

Upon retiring from an active sixty years of Chiropractic Practice, Dr. Miller concentrates on her gift of healing through Counseling, Workshops and Energy Activation.

At the age of 93, she still drives her car, exercises, text-messages, uses her computer and I-Pad and is on Facebook. She looks forward to more years of activity.

INTRODUCTION

Aileen's destiny began over 93 years ago on a farm in Indiana, but she was not destined to live on a farm her entire life. Neither of Aileen's parents had more than an eighth grade education, so they knew how important a college education would be for her.

In Aileen's many years as a woman doctor of Chiropractic, she didn't let traditions, or a male oriented society thwart her ambitions to learn new and better techniques of Chiropractic care. She was always mindful of new healing modalities for the betterment of her patients' health and wellbeing.

Aileen's experiences throughout life point us to the realization that what ever is uppermost in our hearts can be attained.

Stop the struggle. Relax into your work, and let yourself be guided along the journey, was Aileen's philosophy.

INSIDE THIS BOOK

- Aileen's sister, Marjorie talks about her own near-death experience.
- You will read about how the fields were made ready to plant the crops.
- Wash-day was one day a week and it took all day to prepare the water, wash the clothes by hand, then hang them on lines outside to dry.
- Aileen played the clarinet in the only All Girl's Band in the United States.
- Why did the Screech Owls guard the Chicken House?
- Aileen's Mother raised chickens and ducks, and sold eggs to pay for her two girl's education.
- Read about Dr. Miller's experiences with her unusual patients.
- Aileen takes you on her journeys within the United States.
- Travel with her to Europe, Japan, Hawaii and China.
- Find out who visited her at the paws of the Sphinx.

CONTENTS

ACKNOWLEDGEMENTS

My heartfelt love and gratitude go to my Spirit Family who guided me along this journey of writing about my ninety-three plus years.

I thank all of my friends and relatives in the body and in the Spirit, who have encouraged and supported me through out these years, and had complete faith in me that I would bring this book to fruition.

A Special "Thank You" goes to my dear friend, Sarah A. Schweitzer, who spent many devoted hours editing this manuscript, giving me excellent advice. She is also a Trance Channel who wrote several books; among them are: Your Chakra Energy System, The Aura, Your Guardian Angels, Soul Identification, Numerology and many Pamphlets. I have attended many of her Meditation, Aura and Spirit Development Classes. Her contributions, love and faith in me are deeply appreciated!

A Special "Thank You" goes to my dear daughter, Terri Miller who has spent many hours helping me create this manuscript, and pulled me through many computer snags when I didn't know what to do. I am thankful for her willingness to review its contents, and jog my memory concerning certain facts, and offering constructive commentaries. Her loving faith, suggestions, support and urging me on to the final exclamation mark are deeply appreciated. I deeply love her, and appreciate her diligent assistance; without her expertise and love, you would not be reading this manuscript.

EDITORIAL

Memories are present and past experiences of the total person; their feelings, concepts and attitudes, as well as a reflection of the true nature of an individual soul.

Through the years that I have had the honor to know Aileen, I have been impressed with her beautiful soul and her ability to love unconditionally. I feel honored to have been asked for my editing input for her first book.

As I read her words, I never ceased to be amazed at the life experiences this woman has lived. Life experiences that reflect the beautiful light that shines from her soul for all of humanity to see. She truly is a blessing in this world and in my life.

Sarah A. Schweitzer, PhD.
Author of "Your Guardian Angels"

PROLOGUE

George Michael patted the cheek of his big brown horse, Fritz as he hitched him to the four-seated black buggy with side curtains. George and his wife, Ida and their daughter, Alice decided to go for a Sunday afternoon ride from their farm home in Columbus, Indiana toward Seymour, Indiana. Their son, Louis was overseas serving in the Army of WWI.

It had rained all night, but the roads seemed dry enough for travel. The trees were budding and the colorful blue crocuses were already blooming in the bright sun. Just as Ida said, "Be careful, George!" the right rear wheel of the buggy slid off the road into the ditch. As hard as Fritz, the horse pulled, and as much as George pushed, the buggy's wheel was still in the ditch. A door opened on the porch of the nearby farmhouse in Seymour and the man, seeing the dilemma, walked closer, calling out, "It looks like you need some help!" "I sure can use some help," replied George. While introducing themselves, the lady and their son came off the porch to see what all the commotion was about. William Dettmer, the farmer said, "George, I'd like you to meet my wife, Anna, and this is my son, Arthur." (Ever since Arthur's discharge from the Army of WWI, he had been working on a farm away from home in Iowa; he was home now, until the planting season would begin in Iowa.) George immediately introduced his wife, Ida and their daughter, Alice to Anna and Arthur.

William brought his strong brown horse to help pull the buggy out of the ditch. Arthur was not much help; his interest was in Alice. From that day forward he began courting Alice, taking her to dances and the neighbor's BBQ gatherings.

Alice didn't get along very well with her mother and they had an argument, perhaps it was about working at the Tomato Canning Factory; anyway, Ida didn't speak to her daughter for 3 days. Meanwhile, Arthur had asked Alice several times to marry him, but she refused each time. Then Ida accused her daughter of being pregnant. Although Ida had no reason for the accusation, Alice felt insulted. Ida gave Alice an ultimatum; "Either you go to work, or you get married!" Alice was afraid to work in a factory, but she knew all about household duties such as, cooking, baking, canning, and making her own clothes; she also crocheted dresser scarves and tatted handkerchief edges. She accepted Arthur's proposal of marriage.

Alice and Arthur married November 17, 1919. (She was only nineteen.) They set up housekeeping in a nearby city where Arthur earned their living as an Insurance Salesman. Marjorie Anna Elizabeth was born October 1, 1920.

1924-1933

A BABY GIRL OCTOBER 4, 1924

My Dad said he wanted a boy, but here I am, Aileen Etta Martha arriving at 4:40 in the afternoon ---- definitely a blond hair, snuggly baby girl, cuddled in my Mother's loving arms! My father hardly looked at me, and was afraid to hold me; I was so little! My father was angry and said that it was my Mother's fault that she didn't have a boy; "We already have a girl!" he commented.

My sister, Marjorie, who is four years older than I am, was staying at Aunt Lizzie's house for a few days. When she came home she wanted to play with me like a doll-baby. Mother said, "Now be very gentle when you touch her ---- she's very soft." Then Marjorie kept patting my cheek and humming a song in her sweet voice. I learned that my sister was taught to be gentle with babies.

FARM LIFE

After Louis Michael had been discharged from the Army of WWI, he was living with his wife Martha and their two boys, Harold and Floyd, helping his Dad, George on the farm. George relied heavily on Louis's help with the farm work. Louis had been having pains in his abdomen and one day he was doubled over in such severe pain that he was taken to the hospital. By the time that he was admitted and examined the toxic fluid from his ruptured appendix had spread through out his entire body. He died of peritonitis. The death of Louis left George needing help on the farm, so

George asked his son-in-law, Arthur to move his family to the farm so that he could help with the farm work. Arthur agreed even though he preferred being a Salesman. My father respected his wife's Family, therefore the move to the farm was made.

I was around four months old when we moved to Grandpa's farm. Cough, cough, cough! Mother said that I could hardly breath and I felt like I was burning up inside; she thought I was going to die. Mother told my sister that I have pneumonia. Through my early years, I had many bouts with bronchitis. My mother gave me honey with a few drops of whiskey and massaged my chest with mentholated cream. As a baby I intuitively knew that there is a routine to follow and my mother took care of my needs. I didn't always need to cry to get attention.

Spring arrived and Dad started plowing the fields. Mother was strong enough to plow another field to get it ready for planting corn. She would bundle me up nice and warm and put me in a basket and carry me out to the field where she would be plowing. Mother had a favorite horse named Maude. My Dad had already harnessed and hitched Maude to the plow so that Mother could plow the field. Maude was gentle but a very strong horse; she pulled a single edge plow that Mother guided in a straight line from one end of the field to the other. Maude would stop at the end of the plowed row without being told, and ready to turn around. If I whimpered or cried, this horse would not move until I was attended to! Imagine a horse that smart! In those days men and women worked together doing whatever was needed in order for a farm to run smoothly.

There were two bedrooms on the second floor of our house; one was used for a storage room and had an extra mattress, a small brown wood table, a couple of old straight-back wood chairs, some winter clothes wrapped in white sheets, a few dishes and some silverware, a couple of soft pillows, books and lots of magazines. Mother liked to read so she put the magazines upstairs in that room. Sometimes my sister and I would play with our dolls in the spare room too. I was learning to go up and down the stairs, and Mother would say, "Marjorie, keep hold of Aileen's hand when you two go down those stairs." Well, one day I thought I could do it by myself, and managed to twist my hand from hers, and fell all the way down those stairs to the floor! Mother came running and said, "Marjorie, I told you to hold her hand!!" Marjorie said, "But she jerked away from me!" I was crying while Mother felt all over my arms and legs to see if anything was broken. I really yelled when she tried to move one of my arms (my shoulder might have dislocated). Mother did something to my shoulder that made it feel a little better. I had to lie down while she rubbed some kind of salve on my shoulder and elbow, and soon I went to sleep. I was too independent, which caused harm to me at that time because I did not have enough practice going down those steps. However, independence is a strong trait to have which helped me to make decisions throughout my life.

It was nice and warm upstairs in that storage room in the wintertime because the sun warmed it in the morning. I would take my one and only doll up there with me and we would have a tea party, or play Momma and baby. Other times I felt so happy as I would look at the pictures in the magazines and sometimes I fell asleep on those soft fluffy pillows.

During chore time, the chickens had been fed, the pigs had been fed, and the cows had been milked. I had fun while milking the cows and aiming it at the cat's mouths to drink, which usually ended up all over them. Mother poured the milk into a contraption that separated the cream from the milk. The milk was poured into five-gallon milk cans. Mother sold the rich yellow cream to the Creamery in town and bought margarine, (which was much cheaper than butter.) Included with the margarine was a little packet of yellow coloring that I had to mix into the margarine to make it look like butter, but it didn't taste like butter. Yuck. After all the morning work was done, everyone was pretty hungry for breakfast, which was two or three eggs, or oatmeal, sausage or ham, bread or fresh biscuits and margarine or jam or peanut butter. Yes, it was one or the other, never two spreads on the same slice of bread.

I remember the first time I tasted oatmeal I didn't like it, but my Mother insisted that I eat a spoonful. I cried but put a spoonful in my mouth and it came right up. Mother scolded me, and all at once my Dad scooped me up in his arms and carried me down the hallway and showed me the radio and turned the dials to take my mind off the oatmeal. After I stopped crying he sat me down in my chair and said to Mother, in a firm voice, "She doesn't have to eat oatmeal." That was the only time that I can remember, that my Dad ever held me. My dad understood my dilemma about eating and defended me and I felt secure. I later learned that he never liked milk or cheese, yet his mother insisted that he eat and drink both.

In the fall time, my Mother would put on her thin, blue denim jacket with white netting around her shoulders, a pair of my father's blue overalls that she tucked inside of her rain boots, gloves with long gauntlets that came over the jacket sleeves, and a straw hat. Off she would go, into the farthest corner of our apple orchard with a clean bucket, a trowel, a wood frame and some clean white cloths, to "rob the bees". The bees began buzzing and flying all around her, so she quickly pulled the white netting over her straw hat to cover her head. The bees began crawling all over her, but she didn't pay any attention to them. I watched at a distance while mother pried off the top of the beehive and lifted the wood frame with all the honeycombs filled full of glistening amber honey, and began to slowly scrape most of the honeycombs from the frame into the bucket; then she re-inserted the frame and the empty one into the beehive. Mother always left enough honey to sustain the bees during the winter so that they could gather nectar from the flowers in the spring to make more honey. I was amazed that Mother was stung only once, and that was when a bee crawled up under the netting and couldn't get out, so Mother was stung in its confusion to escape. Homemade jam, jelly and honey were always on the table but I usually ate the delicious honey. I realized that mother was willing to get stung and spend a lot of time so that her family could enjoy the luxury of eating honey that would have been an expensive purchase at the store. As I look back at those experiences, I understand that in hard times, farm products must be sold and substitutions made.

SCHOOL TIME

Before I knew it, I was old enough to go to school. There was no Pre-school, or Kinder-garden in those days, so I was in the first grade when I was 5 years old. My sister and I loved riding on the school bus to school;

it stopped at the turn in the road in front of our house! Going to school would be so much more fun than staying home and learning my A B C's from Mother. There was something called "Recess" when we could go outside and play in the middle of the morning and afternoon; all those kids to play with was really fun! During Recess one day I saw a pretty, curly haired girl off by herself, leaning against a tree. She must have been out in the sun all the time because she was really tan! I went over to her and asked her, "Are you sick, or something?" "No," she replied. "Then why aren't you running around playing?" I questioned. It seemed as though she was almost afraid to talk, looking down at the ground, she finally said, "No-one wants to play with me." I said, "I'll play with you, come on, let's teeter-totter!" She looked so surprised as I took her hand, running to the teeter-totter play area.

I wanted to tell my Mother all about my new friend, Daisy as soon as I got off the school bus, but almost forgot about her when I smelled Mother's fresh-baked bread; it smelled sooo good that I wanted to eat some right then! I ran really fast to the house because I was so excited to tell Mother all about my new friend in school. Then I asked her, "Why didn't anyone want to play with her?" Mother took a deep breath, and began a long story while she was preparing dinner (supper, it was called then) about how the African/American people (they were called Negroes then) had been slaves, and they are now free, but most people don't like them, for many reasons. All that was difficult for me to understand, because my new friend was very nice, polite and fun. Daisy and I got along just fine, so every day we played together, and very soon a couple other girls played with us. We became best friends! She moved away so I didn't see her the next school year. I came to the conclusion that others might not make friends because of what they have heard about the African/Americans rather than to befriend them first, and go by their own feelings.

Second grade was fun and another summer has gone by fast. The school bus came down the gravel road to pick me up to take me to school. As I was about to walk into the third grade classroom, the teacher said, "Surprise, you will go into the fourth grade classroom this year." Well, from then on school was not so much fun, sooo much homework every night and weekend. I had to learn what I would have learned in the third grade and keep up with all the other studies in the fourth grade! To make matters worse, I had the same teachers as my sister had three years ago. Marjorie was an "A" student and the teachers remembered her; they expected me to be an "A" student also; they didn't consider the fact that I was two years younger than she was in the fourth grade. I think I would have not made it through the fourth grade without the help of Miss Akins, who was one of my teachers. The reason I was in the fourth grade was because the third grade classroom was crowded; therefore, three students who had the highest grades were chosen to go into the fourth grade. Even though I was one of the youngest in the room, I was also the tallest which caused me to feel self-conscious. I was teased about my height but rather than slouch, I stood tall. I was so thankful that Miss Akins was sympathetic and understanding with me.

I'm thinking now of when my sister loved to tease me when I was in grade school. Have you ever been teased to the point that you cried? My sister loved to tease me, when she did, I would become very angry. Sometimes she would tickle me until I cried; other times she would say, "You don't know how to set the table," even though I had been helping her as soon as I could see over the top of the table and see where the silverware went. I'd say, "yes, I do know how," and she would continue to say, "No, you don't," and then laugh, or change the placing of the knife or spoon and say, "See? You don't know how." The more she teased me the angrier I would get, and the more she laughed, made me even angrier! I tried to hit her but couldn't reach her because my arms were not as long as hers, so I tried to kick her under the table. One time I did kick her, and when Mother came into the house my sister told on me and said it hurt, so I got a spanking. I told Mother how she teased me, but she didn't seem to care. Later in life, I learned that when a person teases someone, he or she is receiving energy from the other person, and feels better as a result of that activity. The anxiety of getting teased stayed with me and I had difficulty in discerning the difference between joking and teasing. I felt inferior and throughout life I was always working toward feeling worthwhile.

WHO WAS THAT?

Lying in bed, looking out the window at that big, full moon, after saying my prayers, I fell fast asleep. Suddenly a big boom of thunder and a crackle of lightening jarred me awake. Boom, boom, boom! What's happening? The sky was so beautiful a minute ago! My parents had told me when I was little, and I'm eight now, that there was nothing to be afraid of when there was thunder and lightning in the sky, but still, I felt a chill and pulled my blanket tighter around my neck. The rain was soothing as it splattered against the window. But just as I turned over in bed my eye caught a brightness up in the corner of the ceiling; at first I thought it was Mother, with her flashlight coming in to check on me. As I looked again, there was an image; just the head, with white hair and a loving smile looking down at me. I'd never seen anything like that and didn't know if I was feeling fear or comfort, or what; never-the-less I pulled the covers over my head trying to figure things out. It didn't look like any pictures of my relatives; anyway, why was there a picture up on the ceiling? Could that image have been an angel, or Jesus? No, not like any pictures that I had seen of Jesus; he didn't have white hair. I was trying to remember what some of the disciples looked like from some of the pictures that I had seen in my Sunday school lessons. I wanted to see the image again, so slowly I pulled the covers off my head, just far enough so that I could see the ceiling. Nothing there; in a way I was disappointed because I was beginning to feel a little braver. I looked and looked but nothing was there. For several nights afterward I looked for the image, hoping that it would re-appear. I never did tell Mother, or my sister; they would just say that it was my imagination. But it was NOT my imagination! The image on the ceiling was real and I later concluded that I might someday know why it was there.

THE SECRET OF THE SNOW

It's been snowing for days, and now it is raining on top of the snow. It's so cold that you can see your breath when you open the door. Jack Frost had printed a beautiful picture of trees and snowflakes on the window. I found a spot to wipe so that I could look out and could hardly believe my eyes! "Mother, come here to look!" I exclaimed. The trees were shiny, silver statues that crackled when the wind blew ever so slightly. The shrubs and grass look so stiff all covered with ice. The fences look like artificial white ropes.

I heard Mother and Dad talking as I was getting dressed by the heating stove in the kitchen, (where we dressed in the wintertime because the house was too cold) and heard Dad say that the "river would surely be frozen over." "Mother", I hopefully asked, "Could I please go down by the river to see if it is frozen?" It isn't easy convincing Mother about anything. My sister, Marjorie was supposed to help Mother bake cookies for the next day, which meant that I could go alone. Thinking for a minute, and with a frown, she finally said, "Well, I guess that you can go by yourself, but do be careful; don't try walking on the ice on the river; it might not be frozen thick enough to walk on, and you would go right through it into that icy water!" I was so happy to be going by myself, that I put on my warm blue winter coat and those thickly lined snow pants as fast as I could. It was so hard to pull on those boots over two pair of wool socks, and tuck in the snow pants in the tops of my boots, but I was determined. "Don't forget your mittens!" Mother called as I pushed open the door. The air is freezing cold, but I didn't care as I began to skip down the driveway toward the lane that goes to the river ----- OOPS! I almost fell on that hard ice; anyway, I couldn't really skip in all of those thick clothes. My dog Queenie with her snow-white chest would have been wagging her bushy tail right along side of me, but she died last fall.

Soon, I saw the river. OH! It nearly took my breath away! The trees and rocks along the river's edge shimmered and twinkled in the sun. Even the ripples of water were frozen and twinkled in the sunlight as if the ripples were actually moving. The ice-covered weeds and sticks shone like jewels tossed helter-skelter, dancing in the sun. I am frozen in wonderment! Soon my thoughts jumped to the neighbor on the other side of the hill from our house and from the river. The other day I heard my Mother tell my Dad that Mrs. Armuth has a new baby girl; I've never seen a baby before. Mother is not very friendly with those neighbors, so I don't know if I will ever see their baby. I looked toward their house; it doesn't seem very far away. So off I went, happy that the lane goes part of the way there before I have to climb those two rail fences before I get to their house. I thought that I could walk on top of the ice covered snow, but down my foot went into the almost knee-deep snow, then another step through the ice and snow; when you're only ten years old it gets pretty tiring. Oh, good, the ice is thicker and I can walk on top of the snow, but now it is up hill and slippery.

I looked back toward the river. Should I go back? I looked toward the neighbor's house; I think I'm halfway there so I kept going. Another rail fence and through another field, I'm getting so tired, and my hands are so cold because my gloves got wet when I climbed that rail fence. My nose is so cold, even under the red scarf that Mother so lovingly knitted for me. I want to lie down and sleep. My thoughts go to my dog Queenie; she was an outdoor dog and she would be so warm that I could warm my hands in her thick fur. I began thinking of the day that she scratched on the porch door and Mother said, "Well, I do declare! I believe that Queenie wants to come in to the house; I heard her scratch on the porch door; she's never done that before!" Mother opened the door and we watched as Queenie came on to the screened-in porch. Queenie came in slowly, wagging her tail and looked around the porch, then into the kitchen and turned left into the dining room. She sniffed into each corner of the room and under the dining table; I wondered if she expected some crumbs to be there. Next, she went into the sitting room walking from left to right around the room, sniffing everywhere, and then into the hall, stopping suddenly, and looked from one end of the hall to the other, before deciding to go into the living room where the piano is. Queenie sniffed every corner, chair and couch; when she got to the piano she looked up at the music and wagged her tail even faster. Could she see something that we couldn't see? Still searching the house, Queenie went into Mother and Dad's bedroom and put her front paw up on the bed; Mother said, "Achhh", so Queenie put her foot down. Next she searched my bedroom, looked over her shoulder at me and wagged her tail fast again. "Mother, what is she looking for?" I asked. Mother just shook her head as Queenie went on to inspect the hired man's bedroom and then the bathroom. My sister, Marjorie's bedroom was upstairs and Queenie did not want to go up those steps. The kitchen got a thorough inspection under the table, under each and every one of the six chairs, and behind the heating stove near the wall. Then she stopped and looked at us and went to the door to go out. What was she looking for? She died a couple days later. I really miss my companion.

No, I must go on, I really want to see that baby. I can hardly lift one foot after the other. Huffing and puffing, I finally made it to Mrs. Armuth's house, now only four steps on to the porch. I'm so afraid that I am shaking! Well, I'm here; I muster up enough courage to knock on the door, but which one? All three doors look alike; I hear a voice in my ears, "That one on the right." Without thinking about where the voice came from, I drew a deep breath and knocked. Actually, that knocking made my fingers tingle, which felt really good. The door opened slowly, and the look of surprise on Mrs. Armuth's face was so funny that I almost laughed. "Come in, dear child, you look half frozen", as she led me into her warm cozy kitchen that smelled like vanilla pudding. There was a pink and yellow flowery, ruffled skirt around a pink basket alongside the heating stove in the kitchen. Mrs. Armuth smiled and said, "I know that you came to see my baby", and pointed to the basket. I looked in; so pink and soft looking; so cute, like a doll baby sleeping there. I stood motionless, even though my heart was pounding. I felt like clapping and jumping up and down, I was so thrilled to see such a tiny baby. I wanted to touch her little, pink cheeks, but I thought I shouldn't.

I shook my head as Mrs. Armuth asked me, "Does your Mother know that you are here?" She smiled and said, "I'll call her right away, so that she knows where you are." I almost shouted, "NO! Don't call her; she'll be mad, so very mad! Don't call her!" I turned to leave and almost forgot to thank Mrs. Armuth for letting me see her cute baby.

As I walked down the steps of the porch I thought about the spanking I would get when I get home, for being gone so long, but it would be worth it. I saw a tiny baby! I had warmed up a bit in Mrs. Armuth's warm house, and going home was not as difficult because most of it was going downhill. I could see my footprint in the snow, so I put my feet in them, which made it easier; but it was colder as the wind was getting rough, and my hands and feet felt numb as I climbed those rail fences again. At last

I came to the lane that goes to my house and it's uphill again, but a little easier since the sun has melted enough ice for the rocks to poke through and not quite so slippery.

I could see my sister, Marjorie coming toward me. "Oh! Oh! they're worried!" I was thinking. Marjorie called to me, "Why were you gone so long? Mother's worried, and sent me to see if you had fallen in through the ice into the river. You're going to get it!" (Marjorie is four years older than I am.) I dodged her question by telling her how cold I am, how my fingers and toes hurt. She said, "Stomp your feet on the ground, and clap your hands; then they'll start to feel warm." Marjorie wasn't always nice to me, but now she was trying to help me warm up. Then I began rubbing my knees to warm them up. I told Marjorie how beautiful the river and everything is, trying to keep her from asking me any more questions. "You should see it!" I exclaimed. When Marjorie opened the door of our house, and I saw Mother, she wasn't mad at all. Was I ever surprised! She and Marjorie helped me take off my heavy, wet clothes and boots. Mother set a pan of water in front of my chair and said, "Put your feet in this water, it will warm them up." The water smelled like vinegar. My hands hurt too when she put them into that cold, smelly water, although it felt warm at first. I was still puzzled that Mother was not mad at me; all she said was, "I guess you won't stay out so long next time." As we were eating supper, I told my Dad all about going down to the river and how beautiful everything was. He didn't like it that Mother let me go alone and that I got so cold. All he said to me was, "Well, did you learn your lesson?" Nobody seemed to appreciate all the beauty that was around us as I described the shiny, silvery fairyland.

Mother seemed to always crochet or knit something when she had a few extra minutes. She's been knitting something with pink yarn and today she said, "Come here Aileen, I have something to show you." Laid out on the dining table, which she used as her sewing table, was the cutest little pink sweater, a pink bonnet with pink ribbon threaded through the edge, and a pair of pink booties with pink ribbon. "That's what you were making!" I exclaimed, "They are so soft and pretty!" (Mother is so talented!) I wanted to ask her whom they are for, but decided not to ask any questions, because she had said to me many times, "You ask too many questions."

After church a few weeks later, Mother said, "We've been invited to the Armuth's house for the afternoon (and she seemed happy about the invitation); we're going to see their new baby girl." (I saw a twinkle in her eyes.) My heart felt like it turned flip-flops in my chest! I wanted to say, "I've already seen the baby", but I didn't dare. Marjorie and I began dancing around the room singing, "We get to see the baby! We get to see the baby!" As we left the house, Mother handed the pink gifts to Marjorie and me, and with a smile and a twinkle in her eyes, said, "Would you two like to give these gifts to the baby?" I felt like jumping up and down with delight as I handed the pink and white box to Mrs. Armuth.

I grew up in an era when children were to be seen and not heard but I had such a strong desire to see the icy river that I risked asking Mother if I could go. After seeing the river, I realized that the risk was worth it. Being afraid that mother would not allow me to see the new baby, I took a chance by going without her knowledge and suffered being extremely cold. Upon reflection, I realized that if I had asked her, she probably would have taken me to see the baby.

GOD HEARS US

Mother wrote in my school Diary, "Smile and the world smiles with you; weep and you weep alone." Mother seldom seemed happy, (so much work to do all the time) yet maybe she was happier than she portrayed. Another time Mother wrote in my school Diary, "Praying without ceasing." For many years I wondered why it was necessary to pray all the time. Actually, when I think of and admire the beautiful flowers, trees, sky; and wishing that God would make someone better; seeing an accident and saying, "God help them!" or saying a prayer before a meal, isn't that praying? When I wake up in the morning asking God to be with me during the day; seeing an intoxicated driver weaving across the road and saying, "I surely hope that the angels watch over him 'til he gets home!" or driving in the snow or blinding rain remarking, "Oh God, I hope I make it!" saying a prayer before lying my head to rest on my pillow at night, isn't that "Praying without ceasing"? As I reflect on the above, I always feel happier after I've prayed or sent a prayer to someone.

ARGUING

In the center of our house was a long hallway from the kitchen to the front door. The dining room and living room were on one side of the hallway; on the other side of the hallway were the stairway to the second floor, my parent's bedroom, my bedroom, which was near the front door, and the parlor. One day when I was in my bedroom reading, I heard Mother and Dad arguing, which they did a lot of, but the arguing became louder and louder and sounded very angry. I began to cry and finally I yelled from my bedroom, "Stop! Stop your arguing! Stop!" There was silence, then a couple of words. I heard the kitchen door open, and I held my breath as I heard my Dad coming down the hallway; I thought I might get a spanking for yelling at them. (Remember? I grew up in an era when children were to be seen and not heard.) My Dad sat down on the bed beside me; putting his arm around my shoulders he said, "Your Mother and I were having a disagreement and were trying to solve it. Everything is all right now, it's all right." As he left the room I took a big breath! At the supper table that evening, they looked at their plates and not at each other, not a word was said. I was sad. I don't like to hear arguing, it makes me feel jittery and sad, and the anger that I felt of that incident, and the fear that I had, stayed with me for many years. After I was married I learned that my husband's parents also argued quite a lot and he did not like to argue either, therefore almost every disagreement that we had we tried to discuss calmly and away from our children's ears.

1934-1944

SAND STORM IN KANSAS

When I was around ten or eleven years old my father's sister, who is my Aunt Etta was planning a visit to Kansas and asked my Mother to go with her. Mother motioned for me to come closer and said, "Aileen, Aunt Etta and I are going to visit some of your Dad's relatives way far away, and you can go with us." I was so excited to think that I would be seeing something else besides the farm and school! "Will Marjorie go with us, too?" I asked. "No," replied Mother, "she has to stay home and take care of Boots (our collie dog) and cook for your Dad." Marjorie looked sad at first, but then was happy that she was in charge of something.

The country looks pretty much the same everywhere: cows and horses eating grass or hay, and once in a while I would see some sheep. We would stop every so often when Aunt Etta and Mother exchanged driver's seats. I thought, "Oh, my! This is a dull trip!" I got to sleep with Mother when we stopped for the night, which was a real treat! Finally we arrived at our cousin's farm; an old two-story gray house, a red barn, and some other gray sheds. I met several men and several women, but no kids my age, only an older boy. In the barn were two horses, and stalls for five cows that were out in the field eating grass. There was a small Chicken House that had two chickens sitting on eggs in their nests hoping to hatch baby chicks; many more chickens were roaming out in the yard and fields.

Near the porch steps was a very beautiful golden brown chicken just sitting there; it didn't move as we approached the porch. I said to my cousin,

Mary, who is about my Mother's age, "Why is that chicken just sitting there? She looks so fluffy." Mary laughed and exclaimed, "I guess that chicken decided that she wanted to be closer to us, so she made her nest by the steps instead of in the Chicken House. She is sitting on five eggs that she is hoping will hatch five baby chicks."

The next day while we were having lunch at the table by the window, Mary excitedly said, "Look out there! Those black clouds look like a storm is coming; we better hurry and shut all the windows!" The wind began to howl through the window cracks and blew the tree branches sideways and the flowering plants were blown right down to the ground! Sand began to blow against the house, and I could see waves of sand blowing every which way when I looked out the window. It was so interesting that I just sat there leaning on the table at the window watching, not a snowstorm, but a sandstorm! All at once one spoon flew up out of the crystal spoon holder onto the table where I was sitting! Five spoons were still in the spoon holder! "Mother, did you see that?" I exclaimed. "Yes, I never saw anything like that in my life!" she remarked. That window had been left open a crack because it was so warm in the house. I said, "It's funny how a gust of wind would pull only one spoon up out of that spoon holder!"

After the storm passed we went outside to shovel and sweep the sand away from the doors. "Mary!" I called, "What happened to the chicken that was sitting on her eggs, I don't see her; did she get blown away?" Mary had started toward the barn to check on the horses, but turned around and came back to the porch. She knew exactly where the nest was supposed to be, so she began pulling away the sand, and found the chicken still sitting on her nest. We both began to laugh and Mary said, "She is so devoted to hatching her eggs, that she stayed right on her nest even though she was being covered with sand." Mary continued to brush sand off her feathers until she was able to shake her wings, what a chicken! She looked so funny! I was amazed at the chicken's dedication to hatching her eggs, which would be her babies, regardless of the sand storm.

Mary, her husband and my Mother shoveled sand away from the barn door; once inside they could see that the horses were all right, and Mary let them out to run around. As Mary's husband looked out over the pasture, he could see that the cows were ok and running toward the barn to be milked. The next day was spent cleaning sand off everything. We even had to clean sand out of the car before we could drive home the next day. I learned that a seemingly dull trip could be interesting and fun after-all. It seemed as though the drive home didn't take us as long as it did to get to Kansas, and Dad was so happy to see us.

TOM BOY?

I loved being outside, and since my Dad had always wanted a boy, I was with him quite a lot. I rode on the flatbed wagon with him into the fields to see if the wheat was growing as fast as he expected it to grow. The ride was so bumpy that I had to hold onto the seat with both hands; I didn't care that my butt was sore at the end of the day, at least I wasn't being teased by my sister or being ordered around by her. Mother was always concerned about me when I was with Dad; she thought I would fall off the wagon and get hurt, or get too close to the horse's feet. I was taught to fear horses rather than to touch them and love them; it was always "Be careful of those horses!" My Dad taught me how to drive a team of horses in front of a wagon; that seemed pretty easy. One day he said, "I think you are ready to drive four horses, let's try it with an empty wagon." I said, "Sure, Ok" He showed me how to hold the reins to each team of horses, and then I practiced driving around the barn lot and then out into the field. The next day Dad said, "I have to load those big bales of hay onto the wagon and it will take all four horses to pull the loaded wagon up that hill; do you think you can do it?" I was excited. "But first you have to drive those horses between those two rows of baled hay; do you think you can do it?" Now, I am a bit nervous! Then I calmed down and suddenly I had the courage to do the job efficiently because I believed in myself. I said, "Get up, horses!" I called each one by their own names and we made it all the way to the end of the row and back, and then up the hill to the barn to unload the hay. I told the horses how strong they were. After we had finished working, my Dad led the horses to a long metal tank of water for their long drink. I ran to untie the release rope on the windmill so that it could start turning to pump more water into the water tanks. After the horses quenched their thirst, my Dad led them into the barn into their individual stalls, where he would take off their harnesses and hang them up on the side of the horse stall. I always had to laugh when the horses would shakes themselves; I guess it felt good to be free of the leather harness. Then we would pull hay down from the hayloft with our pitchforks to feed the horses and the cows. I was tired and ready for supper. Dad told me what a good job I did and told Mother all about it while we were eating. It made me feel good about myself when Dad told me what a good job I had done, and then told Mother all about it. The next day after Dad had hitched the four horses to the wagon, I was proud to show Mother, who was standing at the barnyard gate, that I was not afraid of the horses and that I could drive all four of them. She smiled as I drove toward the field.

HIGH SCHOOL: TYPING, SHORTHAND, SWIMMING, GYM, MUSIC

Typing sounded like fun, so much faster than writing with a pencil, but I didn't want to take Shorthand; you couldn't take one without the other. So I took Gym and Swimming, which replaced Typing and Shorthand classes. I liked Gym, but everyone seemed to be stronger than I. I just couldn't climb those ropes or stand on my head. I really wanted to learn how to swim, but oh, the water was so cold that I could hardly move my arms! Swimming was the last period of the day; there was no time to dry my hair before getting on the bus to go home, and I shivered all the way home with my cold, wet head.

One day Mr. Goucher, the band instructor went into each classroom and asked how many girls would like to play a musical instrument. "Hmmm, I wonder why he's asking that?" is going through my mind. At the last minute I timidly held up my hand. (My Mother played "The Beautiful Blue Danube" so beautifully on our piano that I wanted to play just like her! I picked out a tune of my own, but it didn't sound anything like when Mother played.) He said to me, "You can play a reed instrument." I was so excited that I didn't even care what a reed instrument was. I could hardly wait to get home and tell my parents, "You know what? There's a man at school who knows all about musical instruments and he's going to organize another band!" "Hold on," said Dad, "Slow down! Now what is this all about a School Band? I thought our High School had a band already!" I was so excited that I could hardly explain, "This will be the only band in the United States that will have only girls in it. He wants me to play a clarinet in the band! Can I? Please, please! I would really, really like to; he will teach all of us who don't know how to play anything." Mother and Dad looked at each other and then Mother said, "We'll have to think about it first." I suggested, "There are instruments of all kinds in the Band Room; if there's a clarinet there, maybe I could use one of them. I waited in anticipation while they talked it over and when they said, "Yes," I jumped for joy! Band Class replaced Gym and Swimming Classes.

I was so self-conscious that I didn't want my parents to hear all my mistakes when practicing my clarinet in the house, so I went out into the wooded area of Beach and Maple Trees behind the Granary, sat on the rail fence and practiced the music. (The Granary is a building next to one of the chicken houses, where machinery for harvesting the wheat is kept, and a large wood bin is in there for storing the wheat). My dog, Boots would go down the hill toward the river hunting for rabbits, squirrels or anything that moved, running back to me wagging her bushy tail and then away she would go again until I was ready to return to the house. I always felt like there was someone beside me when I was there; didn't know who IT was, or what IT was, but IT felt comforting.

There were enough girls playing instruments that Mr. Goucher's "All Girls Band" was a huge attraction at all of the football games. The only All Girls Band in the United States! We wore medium blue A-line skirts and white sweaters over a white blouse; the sweaters had our brown Bulldog Mascot over a musical symbol. We traveled with the Boys Band and Football team around the city and to other nearby cities, marching and playing as a separate unit. What fun I had! I would never have been able to see any football games otherwise, because my parents didn't have the money for the games. After the games all of us went to Mr. Zaharako's Ice Cream Parlor for our treat. In those days there were only three different flavors of ice cream -- vanilla, strawberry or chocolate, or a hot fudge sundae. My favorite flavor was vanilla or sometimes I would have strawberry. Mr. Zaharako was so nice and he always turned on his huge organ at the back of the Parlor; it was as high as the ceiling and played automatically. The organ had hand carved roses trimmed in gold, and angels with white wings floating all around the perimeter of the organ. Mr. Zaharako said that this organ was the only one of its kind in the United States. What a treat! Ice cream and organ music!

One year, my Aunt Etta, who was a schoolteacher, was transferred to my school. I was so happy that I could tell everyone that my Aunt teaches at my school! She taught my English and History classes and I studied extra hard to make all A's to show her what a good student I am. I cried when I saw my report card and there were no A's in History or English. When I got home from school I complained to Mother because I always made A's in those subjects. Mother talked to Aunt Etta and she said "I didn't want the other students to think Aileen was "teachers pet", so I didn't give her any A's even though she earned them." I was still very upset.

Looking back over my school years, I realized that when things looked bleak, circumstances can change for the better and I came to the conclusion that everything that happens is a learning experience which helped me grow in character.

MONDAY WASHDAY

Washday took nearly all day and it was done outside of the house. First my sister and I stripped the beds. There were no fitted sheets, we took the bottom sheet off the bed, put the top sheet over the mattress and put a fresh sheet on top and finished making the bed. The only time that both sheets were changed was in the summer when we would perspire a lot at night (no air conditioning). Mother pumped water from the well in our back yard, into a five gallon bucket, and poured the water several times into a large oblong tub that sat on a flat top stove in an outside workroom. While waiting for the water to boil, she, my sister and I took turns pumping the water to fill two other wash tubs, where the white clothes would be rinsed; Mother always rinsed the clothes twice. The boiling water would be dipped from the oblong tub and poured into a different tub outside; that's for the white clothes. The soap that we used to wash the clothes was bar soap that Mother had made from lye and animal fat. The clothes would soak in that boiling water for a few minutes, and then the soiled spots would be scrubbed on a metal washboard; Mother had the toughest hands! She then would use a two-pronged stick to lift the clothes out of the boiling water before squeezing them and putting them into the rinse water. After the sheets had been rinsed twice and wrung by hand, we would hang them, and other clothes to dry on two or three wire lines about twenty feet long, that had been strung from the house to the shed. We always hoped that it would be a windy day. Sometimes it would be so windy that my sister and I would have difficulty holding onto the sheets long enough to get them on the line with wood clothespins, which sometimes popped off. It was a challenge to grab the sheet before it dragged on the ground. OOPS! If that happened, the sheet would have to be washed again, and Mother would not be happy. On a very windy day, the sheets would be dry as soon as the last load of wash was hung on the lines to dry. After the white clothes had been washed, the water was cooled a bit and the colored clothes were washed. All the while more water had been added to the heating water, so that when the dirty overalls/denims, gloves and work-shirts were to be washed, the water would be hot enough to wash the dirt out of the work-clothes.

Now that the wash was done, the tubs had to be emptied. The outside area, where one of the pumps was, and where the wash was done, had been cemented (about 15x25 feet, I think), so Mother just turned over the tubs and let the water run down toward one of the chicken yards, which was adjacent to our back yard. That cement was always clean. The boiling water tub had a spigot in the bottom, which was a big help in emptying that tub of any leftover water. I learned that washday was a lot of work, but with everyone doing her part and co-operating, it goes well. I was thinking, "I certainly hope that there will be an easier way to do the laundry by the time that I get married!"

JEALOUS? OR LOVE?

I thought my sister, Marjorie didn't like me because she was always telling me what to do and what not to do. One day while riding home on the school bus, (some of us had to stand because we were the last ones on the bus) one of the boys was teasing the younger kids; well, he teased me until I was crying. Marjorie, standing next to him said, "If you don't stop that, I'm going to smack you in the face!" and had her hand up ready (she wasn't really going to smack him, it was just a threat). At that precise moment the bus hit a bump in the road and Marjorie's hand hit him hard on the side of the face! Marjorie looked as surprised as he did! He never teased any of us kids again, ever! Did he tattle to his parents about Marjorie? I'll let you guess. As I look back, I concluded that sometimes my sister was jealous of me when I was working with Dad, and other times she was trying to protect me because she loves me. Being teased made me feel inferior and like there was something wrong with me, but as an adult, I concluded that bullies and teasers are the ones who feel inferior and by bullying someone they feel superior and they get attention.

"IN THE GARDEN"

One day, after dark, after the chickens had gone to roost (sit) on their shelves in the hen house, Mother said that I should lock the Chicken-house door so that no stray animal would get in and kill the chickens. Mother thought that I was old enough for that responsibility. "Come on, Boots! I called to my dog, "Let's go lock up the chickens!" The Chicken-house was up by the Granary in a very dense wooded area. The Granary is a red-painted square building, which houses the machinery that cuts the wheat, and holds bins of wheat. The Chicken-house and yard were protected by a high wire fence, with an attached wire gate attached to 2 posts that were about 8 feet high. The gate had a wood latch that fit into a notch on the fence post that must be secured at night. The Chicken-house had a lock on the door that had to be locked at night. Tonight there was a big, beautiful yellow full moon high above me so that I could easily see the latch on the gate. I was just about to open the gate when suddenly, "SCREEEECH ---SCREEEECH"! That sound sooo nearly took the top of my head off! I had goose bumps all over! My dog did nothing and trotted off into the Woods to see what she could find of interest. If she did nothing, then I knew everything was OK, but that Screech really scared me! I looked up and there on each gatepost was a Screech Owl; those Owls are small Owls and are called Screech Owls because that's what they say, "Screech!" I didn't know if they would fly at me or what, so I locked the Chicken-house door and the gate as fast as I could, calling, "Boots!" and almost flew back to the house. Out of breath, flying through the door I said to my Mother, "Those Screech Owls scared me!" She just smiled and said, "They won't hurt you." After that, when I went to lock the gate and the door of the Chicken-House I would sing, "In The Garden". My favorite sentences were:

"The sound of His voice is so sweet",
"And He walks with me and He talks with me",
"And He tells me I AM His own."

I just 'knew' there was an Angel, or some wonderful Being with me, as well as my dog, Boots all the way to the Chicken-House and back. I felt safe when I sang and when my dog was with me, and thusly those Screech Owls didn't scare me anymore. I felt important knowing that my Mother trusted me to do what was an important duty on the farm.

CHERRY PIE & GREEN APPLES

Mother said, "Put on your old clothes today!" "Why, what are we going to do?" I asked. I always had to know what is going on; my sister just seemed to know. "We're going to Grandma's house; the cherries are ripe," answered my Dad." Marjorie and I helped Mother and Dad put buckets and stepladders in the car. I was so excited! We were going across town to Grandma and Grandpa Dettmer's farm to pick cherries. They had apple, peach, plum and lots of cherry trees. Some trees had tart cherries and some trees had dark, red sweet cherries that were much sweeter; those were the ones that Marjorie and I liked to pick. Grandma had a "stoner" that took the stones out of the cherries that was fun to use, except that Marjorie and I had to use a large, curved hairpin to stone them. Grandma canned a lot of cherries, so she needed our help to pick as many as we could before they got too ripe. Dad climbed the ladder and Grandpa used the stepladder to reach the cherries. We were not allowed to climb the trees except at cherry picking time; that was the fun part. Mother cautioned us, "Don't eat so many cherries that you won't want any cherry pie for dinner!" Grandma made the most delicious cherry pies, almost as good as her lemon pies. Of course we ate cherries as we picked them; you know the saying, "one for you and one for me". We ate so many cherries that by the time we went home we didn't care if we ever saw another cherry! Grandma gave a bucket of cherries to Mother that we had to 'stone' the next day. Fortunately for Mother, we ate hardly any.

Our neighbors were miles away, so there was only my sister to play with except when there was a family reunion, and/or during harvest season in the fall when all the neighbors from the surrounding farms would come to help each other husk corn and harvest the wheat. At Wheat Harvest time the women came each day to help prepare a huge meal for the hungry men when they came from the fields at noon. We children helped set the long table and then we could go out to play "catch" and climb trees. We had so much fun! The Mothers were so busy in the kitchen cooking and baking and talking and laughing, that they didn't see us climb the apple trees in our orchard. The apples weren't quite ripe, but we didn't care that they were sour. One of the older boys said, "Hey, I better see if I can get a salt shaker!" Mary, who lives across the fields to the north said, "Why? I don't like salt." (I didn't either.) He called back over his shoulder, "You'll see; wait till I get back." Anyway, I thought I better wait, like he said. He had such long legs that he was back in a flash, and said, "Here, shake some salt on your apple; if you don't you'll have a belly ache." Guess what? The apple did taste better! Mary refused to put salt on her apple, no matter how much Harry coaxed her. Poor Mary! She was so sick in her tummy that she couldn't play with us as she was laying there on the couch the rest of the afternoon; she'll never forget that apple-eating day!

All of these experiences showed me how important planning and cooperation is, not only as a family but also when many people are working together. I also learned that the neighbors trusted each other to do what was expected of them.

MARJORIE GOES TO COLLEGE

Marjorie and I had talked about what we would like to do after graduating from High School. She liked to comb Mother's hair and sometimes liked to put mine in pin curls. Marjorie said, "Maybe I'll be a Beautician and get to style the hair of rich women." I said, "I think I would like to be a Nurse and help people who get hurt, or are sick." Marjorie earned a four-year scholarship to Teachers College but she decided she wanted to be a nurse. That was quite a shock to my parents. How are they going to pay for Nurse's Tuition?

That must have been the year that we had 400 ducks in our apple orchard and 300 baby chicks in the Brooder house. The postal service had delivered over 300 fluffy, yellow baby chicks in cardboard boxes, which we hurriedly put in a wood shed that we called a "Brooder house". It seemed like no time at all and the chicks were ready to be moved to a larger wooden shed called a "Chicken-house". When the "Brooder house" was empty, it was filled with tiny, fluffy, yellow baby ducklings; oh, they were so cute! It seemed that they grew faster than the baby chicks and so they were moved to the Apple Orchard. Selling the chickens and ducks when they were big enough to go to market, plus the extra eggs and cream from the milk, paid for Marjorie's education.

Marjorie had many bouts of ill health after she had all the vaccinations that were required to become a student nurse. She started having headaches; later she had sores on her body, then bronchitis and impetigo. Mother had found an excellent chiropractor near to the hospital, so whenever we visited Marjorie, that's the first place that we went to, because Chiropractic Adjustments helped her nerves to function optimally.

INTERUPTION IN NURSES TRAINING

I'd like to tell you about what happened to my sister Marjorie just three and a half months before she was to graduate as a Registered Nurse. Marjorie told me that she was assigned "Special Duty", and was carrying a special experimental solution in a large basin down the hall of the hospital when she hit a wet spot on the newly mopped floor. She told me, "For a split second I thought that my head was going to fly off into space, as I tried to catch myself from falling and spilling a gallon and a half of soapy-type solution all over me". "In the same week," Marjorie told me, "I washed my hair and it took twice as long to comb and brush it as it usually took; very tired and not hungry, I managed to work with a sledgehammer type headache that meds would not touch. I could hardly walk, and I had to look to see if my feet touched the floor when I did walk." The next day Marjorie was not able to lift her head off the bed and had much difficulty in breathing; couldn't turn over in bed without help, and screamed with pain when her legs were touched. After many tests the doctors didn't know what was wrong with her. One of the doctors said that she probably was succumbing to Hysteria since one of her patients had died within the last week and the other had been discharged. More tests were done which were all negative. The last test was another spinal tap. In Marjorie's own words, "As the spinal needle was pushed into the lower lumbar area, a sharp shooting pain shot down from hip to the heel of left leg! That's NOT good!" In the meantime, she was having so much difficulty in breathing, that she was thinking, "If I don't get some help, I don't think I'll make it throughout the night." The diagnosis was finally made and the treatment was to put her into an Iron Lung. Several doctors came into Marjorie's room and announced, "You have "Acute Abortive Anterior Poliomyelitis"! Marjorie was not surprised at the diagnosis and treatment since this is what she thought all along, but didn't voice it.

She explained to me, "The pain and spasm were increasing in intensity in the legs, the head felt as though it had an Indian Sweat-band around it. The pain came in 'waves', building in intensity like the ocean's surf. It was so severe --- only a few seconds of numbness between 'waves'. I was praying silently to die if the pain couldn't be stopped or lessened in strength and longer 'rest' periods, like if someone poured salt in an open wound; it was unbearable!" Marjorie was a very strong and determined woman, and for her to pray to die, I can't even imagine how terrible the pain must have been! Mother had been summoned to the hospital and was taking care of Marjorie's physical needs, as were the nurses and doctors.

One evening, as Mother was leaving Marjorie to go to Marjorie's room in the Student Nurse's Home for the night, she stopped to look out the window at the clear, bright, starlit sky and smiled. Mother told me much later, "That at the last minute I looked down at Marjorie and I saw her eyes roll up and back, and Marjorie had become very quiet --- I thought Marjorie was dying."

Marjorie told me later that her spirit left the Respirator (the Iron Lung) and the hospital room that night! In her own words: "I was out in space, about halfway between Earth and Heaven; prone, on a narrow, hard board, and there was a microscopic Silver Thread attached to earth at one end, and at the other end, on a 45 degree slant, up into the Heavens. The sky was a soft, deep, velvety blue with a few small stars in the distance. And, although I couldn't 'see' that Silver Thread, I was making contact with it, with only the tip of my little finger of my right hand." Marjorie goes on to explain, "There was the feeling that if I move my little finger away, I'd lose contact with the Earth and if I tried to grasp that thread with my hand, even though it was strong, it would snap in two, and I'd "fly" up Heavenward; with either action, there'd not be any going back down on Earth." What a dilemma Marjorie was in! "Then I heard the most wonderful baritone voice coming from behind my left shoulder, "Marjorie, just let go and come with me, and everything will be fine. You will be all right." "Jesus?" she asked? "Yes," he answered, "come with me and there will be no more hurt, no more pain." "Well," Marjorie answered, "I know I prayed to die if the pain couldn't be stopped; I just couldn't take much more; but, if I don't let go and go along with you, will the pain be less often and bearable, if it doesn't stop completely? 'Cause I feel like I've still some unfinished business left to do on Earth. If I stay on Earth a while longer, will I be able to walk and help others? If not, then I want to go with you now." Jesus answered, "Yes, the pain will be bearable and less often, and yes, you do have some unfinished business on Earth, but, if you come with me there will be no more pain or sorrows, everything will be wonderful." After a pause, He went on to say, "You will walk again, in time, and earn your own living, and I will be with you." Marjorie was so relieved, and she said, "Thank you, Lord! I think I will stay on Earth for a while and finish what I'm supposed to do." "With that I was aware of Mother standing by my head and asking, "Marjorie? Are you all right? Shall I stay a while longer?" "Yes," I answered, "I'm all right. I feel better; you go on to bed and I'll see you in the morning." The waves of pain were much milder and less frequent from then on. Marjorie's "Out-Of-Body" experience took place two days after her twenty-first birthday! None of us will ever forget that.

Marjorie was the only one in a two-bed hospital room. The day after her "Out-Of-Body" experience, I came to visit her on Sunday with our father, his sister, Etta, and our Chiropractor, Dr. Morley. Marjorie said that, "Dr. Morley reached through the holes of the Respirator and, as best as he could, he adjusted my upper cervical vertebrae." Mother leaned against the door because in those days chiropractors were not allowed to treat hospitalized patients. "Improvement was such", Marjorie related, "that on Monday A.M. I was disconnected from the 'bellows' for fifteen minutes, and again in the evening, to breath on my own. The time "on my own" was gradually increased so that on the sixth day the doctor told me, "If you keep on improving as you have, we'll take you out of the Respirator, and put you in that bed, (pointing to the one by the window) in a few days." Marjorie said, "Why wait! Let's do it now!" The doctor wanted to wait, but every time someone came past the door, or into her room, she asked to be removed from the Respirator, until by afternoon, she was removed from the Respirator and moved to the other bed. What a relief! Marjorie thought that if she had hot water bottles on her legs, the leg muscles would be able to relax and there would be less pain. When she asked the nurses for hot water bottles, they thought that was an unusual request, but because they had been told to give Marjorie anything that she wanted, they obliged. Yes, the hot water bottles did help the muscles to relax a little, therefore less pain.

Now that Marjorie was in a regular bed, a footboard was placed under each foot, to help prevent a 'foot-drop' condition. These must be placed exactly so, which also helped to ease the leg pain. There seemed to be a problem in being able to position the right footboard in the correct manner, which some nurses could not understand the importance of, and would not or could not always comply. Was this the reason Marjorie had to live with a right foot-drop all the rest of her life?

Twenty-seven days after being stricken with Polio, Marjorie left the hospital weighing 115 pounds instead of her usual 175 pounds in a "State of The Art" Ambulance to Dr. Striplin, a Chiropractic Specialist, for spinal X-Rays and to have her spinal vertebrae adjusted. From there the ambulance drove Marjorie to our home in Indiana. She said, "Does it ever feel good to be put to bed in my own bed!" She went on to say, "Mother had changed our dining room into my bedroom. Grandpa Michael, (Mother's father) made a backrest so that my shoulders and head could be elevated. After having had my spine adjusted again so that the nerves could function properly, I began to gradually gain strength."

During the time of Marjorie's recovery, I was in Beauty And Barber School. I came home a few times to massage my sister, since I had taken a course in Body Massage. I massaged her and watched her expressions and sometimes she made a frowning face. I said, "Am I hurting you?" and she would say, "Yes, but it hurts good; go ahead and massage." Marjorie sat at the table for Christmas Dinner with Grandma and 'pa Dettmer, Aunt Etta Dettmer (our father's sister), Dr. Morley and me. Improvement continued and in April Dad drove Marjorie to visit me for a week where I was working as a Hairdresser and Masseuse in the lovely Salem Beauty Salon. (I'm sure that Mother enjoyed a much-needed rest away from the care of my sister.) I was surprised that Marjorie was able to walk up the flight of stairs to my apartment without help. Marjorie learned to write again by hemming and embroidering dishtowels, and/or appliqueing them, which helped with dexterity of movement of her fingers. Mother had been massaging her back and legs every day to stimulate the circulation and helped her with exercises.

A year and a half after having been diagnosed with Acute Abortive Anterior Poliomyelitis, Marjorie, Mother and friend, Ella made a surprise visit to the Hospital Nursing School. Mother told me that when one of the Head Nurses saw her coming down the hall un-aided, her face turned white. You see, Marjorie had been told by the doctors on her case, (before leaving the hospital) that she would never be able to walk again, that she might be getting around in a wheelchair. While talking to the Director of Nursing, she said, "You ARE the best student nurse that we've had in the last fifteen years; we'd hate to lose you! I look forward to you coming back to complete your Training!" Marjorie finished her last three and a half more months of training on her 23rd. birthday. My family and I are so proud of her.

When I was told that my sister was stricken with polio, my heart sank. I felt almost hopeless for her. I was so proud of my Mother for staying at the hospital helping to encourage my sister. I was amazed at the strength, endurance, and determination that Marjorie had, and the hard work that it took along with Chiropractic Care for her to recover. I realized that she was an inspiration for me to always do my best in whatever my goals were.

MY HIGH SCHOOL GRADUATION, WORKING & COLLEGE

Mother made all of our clothes except for the overalls (denims); I grew into most of my sister's dresses. A package arrived from a Mail-Order House that had dress material in it for me. Mother said, "Come over here, and look at these dress patterns; which one do you like the best? I'm going to make your dress that you will be wearing under your cap and gown when you graduate." It was a tough decision because I rarely was allowed to make a decision. I picked the one that had a wide collar with a round neck and an A-line skirt. "Now," Mother said, "which material do you like the best?" Oh dear, now I have to make another decision! The ivory material is so beautiful and would look perfect the day of graduation. As I was about to say, "This one", I felt the fabric and it felt sticky and it was nubby, not smooth and soft as I expected it to feel. The other material was sky blue with little white lily of the valley flowers here and there; as I felt that material it was oh, so soft and smooth! I knew right away that I wanted that material to be my dress. I looked at Mother's smiling face and said, "I like this one". Mother's expression changed and she said, "Are you sure? Be sure which one that you want." I could tell that she wanted me to choose the ivory material; it probably was the most expensive and I later learned that it was silk. I always tried to please my Mother, but this time I was actually given a choice, and I wanted what I wanted; I did not want that nubby, sticky material on my body! I said, "Yes, I really like the blue one, can I have this (as I pointed to the blue material) for my graduation dress?" "All right," Mother replied, as she folded the ivory silk material in the tissue paper. I felt so sad that I had not pleased my Mother, and almost changed my mind, until I thought about that sticky feeling; I would be so unhappy every time that I wore that dress. Graduation day came and I felt so pretty in that soft blue dress on graduation day and every other time that I wore it. I was satisfied that I was true to myself in my decision.

A few months after I graduated from high school I enrolled in Indiana Beauty and Barber College in Indianapolis, Indiana, about 45 miles away from home. I loved learning how to set hair in waves and give permanents and to dye the hair. I didn't even know that women dyed their hair until I was learning how to do it, and it was fun. While there, a special course in body massage was offered, which gave me another opportunity to learn something else. Four of us had so much fun practicing on each other.

A group of us students were standing in the balcony watching the younger students master haircutting, when one of the Instructors, who was standing next to me said, "Let me see your hands". I wondered if I still had some hair dye on my hands, or what. She looked them over and then said to me, "You will be doing something more important some day than giving permanents and setting hair." I didn't know what she meant until one day when my parents took me for a spinal checkup by our Doctor of Chiropractic, Dr, Aumann and he said, "Let me see your hands." As he took ahold of them and turned them over Dr. Aumann said, "You would make a good Chiropractor". I said, "Oh, No, I'm not smart enough to be a doctor". He responded with, "Oh, yes you are. I'll be right back", and he went into the waiting room to speak to my parents. Mother began selling more eggs and bought more baby chicks to help pay for my education. Apparently, I would be attending a chiropractic college in the near future, but first I had to go to work.

Because I was not yet seventeen, I had to get a work permit before I could work in the Beauty Shop where the Beauty School sent me. I was really nervous because I was to work there for three weeks, and if I didn't work according to Miss Margaret's, the beauty shop owner, standards, I would be sent home. Since I had taken a special course in Body Massage while I was in Beauty School, the clients began to ask for my massages as well as hairdressing, so I was "in like Flynn". A doctor's wife had her hair styled by Miss Margaret every Saturday at 10:00 AM, and I wondered why she came in early this particular Saturday. Miss Margaret said, "Aileen, Mrs. Smith would like for you to give her a massage before I set her hair today". I was elated! I massaged her exactly as I had been taught; she almost went to sleep. After she had dressed, she said, "Young lady, that was an excellent massage!" I replied, "It was my pleasure, Mrs. Smith!" She smiled so sweetly and said, "Here is a tip". I could hardly believe how much she put into my hand; it was a dime! A dime tip! I nearly jumped up and down! Miss Margaret said, "Aileen, you are becoming quite popular with your reputation as a massage therapist!" After the first four weeks she gave me a raise of two cents, which totaled twelve dollars a week.

I lived in a Boarding House with three other people. Charlie, one of the boarders asked Polly, a hairdresser I worked with, "Polly, would you like to go with me out to the edge of town and shoot some limbs off some of those trees?" "Sure, Charlie; that sounds like fun; can Aileen to go with us?" she asked. This sounded exciting since I had never shot a gun before. Polly drove us to the edge of town and Charlie showed us how to shoot a BB gun. We were aiming at little limbs and after a while Charlie said, "Aileen, I don't believe that you never shot a gun before now; you're really doing good!" Charlie was a lot of fun and we went out with him on our days off from work to either shooting his BB gun, or sitting in his rowboat on the nearby pond.

Mother had written a letter to me, "I think that Dad has found a new job for you to investigate". It was a sad day when I left to go back to my hometown; all those "Goodbyes" to my new friends, yet I was glad a new experience was coming up. Dad put my things in the car and on the way home, I chatted about my clients and the fun I had with Polly and Charlie. Suddenly he interrupted me and said, "I have a friend who works at this Engine Company in town", he continued, "The company is hiring again; they just got a big job with the United States Government." I wondered what that had to do with me. Dad said, "They are paying good money. You could make a lot more there than at Salem Beauty Shop; why don't you go apply for a job?" I said, "But I don't know how to do anything other than work with hair and massage." After we arrived home, Mother said, "You could apply as a file clerk ---- you could do that." So the next experience in my life was working for this Engine Company in the Architectural Department, filing blue prints in a vault. Over the loudspeaker came a voice, "Does anyone want to work over-time?" I always volunteered. Then it was double-time; I never saw so much money in my life! I was so happy that I could save so much to help pay for my college education; while my parents were busy raising 300 extra baby chicks and selling more eggs to also raise money for my tuition.

I had been living in Mauzey's Room and Board House with some of the other company employees. I finally had a Saturday off from work, so I decided to ride my bike out to visit my parents in the country. After I turned off the highway onto the road that leads to my parent's house, I heard this big truck turn off the highway also, and it was soon right behind me and was slowing down. I pulled to the side to let the truck go past me, but it shifted gears and just stayed right behind me; I had chills come over me; was I in danger, what should I do? "Hey, there! Hi Aileen!" came the voice which sounded a bit familiar! I turned around and saw that it was my 'dreamboat' from high school days! I felt my cheeks flush a little; he didn't know that I had a crush on him ever since he walked into class a little late his first day in high school; this tall, dark handsome guy with the most beautiful blue eyes! I came to my senses and said, "Well, Hello, Joe! What are you doing out here?" He said, "I'm hauling a load of pigs to market in Indianapolis. When I saw you turn off the highway, I knew for sure that it was you, and just had to say, "Hello!" We chatted for a while and I ended up agreeing to ride with him in two weeks when he would be hauling another load of pigs to market; that is, if I didn't have to work that day. I was happy while taking those fun trips with him, which continued through the summer until I went off to Palmer School of Chiropractic in Iowa. He hated to see me leave, and I hated to leave him; and I didn't even know if he was a good kisser; we were just friends.

I learned in the beauty and barber school to always do your best. I observed that otherwise you have to do it over which wastes time and patience. I concluded also that a smile and a pleasant attitude wins friends.

PALMER SCHOOL OF CHIROPRACTIC, HERE I AM!

The long drive to the college was filled with clothes, enthusiasm and trepidation. Dr. Sherman, one of the college professors had an apartment in the rear of his house, which he rented to students and that's where I met my brown-haired, happy roommate, Virginia. Dr. Sherman rented one of his upstairs rooms to my Dad for the weekend; Mother needed to stay home to take care of the livestock and chickens. On Monday I enrolled; there was no choice of what classes to take, they were decided for you. It seemed that all of the walls and some of the ceilings had Dr. B.J. Palmer's favorite words of wisdom, ie: "Miracles happen every day."

This whole Chiropractic Movement began when Daniel David Palmer adjusted a vertebra on Harvey Lillard's upper spine and Harvey could hear again. Harvey was a man of color who worked for D.D. Palmer, as he was called, and had been deaf for many years. He came to D.D. Palmer and said that his neck and upper back hurt, so D.D., who had been studying Anatomy, especially the skeleton, had him lie down on a padded table and adjusted a vertebra that D.D. Palmer felt to be out of alignment.

D.D. Palmer's son, Dr. B.J. Palmer continued on with the premise that there is a connection between the nerves of the spinal column and the organs of the body. Dr. B.J. Palmer is considered to be the Developer of Chiropractic. I was fortunate to be one of Dr. B. J. Palmer's students, and once a week it was mandatory for all of the students to attend his lecture in the Auditorium. I guarantee that no one ever fell asleep during that time! He would pace the floor, and pound the podium, and shout, and stamp his foot, and then almost whisper returning to a shout in order to put his point across. I learned so much from his lectures about how the body relies on each and every bone, muscle, nerves, brain, organs, blood and even the skin, so that our bodies can function properly. Also, I soon learned that all chiropractic colleges teach the same classes that are required by medical students, except for prescribing medication. Instead of medications, we were learning how the organs of our bodies receive nutrition through the blood supply, and nerve supply by way of the nerves in the spine and the brain.

B. J. (as he was also known) traveled extensively bringing home many artifacts, gems and artwork, which he would often include in his lectures. Between his home and one of the classroom buildings was a section of property that was called "A Little Bit Of Heaven." At one side was a waterfall that was built of various boulders and stones and gems from all over the world. There were various animal statues such as a lion, tiger, monkeys, an elephant and a statue of a Buddha, a huge rose quartz crystal, purple amethyst, green tourmaline and other beautiful crystals, large colorful hand-painted vases from Japan, China, India, Italy and other countries. There were flowers, plants and small trees from all over the world interspersed among all of these treasures. The atmosphere was so fresh and calming, truly a "Little Bit Of Heaven".

The Bulletin Boards in the entry Hall of Palmer College had notices of after-school happenings, and lost and found, and jobs available. I found one notice that said, "Elevator Operator wanted in Mississippi Hotel." Hmmm, I thought that sounded interesting. I had been in an elevator twice and to operate the wheel from floor to floor looked pretty easy. (I had to work to pay for my room and food.) I applied for the job, and when I got there the manager of the hotel said, "Our PBX Operator is ill today, so you will be answering the switchboard as well as operating the elevator." Wow! I didn't know anything about either, but I said, "Just show me what to do." Both jobs were really fun, once I got the hang of it. The Hotel had many permanent residents, so it was not very busy therefore I had time to study during working hours. Classes were eight hours a day five days a week, and I worked every evening three to four hours, and eight hours on Saturday and sometimes four hours on Sunday as well, so there wasn't much time to study, except at work.

Some of the men students were older, or had already been discharged from the Service. There were very few women students and most of the men did not welcome us; I guess they thought that we were too frail, but it doesn't take brute force to give a proper adjustment to the vertebrae. I wanted to be a Doctor of Chiropractic, but what does Neurology, Science, Chemistry, Anatomy, Physiology and more have to do with giving a spinal adjustment of the vertebrae? Finally I was being shown how to give a proper effective adjustment. Wow! It's not as easy as I thought it would be, so Practice! Practice! Practice! And Study, Study, Study! I learned that what's in all those books IS important after-all, no matter what the subject matter may be.

A dress shop was advertising for "help wanted". If I had that job, I'd get a huge discount on clothes. So I quit the hotel and began work at the dress shop. I needed a better winter outfit to go to church in, and there was a cute emerald green bolero suit that I just adored. One of the little gray-haired sales ladies took a 'liken' to me and said, "I see you eyeing that suit over there, have you tried it on yet?" "Well, no," I answered. She smiled and said, "We're not busy right now, so go ahead and try it on." Well, it fit as though it had been special made for me. "Little Miss Gray Hair" clapped her hands and said, "The store is going to have a Sale soon, so I will put this outfit back in the stock room, and when it goes on Sale, you will have your perfect outfit!" I couldn't believe that she could do that, but she did, and soon after the sale, I came home with a real bargain.

The college surrounded a Courtyard on three sides, with the street on the fourth side. In-between classes we would stand on the balcony for a couple minutes. Across the way I saw this cute, tall, slender curly brown haired guy. Mary said to me, "I see who you're looking at, the one with the baggy pants, he's really cute isn't he?" I think I blushed and said, "Yes, but he's not in any of my classes, I'll probably never meet him." There was a saying at the school, "if you're not married when you get here, you'll be married by the time you graduate, and if you're already married, you'll have children, or more children, by the time you graduate."

Some of the students were married and they both worked. One couple that I really admired had five children. Norman worked in a hotel underground garage checking cars in and out. His wife managed a laundry/dry-cleaning service across from the Chiropractic College, and her young children helped sort clothes and do whatever to help when they were not in school. The location was perfect for the students who didn't want to wash their own clothes. I would stop on my way home from work in the evening to chat with Norman. This one particular evening as I was riding my bike up Brady Street hill, I saw that there was a fellow talking to Norman; as I drew closer I could see that it was the guy who I had my eye on from across the Courtyard, and I became a bit nervous. "Hi Aileen," called Norman, "come here." As I came closer I heard him say to this guy, "This is the girl I was telling you about; she stops by every night on her way home from work. Turning toward me he said, "Bob, meet Aileen." Then he said, "Aileen, meet Bob ---- he's in my Anatomy Class." We shook hands and talked a minute and then I said, "I must get home, I have some studying to do for a test." The next night Bob was there again, and the third night when Bob was standing there talking to Norman, he asked me, "May I walk you home? I don't have a bike yet." I said, "Ok." (At a much later time I learned that Bob had been telling his buddies, "When I saw Aileen riding her bike, I knew that's the girl I am going to marry!") As we walked the rest of the way up Brady Street Hill I asked Bob, "Why are you here at Palmer?" He began, "When I was a little kid I had asthma attacks and my Mom took me to her Chiropractor and I was cured. Then when I was in the Navy, I began having asthma attacks again. After I got home I went to our Chiropractor and was cured again." After a moment I said, "So you want to cure everyone who has asthma?" Bob laughed and said, "Well, if asthma is cured, chiropractic adjustments probably cures other ailments; don't you think?" Then he asked me, "And what brought you here?" I took a deep breath and said, "It's a long story. When I was in high school my Mother suffered with severe sinus congestion/infection and nothing would help. She finally went to a doctor of chiropractic who brought her here to Dr. B.J. Palmer's Private Clinic for Mother's neck to be X-Rayed. Dr. B.J. Palmer adjusted her neck and she began to improve until she didn't have anymore sinus congestion. After a while she noticed that her varicose veins were gone." Bob listened intently. I continued, "When I was in high school I began having sinus congestion and abdominal cramps, which all disappeared after getting some chiropractic adjustments of my spine. When I was in Beauty and Barber School my chiropractor encouraged me to become a Doctor of Chiropractic." Bob exclaimed, "That's really something! And your Mom was actually adjusted by Dr. B.J. Palmer!"

On the bulletin board at school was a notice asking for help at Walgreen's Drug store; I could make more money, so I applied and got the job. I was to tally up receipts of the different departments at the end of the day. "OH, NO!" I said to Bob. (Yes, he met me every evening after work.) "There is no adding machine and I'm terrible with figures." After a couple of days I asked the manager, "Could Bob please come in and help with the adding? He's a whiz!" He at first said, "No, it's after hours and he doesn't work here." The next night, when the manager saw how long it took me, and Bob was waiting outside the door, he said, "All right, but he must stay in that section of the department." I was so embarrassed, but glad that Bob could help.

Another year later the Arsenal across the river from the college placed a "Wanted! File Clerk. Best wages!" notice on the school bulletin board, so I applied and now I have another new job making more money than at the drug store. The downside was that now I must take a bus to work, and there is no time to study at work. I sure am learning how to do a lot of things in a short period of time! By working so many different jobs and meeting so many people who had a lot of health problems and were unhappy, I was even more determined to become a doctor of chiropractic and help people to have a healthier life. I also came to the conclusion that there are many nice employers who make an effort to hire students part-time so that they are able to continue their education.

1945-1954

TOO MUCH FUN TIME ?

Who? Me? Imagine! Me? Called into the Magistrates office! Bob and I were told to spend more time on our class work; our grades had fallen a bit. I was nervous and embarrassed. Bob and I probably spent too much time riding our bikes in the park, instead of studying. And Dr. Sherman, my landlord and also one of my professors, probably saw Bob hanging around the apartment and taking up too much of my time, so he might have reported me to the Magistrate.

I was busy studying in my apartment when I heard noises out in the yard -- it was Dr. Sherman practicing Archery. Archery looked very interesting so I went out on my porch and said, "Hi, Dr. Sherman, I looked up from studying and saw you out here and you seem to hit the bulls-eye almost every time. Have you been doing this for a very long time?" "Hello, Aileen. I hunt pheasants whenever I can get away during season, and the season is almost here," he responded. "Have you ever used a bow and arrow?" he asked. "No." I replied. Dr. Sherman handed the bow and then the arrow to me and said, "Would you like to learn?" I was thrilled that he would teach me, and he said, "One important thing to remember is to keep your wrist very straight with your arm." I learned right away what he meant when the bowstring stung my wrist. Archery was especially fun when I saw how many times I could hit the bulls-eye. He left the bale of straw that had the bulls-eye painted on it in the yard and said, "I'll leave the bow and arrow here on my porch, feel free to practice anytime." I was thrilled. Even though I was reprimanded because my grades were not satisfactory, I noticed that the Professor's philosophy was "all work and no play make Jack a dull boy/girl".

None of us in school had time to make many close friends, we were too busy studying and working, and now dating whenever possible. How then did I have time to be initiated into the Sigma Phi Ki Sorority? In-between classes or during a study hour I would sometimes be found in the Sorority Room. Our Sorority Mother was Dr. B.J. Palmer's wife, Mabel who was a lovely, gentle person. We gals called her "Mom" because she always had a shoulder that we could lean on and an ear to hear our "troubles". She seemed to know how difficult it was for us girls to be away from home and not be able to confide in our Moms, so there she was; listening to silly stuff, like, "Do I look good with my hair like this?" as well as important things, like, "If I take this other job, do you think it will interfere with my studies too much?" I even asked her about Bob and she said, "He's a good guy; he seems to have his head on his shoulders". Knowing that I could trust my Sorority Mother, I asked for and received her opinion of my boyfriend, which I really appreciated.

I often received letters from my sister, Marjorie and in her last letter she said, "We've talked of living together; now is the time that we could do this. I've written to the Director of the Palmer Chiropractic Clinic, and since I am a Registered Nurse, I have been accepted there, to work in the Science Lab." I was elated! My sister is a Polio survivor and using Sister Kenny walking Sticks; she was physically limited, so this would be a good job for her. Soon we moved in together and Marjorie suggested, "I'll do the cooking, dusting and ironing, and you do the other cleaning, washing, grocery shopping, etc., OK?" "That sounds good to me." I agreed. Yes, she was still telling me what to do and how to do it. Soon, Marjorie asked Bob, "Would you like to come for a home-cooked meal on Sunday, cherry pie for dessert?" Bob loved my sister's cooking, especially her cherry pie, maybe that's why he continued to date me. During Bob's visits my sister was able to assess Bob's demeanor and intentions. Was he the right one for me? Living with my sister required a lot of patience and I was determined to make it work for peace of mind for us both.

Bob bought an old car and surprised me by picking me up at the Arsenal where I worked as a Special File Clerk after school. He worked at a jewelry store and was off work by 8:30 PM, so he could drive me home after school and on Saturday. I was so glad not to have to take a bus anymore! Of course we did a little smooching on the way home. One evening as he was driving me home he stopped in front of a house along the way. I said, "Why are we stopping here? Do you know someone who lives here?" Bob grinned his winning grin, put his arms around me and said, "Will you marry me?" I was thrilled as he placed the most beautiful diamond ring on my finger! I really was in love with him! (The second time that he kissed me heaven lit up, and I saw beautiful stars of all colors! I knew that he was THE ONE for me!) That very night he called my Dad, getting him out of bed, and asked him if he could "have Aileen's hand in marriage". My Dad said, "Yes". I was thrilled that Bob wanted to marry me and was determined that I would be a good wife. I knew that he was a good man since he showed respect for my parents by asking my Dad if he could marry me.

MY WEDDING

Six months later I went to the same dress store where I had previously worked, and looked for the same little gracious lady I remembered who helped me purchase that green suit. I said, "I don't have the money for a bridal gown, but I would like a wedding dress that I can wear to church and other places after the wedding." "Oh, my dear" she said, with a twinkle in her eye, "I think I know exactly which one is just for you," as she showed me this baby blue dress with ruffled pockets; it fit perfectly! Then I shopped for just the right hat with a veil and some dress shoes.

I had just graduated and Bob was still in college, so we decided that Labor Day weekend would be a good time to get married so that Bob wouldn't miss any classes. Bob's Dad said, "Bob, you promised not to get married until you had graduated!" "Well, one of us did," Bob laughed. (Bob graduated six months later.)

My Mother could not come to the wedding because her Mother was quite ill and needed care. My Father, my Aunt Etta, Bob's Father and Mother (Richard and Rose Miller), Bob's Aunt and Uncle, my two dearest friends from College and Bob's Best Man and his wife attended the wedding.

My sister, Marjorie was my Maid of Honor, Bob's best friend in college, Johnnie was his Best Man. Bob said to the Minister, "We would really like for you to join us at the Reception at the hotel." The Minister was delighted to be part of the family. We relied on wedding gift money to pay for the dinner, and had twenty-five dollars left over; otherwise we might have been washing dishes that night! (No, our parents did not pay for our wedding.)

We worked, and lived, in our office that we had found near the college. We used our bedroom as the waiting room and it sometimes was a challenge to get it ready to greet our patients. We built our Practice by walking door-to-door distributing Chiropractic literature. Soon we hired local Boy Scouts to help us distribute the literature. We met and got to know some of the neighbors face-to-face and soon had a thriving Practice.

September 1, 1945- Aileen and Robert Miller, the happy newlyweds, married in Davenport, Iowa. Bob's holding a "Just Married" sign.

MISS AILEEN DETTMER

MISS Aileen Dettmer of 208 East Eleventh street, Davenport, daughter of Mr and Mrs Arthur Dettmer of Columbus, Ind., will become the bride of Robert C. Miller of 3202 Harrison street, Davenport, son of Mr and Mrs Richard Miller of Detroit, Mich., at 5 p. m. today at Holy Cross Lutheran church, with the Rev. Theodore Schulz officiating. Miss Marjorie Dettmer, sister of the bride, will be maid of honor, and John Prizer of Davenport will serve as best man.

The bride will wear a crepe afternoon dress of pale blue with white trim and fuchsia accessories. She will carry a bouquet of white roses. Her sister will be attired in a rose colored dress with gold and brown trim, with which she will wear brown accessories. Her corsage will be of roses.

Following the ceremony a dinner will be held at the Hotel Blackhawk for members of the wedding party and relatives.

The bride is a graduate of the Columbus, Ind., high school and until recently has been employed at the Rock Island arsenal. She was graduated last week from the Palmer School of Chiropractic.

Mr Miller is a graduate of a high school in Detroit and was in the navy for more than a year before receiving a discharge about a year ago. He is now a student at the Palmer school. They will make their home in Davenport.

9-1-45

My Wedding Announcement in the newspaper

Upon reflection, I could see how good Bob was at planning; working at a jewelry store to get my ring at a good price, marrying on a holiday, living in our office, and how to advertise.

ARIZONA BOUND

One day, after taking care of patients, Bob had an idea, "Let's sell the Practice, go visit Johnnie (Bob's best friend), who was already in Chiropractic Practice in Arizona, and find a place to open an office." I was surprised, but agreed, "Good, neither of us like cold weather here in Illinois, and it's warm in Arizona, let's go." Since we had not been on a honeymoon since our wedding, this trip was it. Oh, it was so nice to be where it was warm!

I found a job with another doctor of chiropractic, who said that he needed help with his patients; however, we went into the lower level of his office building and he showed me his Nutrition area. He had bought vitamins in bulk and asked me to count out so many per bottle; he would seal the bottles afterward. The doctor said, "Do not come into my office, I don't want my Patients to see you." I asked, "Why not?" His answer was, "I'll keep you busy with these vitamins." My assumption was that since I am a female chiropractor (my husband had told me that there were no women chiropractors in that city) he didn't want his patients to ask for me to take care of them. Bob looked for an office location, but mostly played golf with his friend, Dr. John when he was not in his office. He didn't find a location there that was within our budget so we left Arizona and headed back to Michigan where Bob's parents lived. On our way back to Michigan we liked the looks and feel of Tyler, Texas as we investigated that area, but found no suitable office there; (Tyler is the Rose Center of the United States), but we kept on driving to Michigan because our money was running out from the sale of our practice in Illinois. We had no place to live except to move in with Bob's parents until we could save enough money to have a home of our own.

Even though Bob's idea was not fruitful, I came to the conclusion that if we had not investigated various locations, the thought of "what if" would have always been on our minds.

UNHAPPY MOTHER-IN-LAW

I felt that my Mother-in-law, Rose didn't really like me because she talked to me in a gruff unfriendly manner, which was very upsetting to me. Before Bob joined the Navy, he had been dating a really lovely girl and my Mother-in-law had told me how much she liked her. As soon as he was discharged he went to Palmer Chiropractic College. While there he had no more contact with her, met me and the rest is history.

A friend suggested, "A good way to change her mind about you is, to visualize her in front of you, and say the Lord's Prayer to her; do this everyday." It was not long afterward that I noticed a change in her attitude towards me, or perhaps it was my attitude of LOVE, rather than my thinking, "What did I do wrong?" It was only after I had no more fear of her that she finally accepted me.

Now that we are definitely living in Michigan, Bob began pouring cement driveways to earn a living. I began my Chiropractic Practice while sharing a building with a realtor named George. "George," I said, "Will you help me set up a dark room for developing X-Rays? In exchange I can help you with secretarial work." So, that's what we did. While sharing a common reception room for my patients and George's real estate clients, I came to the conclusion that it was an asset; George's clients would talk about selling or remodeling their home and talk to my patients; my patients would talk about how chiropractic improves their health. His business and my practice flourished. In Practice again, helping patients regain their health; what a wonderful feeling! Every once in a while when massaging a patient's back, the patient would say, "Your hands feel so hot I had to look to see if you were using a heating pad on my back, but the warmth kept moving with your hands!" We'd laugh and I'd just say, "Yes," or I would say, "That could be the Angels working with us".

Bob's Dad quit his job at Packard Motor Car Company where he was a Tool and Die Maker, so that he and Bob could build garages as well as pour cement driveways and sidewalks. Bob came home waving a paper and announced, "I've passed my Masonry exam and got my license!" Soon he came home waving another paper and said, "I've passed the Carpenter's exam and here's my license!" We danced around the kitchen singing, "We can build houses!" Relying on his experience in architectural drawing in high school, Bob designed and drew up the plans to all of the houses he built. No two were alike. They were one story, built of cinder block with a wider over-hang than most houses, and painted white. People would drive by one of his houses and say, "Hey, that looks like a Miller Home!" Bob loved working-out-of doors rather than in an office taking care of patients!

I want to tell you how Bob surprised me with our first house. One day Bob said, "Come here a minute, I want to show you something." On the table was a blueprint of a house. Bob said, "I'd like for you to give me your opinion of this house plan, (as he sometimes did ask for my opinion)." I had a strange feeling that this was a SPECIAL blueprint. I became excited! "Is this our house?" After examining it thoroughly, I excitedly said, "I love it! It's perfect! Where is this going to be built? When can you start building it?" I was talking so fast that Bob could hardly get a word in edge wise and interrupted, "Honey, I've already purchased a lot on the same side of the street that my construction business is on and I can walk to work. I'll order the materials and get started right away." Three months later, we moved into our first house. What an exciting day! Our first house!

Now, I didn't need to pay office rent anymore! Our living room was the reception room with a sleeper-sofa that Bob's cousin gave to us, and one chair. (Since we had no bed, that sleeper sofa did double duty). One of the bedrooms was my office, with an X-Ray machine, adjusting table and a desk. I said, "Honey, I need a Dark Room in which to develop X-Rays." Looking perplexed, Bob said, "Oh, I never thought of that. Hmmm, I think I can convert the shower stall that's in the garage into the Dark Room." The dining area was furnished with a card table and milk bottle crates for chairs. Bob's parents then furnished our bedroom. We didn't have much, but we had love.

I learned when to be dependent and when to be independent by careful planning, saving, and working together with what we had. By discussing the ideas we had for the future we accomplished much in a short period of time.

"HONEY, WE'RE HAVING A BABY!"

We'd been married nearly three years and we have a house all our own. Bob's dad said, "Hey, Bob, when am I going to be a grandpa? You're all settled in your house and have that extra bedroom!" Bob and I began planning and soon I said, "Honey, I think we're going to have a baby". He was so delighted! We both were hoping that our first baby would be a boy. We were so happy, floating on a cloud! The third bedroom was getting furnished with a baby bed and dresser. Bob's Mother said, "I'm giving you a baby shower!" "Oh, My!" I stammered, "But, Thank You!" I had never been to a baby shower; I was so nervous and so excited! My Mother-law invited all her friends who brought so many gifts, and food to go with her beautiful pink and white cake. It was an amazing lovely, sunny day while I opened many gifts! I was so thankful to have a caring Mother-in-law!

"Marjorie," I called on the phone, "Will you come to Michigan to be with me when my baby is born? We'll pay for your plane ticket." She was delighted that I asked her and came a week before our baby was to be born. My sister was a Registered Nurse who worked in the Premature Baby Section in a hospital in Dallas, Texas. If anything would go wrong, I wanted her to be there. I wanted my Mother to come also, but we didn't have the money for two tickets. I felt that my Mother was disappointed even though she didn't say so.

I looked up from planting geraniums and said to sister, Marjorie, "We'll drive to the hospital this afternoon where my baby is to be born, so you'll get an idea of how long it takes to get there." The baby wasn't due for around another week. During that night I awakened Bob and said, "I think we'll be going to the hospital soon, get your pants on!" So our beautiful son, R.C. Miller, III was born. Later one of the nurses came in laughing, "The staff was concerned that your husband would wear out the carpeting in the waiting room; he rocked so hard and so fast!" (Husbands were not allowed in the delivery room in those days).

My sister was an angel, helping take care of little Robby, washing diapers in the bathtub because we didn't have a washer, and then hanging them outside on the clothesline to dry. She said, "I sure wish that you had a washer!" "I'm sorry, Marjorie," said Bob, "but I don't have quite enough money, maybe Dad will help me get one tomorrow, and hook it up." And he did! She and Bob's Mother prepared delicious meals while Bob worked. We hated to see Marjorie leave but premature babies in the Dallas hospital need her also.

My sister had told me, "Make sure that the house is quiet when the baby sleeps." I had seen only one other tiny baby, and had never taken care of any little children except the three year old I helped with when I was in Beauty and Barber School, so I believed everything that my sister told me. After vacuuming the living room, I had the hallway to vacuum before putting baby Robby down for his nap, so I laid him on my bed while I hurriedly finished vacuuming with the very noisy vacuum cleaner. Rushing in to put him in his own bed to take his nap, I found him fast asleep! From then on I was not concerned about whether the house was quiet or not. My sister took care of pre-mature babies, so perhaps she thought all babies should have it quiet while napping.

I had heard so many stories about unhappy relationships with one's mother-in-law, but after living with my mother and father-in-law very compatibly, I concluded that there are those who can be nice and helpful. None of my family lived anywhere around here, so I was very appreciative of the fact that my sister could take time off from her work to help me. Since her duty as an R.N. was to care for premature babies, I knew that I could trust her to take proper care of my baby. I was also aware that sometimes a change in usual procedure is the one that works best.

It wasn't long before I was again happily taking care of patients in my Home Office. They were so happy to have their spines aligned again. Bob and his Dad were working very hard and their construction business was thriving. At dinner one evening Bob said, "I have a buyer for our house. What do you think about us moving into that house that I'm building a few blocks from here? It has a basement with a shower room, and there will be more place for little Robby to play when the weather is inclement." I said, "Sure honey, I'll have fun decorating another house; I'm sure that my patients won't mind going to a new location," Our new house was on a corner, so my patients had more space to park. Robby loved running around in his new yard and playing with the neighbor who lives across the street. "I always wished that I had a brother or a sister," Bob said as he finished dinner. "I think that Robby should have a brother or a sister, so he won't be an only child." I agreed and said, "Maybe it will be a girl next time." About three and a half years after Robby was born, I was happily announcing, "Yes, Bob, we're having another baby!" We were as excited as when I was pregnant with Robby!

NAME CHANGE? MIX UP?

Cheese Cake Factory! Have you ever eaten in a Cheese Cake Factory? We were so looking forward to eating their delicious dinner on Mother's Day. Instead, we were driving to the same hospital in which Little Robby had been born; I was in labor with another baby. Suddenly, in my head I heard, 'Debra Carol'. I knew that it was my Spirit Guide talking to me. I said, "Honey, I just heard 'Debra Carol'." Smiling, he said, "Pretty name!"

While in the hospital the nurse brought our babies in to us to feed. I had a strange feeling come over me when the nurse handed the baby to me! She was so cute and cuddly, and as I hugged her tightly my eye caught the name on her wristband and it was not the correct name! WHAT?! It seemed like it took the Nurse forever to answer my call bell. She was sooo embarrassed as she read the name, "Baby Smith" on the wristband of the baby I was holding! She practically ran out of the room and brought my own sweet, cuddly baby to me. "Please don't tell the Supervisor! Please!" she begged! I knew that the nurse didn't intentionally bring the wrong baby in to me --- they looked so much alike. She was so embarrassed and apologetic that I felt that in the future she would be more careful, therefore I didn't report the incident.

A day later a nurse brought in a document stating the baby's name, since both parents were to sign it. The name said "Betty Carol Miller"; "Betty?!"

I exclaimed! "Where did THAT name come from?" "Well", the nurse said, looking very surprised, "that's the name your husband, that man out in the waiting room, gave us." "Oh NO!" I exclaimed! "Her name is NOT Betty, it is Debra! Where IS he?" The nurse went to call him into the room, and responded, "He's already left; we'll contact him." I don't get upset very easily, but I was angry! You see, the girl that my Mother-in-law was hoping that her son would marry was named "Betty". He had been dating her and then he joined the Navy. The family liked Betty, and they were expecting that Bob would marry her. Well, no way was our daughter going to be named after his former 'flame'! Bob agreed with me and our baby girl was named Debra Carol. I came to the conclusion that Bob gave his former girlfriend's name as our baby's name just to get my reaction; he always had a good sense of humor.

MICHIGAN STATE CHIROPRACTIC ASSOCIATION

Once a month the doctors met in a hotel room in Detroit, and the Women's Auxiliary of The Michigan State Chiropractic Association met in a room next door. Some of the men didn't especially like us women chiropractors, even though there were very few of us in the mid-1900's. When our meeting was ready to convene, one of the doctors said to me, "The women are meeting next door." I just smiled and said, "Yes, I know, I've already said "Hello" to them. Your wife isn't here tonight, is she?" and I proceeded to take a seat next to him. Since there was much prejudice toward women professionals and toward the chiropractic profession in the 1900's, I concluded that this was progress and didn't take this doctor's insinuation as a personal affront. Never-the -less, I was voted in as their secretary for a couple of years. When I was nominated as President of District One of the Association I declined; I had recently given birth to my baby girl and felt that I could not do the job efficiently. Although the would-be Past President encouraged me by saying that he would be as helpful as possible, I thanked him for his confidence in me, and still declined. It would have been easy to let the ego win, however I realized that it would be best to have a president in charge who could give full attention to the duties at hand.

ANOTHER NEW HOUSE

"Honey, our third house is ready to move into", announced Bob. Debra was still very little. Bob said, "Don't worry, you won't have to do a thing, I'll take care of everything!" I was excited! The neighbor's baby next door was about a month older than Debra. Emerson, our neighbor in back of us had two girls, about two years and four years older, and their boy was the same age as our son, Robby. Our boys, as they grew older were always climbing the fence that separated our yards, so Emerson said, "Bob, let's put a gate in here before they ruin the fence, besides, we won't have to go through the neighbor's yards to get back and forth." The kids were thrilled, and so was I! Even our poodle dogs were thrilled; before long baby puppies were running around. I am so thankful that my husband was so thoughtful about moving us to our new house, and that I have friendly neighbors.

When Debbie (as we call Debra) was older she loved running around in her walker. While I was in the kitchen making lunch, I heard a crash and a "scream"; turning, I saw her lying upside down under her walker, at the bottom of three stairs at the back door. (I had left the door open to the stairs to let more light in, and I didn't think she could get through it with the walker.) My heart was pounding in my throat! I pulled the walker off her and held her close; she was so frightened and crying. I checked for anything broken, bruised and/or scratched; she seemed pretty much OK. She landed on her head, so I checked her spine and found a couple vertebrae that needed to be adjusted into proper position. Now she was calm, ready for lunch and a nap. I'm reminded of the time when my son was still crawling and he picked up the vacuum cleaner extension cord; just as I yelled, "Put it down!" he put it up to his drooling mouth and screamed as he got an electric shock. I picked up my crying baby, and holding him close I checked his spine. The electric jolt shocked a couple of vertebrae out of proper alignment, so I immediately corrected the subluxations so that his nervous system could continue to function properly. I am so blessed by following my desire to be a chiropractor, and knowing how to adjust my family's spines when needed -- especially in emergencies.

PATIENT CARE

"Please tell me, what really happened to you?" I asked my new patient as I viewed his X-Rays. "Well," he began, "About two years ago I was standing in front of a cement wall; a trucker was maneuvering his truck, backing it into a parking space when suddenly his foot slipped and the truck pinned me against this wall. I was taken to the hospital with a smashed face and other broken bones. I finally healed but I've had many health problem ever since." He continued to tell me in detail about his headaches, heart problems and other problems. After analyzing my patient's X-rays I saw that he had many vertebral subluxations, as well as some fusions; his case looked almost hopeless. I decided to take on the challenge of removing nerve interference as much as was possible so that this man could be healthier; he was one of my most difficult challenges. After the first week of vertebral adjustments his headaches were less severe, and as time went on, he had fewer health problems. After about a year and a half he and his wife moved many miles away, but he managed to come to my office for a spinal checkup about twice a year to keep those nerve channels open. I learned to never say, "I can't help you." I felt very grateful that I was able to help this man when no one else had succeeded.

1955-1964

RUNNY EARS

"Good morning, Mrs. Martin; Hello Johnnie. What may I do for you today?" I asked. "Good morning, Dr. Miller. You've done so much for my husband's backaches, I thought you could help my little Johnnie with his stomach aches." "Of course, Mrs. Martin; come in here (the spinal adjusting room), and I'll check Johnnie's spine to see if he has any vertebrae that are out of alignment," I replied. I checked his spine and continued with Johnnie's history, learning that he had tubes in his ears due to exudate coming from them for the last three years. (He is only seven years old now). His ears smelled as though there was something rotten inside of them, and he was wiping them as we talked. "Johnnie," I asked, "Do your ears hurt?" He said, "They feel itchy all the time." I took some spinal X-Rays, adjusted the involved vertebrae, and asked Mrs. Martin to bring Johnnie to my office in a few days to see if the vertebrae needed to be adjusted again. Mrs. Martin brought Johnnie in for Chiropractic care every week for the next six weeks. After the second week he had no more stomach-aches, but Mrs. Martin continued to bring Johnnie in for his spinal check-ups because she said, "Dr. Miller, there is less "runny stuff" coming from Johnnies ears! That's amazing! They don't have that terrible smell anymore. I can't believe it! To think that I brought Johnnie here for his stomach aches and now his ears are being healed!" "I am so glad, Mrs. Martin! You see, when all of the nerves of the spine can function without any interference," I explained, "the body heals itself. His vertebrae are staying in place now, so bring him in four weeks from now for a check-up." After a couple more months there was no more discharge from Johnnies ears. Mrs. Martin and Johnnie we elated! Mrs. Martin said, "I am so glad that I don't need to put towels on Johnnies pillows at night to catch the discharge, because there is no more discharge." Johnnie added, "I'm sure glad they don't itch anymore." I wasn't sure if Johnnies ears would heal since they have had the discharge for at least three years, however it was proven to me again, and to the patients that once the nerves are free, they can function optimally. This is another reason why I love being a Doctor of Chiropractic.

AN UNUSUAL VACATION

WORLD'S FAIR!? I was excited! The 1958 World's Fair was to be held in Belgium. I was especially excited because I had been to the 1934 World's Fair in Chicago when I was ten. Uncle Bill lived in Chicago, so we stayed with him and the family. I don't remember much except that there were so many new inventions; everything was so big and beautiful and fantastic!

Bob's Dad had passed away the year before due to his heavy smoking and drinking. After Bob's Dad passed away, his rocker would rock and the lights would turn on and off by themselves. Those things made Bob's Mom nervous and I suggested to her, "It's probably Dad's spirit hanging around and doing what he always did when he was alive." I stayed with her at night until those strange happenings stopped. Bob and I thought it would be good for his Mom to go with us to the World's Fair. Bob said, "How about it? We'll fly over together, it'll do you good." She smiled and said, "That sounds good; I've never been to Europe, but I'll never fly." Bob countered, "It takes much longer by ocean liner and that would take away a lot of time from our vacation." Mom said, "I'll never go on one of those ocean liners either." After much coaxing, Mom decided to fly with us <u>and</u> come back alone on one of the largest ocean liners there was. How we did laugh!

Before we could take the trip, we were required to be vaccinated. Vaccinations! Mandatory! My family will NOT be vaccinated! We explained the dangers to Mom. The ingredients of vaccinations are supposed to trigger the immune system of our bodies to develop adaptive immunity to a pathogen. Vaccinations introduce a foreign substance into the body. When a person is healthy, their own immune system will kill the bacteria and viruses, therefore a vaccine is not needed. I prefer to put only healthy substances into my body. Mom agreed and said, "I won't be vaccinated either." I obtained the necessary papers from the local health board; the papers give you a choice for not wanting to be vaccinated: "allergic reactions" or "religious reasons". One day, Mom came to my house with a frantic look on her face. Her arm was huge, red streaks going up and down the arm, and so painful that she could hardly bear it! I told her, "Call your doctor and explain it all, and he will know what you need to do." "Why?" I asked, "did you go ahead and get vaccinated? You had agreed that it would be best not to!" "Well," she responded, "I was telling my friends at the Garden Club that I go to, about my trip, and they were scared for me and convinced me to get the vaccinations." Apparently Mom was allergic to the vaccine. The doctor gave her a counter-active shot, and told her to keep her arm above her heart, using ice packs day and night; this went on for over a week. Mom recovered in time for us to leave on the plane to the World's Fair!

After enjoying the fantastic World's Fair (which held so many experiences and memories too numerous to write about at this time), we accepted my high school Pen Pal, Piet's invitation to visit them in Holland. Piet and his wife, Meena were so excited that we were coming! (He had visited us a few years prior.) They had a boy and a girl near the same ages as our children who got along very well playing ball and hide and seek in their yard. Meena spoke no English, so there was a lot of translating from her husband. She gave me a pan of cream and sugar to whip and I said, "Piet, this cream will not thicken." "That's yogurt that Meena made," replied Piet, "to put on our wild strawberries. She just wanted you to mix the yogurt and sugar to sweeten it up." I was so embarrassed, but then we all laughed and laughed.

Bob had rented a car as soon as we arrived in Europe. Piet asked Bob, "How much are you paying to rent that little car?" After Bob told him, Piet was upset and talked to the rental agency; the outcome was for Bob to pay nearly half as much. We were so grateful! We had so much fun with Piet as he took us to local places for excellent food and singing. Piet was a high school professor and school was still in session, so he couldn't join us, but told us about certain places to stop as we drove on to Germany.

On the way we met one of my patients, who was visiting her husband, who was stationed in Germany. She was telling us about all the other places that we could visit while in Germany, such as Heidelberg. I respected this woman and her opinions and knew that I could trust her, so I asked her, "Would you like to go with us down through Italy and up into France before you go back to the States?" She excitedly said, "Oh, would I? I'll pack my bag right away!" In that little car we had my Mother-in-law, our son, our daughter, my husband and me, and our luggage for a six-week vacation, AND now Sylvia. Six of us in that little car! We were packed in like sardines in a can, but no one complained. Sylvia was a wonderful traveler with a great sense of humor, and told us what roads to take to see more of the countryside, and what else to see. Sylvia said, "If we want to eat lunch, we better eat before one, or we won't be eating until after three in the afternoon; everyone stops for a siesta. The food was delicious whether we ate on the roadside or in a restaurant. In a restaurant one evening my daughter was ready to bite into a fresh peach, when a waiter said, "Here, my little one, this is how to eat a peach," and proceeded to show her how to peel a peach with a knife and fork, and then eat it with a knife and fork. We learned that in those days, in any restaurant in Germany, you don't pick up food with your hands. I thought that's a much neater way to eat, so I began eating with a knife and fork also. LOL! I concluded that fun is what you make with everyone being positive and helpful.

The trees were so tall and so thick in the Black Forest that we couldn't see the sky on a bright, sunny day; it was rather spooky! Otherwise the green pine trees were so beautiful! Just ahead, in the middle of this huge forest was a brown building, with ornate carvings around the window that framed a magnificent cuckoo clock. It looked like it had been there for over 100 years! "Oh look," I called out, "Cuckoo clocks! We love them; let's stop." Inside were hundreds of magnificent cuckoo clocks of all sizes, and Bob fell in love with five of them. "No problem", said The Proprietor, "We'll pack all of them and ship them right to your home; guaranteed in perfect condition when they arrive."

Our daughter, Debbie, was falling in love with a cute, curly black-haired doll dressed in typical ethnic clothes. It was rather expensive, but I thought where would she ever see a doll that she loved that much! Of course our son was walking all around the store trying to decide what he wanted. So many choices! He finally walked around the corner wearing a green velvet hat with a red and green feather in the headband! I said, "You look so cute and handsome!" The kids were so happy to take their treasures home!

We were getting hungry, so Bob asked The Proprietor and his wife, "Are there any restaurants anywhere nearby, and a hotel?" These people had figured that we would soon be hungry. "Come into our dining room," invited The Proprietor. There, on the dining table, was a roast chicken with all the trimmings and an apple pie with cheese! The husband and wife were pleased to hear us giving "Thanks for our food". The food was so delicious and I was so full. Afterward, his wife said, "Upstairs are your bedrooms, ready for a good night's sleep; if you need anything, just ring the bell on your nightstand." How wonderful! We didn't even need to look for a hotel! In the morning I could smell breakfast as I came down the stairs, eggs, potatoes, bacon, sausage, toast made from her freshly baked bread, freshly churned butter, hot cinnamon rolls fresh from the oven, wild strawberries and strawberry jam; mmm! Oh yes, milk, hot chocolate, coffee and tea were included. I was so full that I thought that I wouldn't want to eat lunch that day. What wonderful hospitality!

Hummel Figurines seemed to be in every store in Heidelberg. My mother-in-law (Mom) was so struck with their beauty, she got me all excited, and needless to say I went home with quite a few of them; my favorite was the large Umbrella Boy! As we drove up to the Heidelberg Castle, our son asked, "Is that really a castle? Who lives there?" (He was eight years old). I said, "No one lives there anymore." We joined a tour group and learned that the castle was built in 1214. I was intrigued by the fact that only kings, emperors and popes had ever lived there. A 30-year war, a 9-year war and other battles had damaged some areas of the castle. In 1764 lightning set the castle on fire destroying much of the 500 year-old-castle, and it became a tourist attraction. In 1815 Johann Goethe gave his lady friend two leaves from the Ginkgo Biloba tree that was growing in the castle grounds.

Hmmm, to think that I take Ginkgo Biloba for my health; apparently Ginkgo was considered valuable way back then! My interest in Germany is probably due to the fact that my ancestors came from Germany. Seeing the snow glistening on the trees, and the ground covered with almost knee-deep snow as we drove up the Swiss Alps, I expected it to be cold. As we got out of the car and I took off my coat, I said, "It's warm! Feel how warm it is!" Robby picked up some snow and threw it at us, and then said to Debbie, "Bet you can't hit me!" The children had so much fun throwing snowballs at each other, and us, on the 4th of July in the Swiss Alps; something they will always remember, as do I!

We drove on to Rome, Italy and to the Colosseum. The Colosseum was immense; why can't we build something like that here in America? The Trevi Fountain! I marveled at how many pennies were in it. I talked to people who were standing nearby and I learned that all those pennies were gathered weekly to support food programs. St. Peter's Square was huge; beautiful buildings with so many ornate decorative designs; so many pigeons having a "hay-day" eating all the morsels of food tossed out to them. It's a good thing that I'm not afraid of birds flying so close to me!

Before going into the Vatican we were told by The Guard at the door to cover our shoulders. Sylvia, luckily, found a small shawl in her bag to cover her bare arms. I was glad that my blouse had sleeves. I looked for seats and said to Bob, "I wonder where we sit." Then I realized that we were standing shoulder to shoulder! Luckily we were being pushed closer to the Pope so that we could almost touch him, and received his blessings --- quite an experience! We saw the beautiful Michelangelo's painting in the Sistine Chapel. Wow! I could have looked at the beauty of it for hours!

It was a beautiful drive thru the countryside from Rome to beautiful, unusual Venice! The Artists' World! There is nothing like it anywhere in the world that I know of. Bob's Mom said, "I'll stay with the children, and you two go out and see the sights tonight." We looked at each other and Bob said, "But we would like for you to see the sights at night also; we didn't bring you along as a babysitter." "I know", she said, "but you go ahead and enjoy the evening." Bob and I had a romantic full moon

Gondola ride on one of the canals, with a tall, handsome Gondolier singing love songs to us, and Bob telling me how much he loves me; I felt as though I could be in Heaven. The houses had beautiful scenes painted on them, so it was like we were going through an art gallery all the time. The next day we shopped the stores and I bought a beautiful Venetian green glass vase, a shell colored beautifully embroidered tablecloth and napkins to fit my large dining table. I really liked some of the paintings but didn't know where I would hang them. I'm laughing now because wouldn't it be fun to have a Venice, Italy painting hanging in my Venice, Florida home right now?

As we were driving from Venice across Italy to the Italian Riviera, Stella suddenly realized that it was time for her to meet up with her husband in Germany. It was a sad "Goodbye" because she was such a joyous and helpful companion. I was a bit disappointed when we arrived at the Italian Riviera because the beach was mostly stony, not much sand.

Ahhh! The French Riviera; so beautiful with the clear blue-aqua water! "We didn't pack any bathing suits," I said to Bob. "Well, I need a new one anyway, so we'll find a store close to the beach", replied Bob. Soon the kids were in their new suits and were waiting with their Dad. I came out side the store and said, "I can't find any one-piece suits; I don't want people looking at me in a two-piece suit!" Bob laughed and said, "If you wear a one-piece suit here, you WILL have people looking at you! Look out there on the beach; do you see any one-piece suits there?" OK, I finally decided on a cute yellow and white checked two-piece suit that Bob just loved. I felt very uncomfortable in that two-piece suit, but I soon became accustomed to it because all the other women wore two-piece suits that were hardly on them--Ha! Ha! Ha! I enjoyed the fun of body surfing with our children and/or jumping the waves off the coast of France; an experience I shall always remember. "How do we dry these suits?" I was wondering. Bob's Mom to the rescue! She had brought clothespins and a clothesline upon which clothes were already drying. How did she know to bring a clothesline and clothespins? She's always thinking ahead. After we were home in the U.S.A. and I told my friends that I have a two-piece bathing suit; they laughed and said, "We can't wait to see you model it!"

No one in the States had a two-piece at that time. It was two years later that I had the courage to wear that suit again.

Over all, our trip took us to many interesting places, such as:

- The Eiffel Tower, which was built in 1889 and named after the architect and builder, Alexander Eiffel; the Eiffel Tower was the entrance arch to the 1889 World's Fair. I didn't expect it to be so tall as I looked up at it.
- The Arc de Treomphe was built in 1806 to honor the dead who fought for their country.
- The Tomb of The Unknown Soldier is beneath the Arc.
- The Louvre became a Museum of At in 1793 of famous artists, housing such famous artworks as the Venus de Milo, the Mona Lisa and many other famous painting of famous artists.
- Notre Dame was still being repaired from damage during World War II.

Restaurants are everywhere and the food was delicious! Desserts? Not so much, the same as in London, the desserts were quite dry and tasteless, which was probably a good thing for all of us, especially me, since I had been enjoying so much delicious food ever since leaving the States.

Our flight back to America from Paris was uneventful. All the way home I was thinking about the wonderful vacation I had with everyone on our trip, and how happy we all were!

On the appointed day my husband met his Mom in New York as she disembarked from a Queen Ocean Liner. She said, "I was thinking out there on the sea; I am so glad that I chose to travel by plane <u>and</u> by ocean liner, because I will never have another chance like this; I loved all of it!" We had another good laugh about her choices.

Yes, we all had a wonderful vacation! No matter how perfect a plan seems to be, I noticed that throughout the entire trip changes had to be made for accommodating others, as well as for our own peace of mind and happiness. When my high school Holland Pen-Pal and I were exchanging letters, I was helping him to learn and better understand our language. At that time I didn't have the faintest idea that I, with my family would ever be visiting him and his family in Holland. That was the first time that I had the experience of trying to communicate with a foreigner who didn't speak my language (Piet's wife); it was a bit frustrating. This experience was valuable to me as we traveled through other countries and met people who didn't speak English. This trip has taught me a lot about people of different nationalities; their way of life can be very different from ours, and still be good. No matter the choices that we make to our destinations in life, it is all in Divine Order; I realize that when following Divine Order, every one wins. This was shown to all of us as we each had a beautiful vacation of fun; friends and family bonds were deepened.

NINE MONTHS LATER

Bob, Bob's Mother, and I were talking. I said, "Wouldn't it be nice if this baby is born on the tenth, the same as our other two children?" Bob's Mother said, "Maybe it will be born on my birthday, the twelfth, I'd like that!" On the way to the hospital, Spirit whispered to me, "Theresa Marie". We had not really chosen a name yet; Bob said, "Yes, I rather like that name, how about you?" I loved that name. Theresa Marie chose to be born on a bright, sunny day --- Friday the 13th! That was the very day that SHE wanted to come into this world! She's been an independent personality ever since! Her independent nature has been an advantage throughout her life. Babies intuitively know when it is their correct time to enter into this world. I was so happy to have a healthy, beautiful baby girl!

ALTERNATIVE MEDICINE

Portia, a girl of about ten years old, who lived on the block behind our house called through the screen door one day, "Can I take Theresa (who was about six years old at the time) for a ride on my bike?" "Sure, Portia, come on in," I invited. Riding the bike was so much fun for both of them. After awhile, I heard Theresa screaming as Portia carried her into the house. "Portia! What happened?" I asked, as I took Theresa into my arms. Portia was so scared and upset that she could hardly tell me what happened, "I think her foot got caught in the spokes of the bike wheel!" I saw that a couple of inches of flesh were torn off the side of her foot. "Don't worry, Portia, she'll be O.K." I quickly told my secretary, "Reschedule my patients; we're on our way to Canada." I said a prayer as I drove across the border to Canada to my Naturopathic Physician, who I knew would use natural medications to treat my daughter. He applied Natural Antibiotic Lotion on Theresa's foot that also helped to take away most of the pain, then an aloe-based crème to help promote healing. Theresa had been crying with pain; now she was mostly relaxed and calm. Then the doctor placed a plastic cover over the injury to prevent anything from touching it. The doctor gave me instructions on care of the foot, and to keep Theresa from running and jumping around, which could re-open or irritate the wound, and to return in a few days. Portia heard my car drive up the driveway and was waiting in our sunroom to find out how Theresa was; she was very upset that she had hurt her little friend. I assured her that, "accidents happen and not to worry; she just can't run around and play for a while; she'll be all right." Theresa was only about six years old, so you know how active children are at that age, and how difficult it is to keep them from running around. When I took Theresa to the doctor for a checkup a few days later, the doctor was surprised at how much the foot had healed already. I have learned that natural methods of healing usually are the best. This experience has made me realize how important a home office is, especially when raising a family; emergencies can be taken care of immediately.

REAR-ENDED!

In the early days of my Practice an acquaintance named Sue came rushing into my office in a panic holding an ice pack on her neck. "What happened, Sue?" I asked. "I was on my way to the grocery store," she explained, "when this car didn't even slow down and plowed right into the back of my car. My head went back and forward with my glasses flying off into the back seat. My neck is killing me!" I could tell that she had been crying. I took x-rays of her neck and analyzed them right then and there. "Sue, lie down on this adjusting table and I will adjust those vertebra back in place before the nerves and muscles have much chance to do more damage!" Afterward I had her lie down on the couch in the adjoining room to let those muscles relax before she drove back home. Two days later she returned for another session and said, "Oh, I'm so glad that I came to you right away; I'm feeling so much better already." It is so important to have the misaligned vertebrae adjusted back into their proper position as soon as a trauma happens. Sue could have ended up having severe headaches and stomach problems later on and not even realize that they were caused from the misaligned vertebrae due to the accident.

EDGAR CAYCE AND THE "I AM"

After I became friends with a little lady in our church named Isabel, she invited me to her house for lunch. "Have you ever heard of Edgar Cayce?" she asked. "He's the man who would lie down, go into a sleep-type condition and tell people what to do to help themselves get well." This really fascinated me, so she gave me a book called, "There Is A River" by Thomas Sugrue, mostly about Edgar Cayce. That was the beginning of my interest in Metaphysical Studies. This interesting lady was a Spiritual Medium and gave me a message from Spirit about when I was a teenager, and in the near future as she saw it happening. I was amazed at how accurate she was about the past in this lifetime; things she couldn't have known about me! As time went on, things that she had predicted did come true, such as having three children and my holding office in three different organizations.

During another one of my visits to her home, Isabel explained the "I AM" teaching (not a religion). I decided to investigate this unusual teaching and as soon as I walked into the I AM Temple I knew that this is something special. The atmosphere was so light and uplifting; I felt so good and decided to attend every week. My husband noticed the positive change in my personality and was so impressed that he decided to join me. We were given positive affirmations from St. Germain's "I AM Decrees of Violet Consuming Flame and Healing" booklet to repeat every day, ie: "I AM the Perfect Intelligent Activity of this body," and many others. After saying many I AM decrees on positive affirmations, I noticed that my husband's business was more successful and so was my Practice. We both had changed our attitude about everything in a much more positive manner of living. These positive affirmations brought back the remembrance of what I had learned a few years ago and forgotten about, from Norman Vincent Peale's book, "Positive Thinking". I previously had read W. Clement Stone's book, "The Other Side of The Mountain", Napoleon Hill's book, "Think And Grow Rich", and attended their lectures, as well as Og Mandino's lecture on "Success". I've come to realize how important it is to continue to educate myself, and to review the important things and use them in my life, and to believe in myself.

EMERGENCY AT MARTZ'S FAMILY REUNION

Our dear friends, the Martz family, invited us to join their family reunion at a large park. The boys were playing baseball when suddenly I heard a scream and shouting! "Robby's down! He's not moving! Come!" I felt like I was flying down that hill to get to my son's motionless body lying on the ground! I asked, "What happened?" but everyone was talking at once. My dearest friend, Marie was now kneeling beside me praying, and other joined in. Someone backed a truck up to us and two guys lifted my son's motionless body onto it and away I went with them to the hospital. On the way to the hospital the driver told me that, "Robby was running to catch the baseball when he ran into a metal pole, possibly a flagpole". At the hospital I paced the hallway until I was told that Robby had a concussion and was in a coma; his blood pressure was fluctuating and needed close monitoring. Of course I stayed overnight with Robby in the hospital; unable to sleep, so very worried. In the early morning he regained consciousness. The doctor wanted Robby to stay for a couple more days, but I convinced him that I would keep my son quiet for a few days to a week at home, which isn't easy for a teenager. One of the first things I did upon returning home was to X-Ray Robby's cervical spine. With a fall so severe that he was unconscious, I felt that some of his vertebrae had probably been jarred out of their normal position. The X-Rays showed that several vertebrae needed to be adjusted so that he would have normal nerve supply, especially to the head. After I explained to Robby what the X-Rays showed about his neck and skull, he decided that it was very important to follow doctor's orders. I adjusted his spine, fed him good wholesome food and his recovery was quite fast. Everyday I am thankful for all of my wonderful friends and even those who I didn't really know, who helped when needed; and that I am a Chiropractor and knew what needed to be done.

1965-1979

40 LB. WATERMELONS

My Dad, (Robby's Grandpa Dettmer) called on the phone, "I'm coming up to Michigan with those big black diamond watermelons, and we'll celebrate Robby's birthday with mine". He would sell watermelons to gas stations and small grocery stores on the way from Texas to Michigan to help pay for his trip. Those watermelons were so large that they would not fit into anyone's refrigerator; some weighed up to 40 lbs. In those days you could not buy a quarter or a half of a melon in the stores, only a whole melon and of course a 40 lb. watermelon could not fit! People along his route looked forward to his annual trip and called each other, "Hey, here comes that guy with those mouth-watering green striped watermelons! Hurry UP!" Then they would divide one melon amongst three neighbors, or buy more than one and have a neighborhood picnic, saying, "They're the best ever!" I realized how much fun my Dad had selling those huge melons! We could not wait to sink our teeth into those juicy, sweet red melons! I always looked forward to my Dad's visit because he has such a positive attitude, and I always made sure that I have a birthday cake for him.

A BABY PATIENT, AND A FALL

"Dr. Miller, I've never been to you, but my neighbor thinks that you can help my baby," offered Mrs. Jones. "What seems to be the matter?" I asked. "I've had to give Billy an enema every day since he was born and he's ten days old today, and I know that is not normal. My neighbor said that maybe there is something wrong with his spine; I don't see anything wrong, but she says I should bring him over (to you)." Upon examining Billy, I said, "Your neighbor is absolutely right; I believe that I have found the problem right here in his back." "Why? What's wrong?" the concerned Mother asked. "Right here," I showed her, "is a vertebra that is not in proper alignment and needs to be adjusted back into its proper position." She asked, "Will it hurt him?" I responded, "Not at all; it's a very gentle movement." I showed her how to hold him so that I could give a very tiny adjustment of that vertebra so that complete nerve flow into the intestines could be accomplished. The baby actually smiled at me. "Now, Mrs. Jones, be prepared for a full diaper by the time you get home. Please call me afterward, Ok?" After a couple hours the phone rang and it was Mrs. Jones, "Dr. Miller! Oh, my goodness! I don't know where all that stuff came from; about the time I thought he was through and I had him all cleaned up, there was more; but he sure is clean now, and looks so happy. How can I ever thank you?" I just said, "Go thank your neighbor; what would you have done without her suggestion?" I added, "And bring your son in and your family in for regular spinal checkups."

Many of my patients came in for low back pain, and many with a diagnosis of arthritis of the hands and/or knees. What can chiropractic care do for low back pain and arthritis when it's so far from the head and neck? All of our nerves originate in the head; most of the nerves travel through the neck before they end up anywhere else. Any misalignment there can cause a malfunction along that nerve pathway which doesn't allow that part of the body to function at full capacity. When that misalignment is corrected, the body sends more blood supply and a better nerve supply to that area and better health is the result.

One day Mr. Thomas came in all bent over and said that his arm also felt very weak. He said, "When I jumped off my tractor yesterday morning I twisted to keep from landing on a tree limb. I felt a twinge but I didn't give it much thought at the time; today I can't straighten up and boy, does my back hurt!" I X-Rayed his spine and found the problem. Before adjusting his spine I applied an ice pack on his lower back and shoulders, then adjusted all of the vertebrae that needed realignment. He said, "Wow! My arm doesn't feel weak anymore!" He walked out of my office in much less pain and could stand almost straight. I told him to not work the remainder of the day and to return in two days. It took a few more sessions before Mr. Thomas was able to work again at his strenuous job. During one of those visits he said, “Dr. Miller, I’ve had high blood pressure for quite a few years; the other day when I saw my Cardiologist, he reduced my medication. Those adjustments sure do work!” He continued coming to my office for regular chiropractic care to maintain his health.

I had a “Chiropractor” sign in my window at my Home Office, but I realized that it’s just as important to talk to all of my neighbors and explain to them what Chiropractic is and how the adjustments of the spine are so beneficial to maintain good health.

WHERE IS OUR SON?

One morning it was very quiet in Rob’s room; had he gone to school early? If so, why? (He was a High School Senior.) He always ate breakfast, but there were no dirty dishes. As I opened the door to his room I noticed that the window was open, and his pillow was gone. I ran to the driveway, no car. He had been working on his ‘pride and joy’, and he got it running just the day before. I called his buddy’s Mother, “Did Rob go to school with your son this morning?” “No”, she said, “He told him he wouldn’t be in school and not to look for him after school”. Oh, my word! I called Bob, who was already at work, “Rob’s run away from home! But why?” Bob came home immediately saying, “No matter now, we must find him; but where would he go?” We called his Grandma Rose; we called his other buddies; nobody knew he was gone. His girlfriend called after school and asked, “Is Rob ill? I am worried; I didn’t see him in school.” We thought maybe she was acting innocent, “Did he talk to you about going anywhere?” She seemed sincere when she said, “No, this is all news to me. What can we do?” We kept asking others, and thinking maybe his best buddy was sworn to secrecy. Bob said, “You go ahead with your patients today and I’ll try to find him.” I had difficulty keeping my mind on my patients; I kept thinking of my son’s whereabouts. I thought maybe it was my fault that he left, but why?

That night I got out the oil paints that I had never used and decided to paint a picture of the “all seeing eye” and asked God to help us find Rob.

My intuition (which is God speaking to me) directed us to Norfolk, Virginia, where cousin Marvin is in the Navy. It took some persuading to convince the Naval Commander to let us talk to Marvin. Well, Marvin was sworn to secrecy, "I told Rob that I wouldn't tell anyone where he is, and if they guess that he's here, I won't tell just where." Finally the Naval Commander explained to Marvin that there are times that it is more important to the parents, and the child's welfare, to reveal a secret. Marvin caved and said, "Well, he has a job at a fast-food restaurant," and gave us the room address where he was living. Rob was not at either place; it was his day off at the restaurant. The Manager said, "I don't want to give you any information, how do I know that you are not violent parents?" Bob convinced him that we would not cause a disturbance, and then the Manager said, "He gets his hamburgers free, so he will probably come here around 5:00 or 6:00 for his dinner." We parked where he couldn't see us and waited. "Shhhhh, there he is ordering his hamburger; oh, he's ordering a milkshake too, and then I'll go up to him," Bob suggested. Bob went up to Rob and said, "Hi, I want to talk to you." Rob was surprised and shook his head, again Bob said, "I want to talk to you. Your Mother is in the car, come on to the car." Bob told the Manager the story and Rob verified it. The Manager said to my husband, Bob, "I really hate to see Bob (Rob) leave; he's a good worker and never swears, which is unusual for most kids who come here for a job." Looking at Rob, he said, "Your Dad knows what's best; go finish your education. I'll mail your check to you." There was very little communication on the way home; Bob did most of the talking. I was so angry with him that I hardly knew what to say. We did stop at a few places of interest to cut the tension. I didn't know that my son disliked school so much that he needed to run away from it. Earlier in high school I had taken him to a hypnotherapist to help him remember what he had studied and his grades had been improving. It was near the end of the school year and Rob could not catch up on his studies in time to graduate, so to Summer school he went and then Rob received his high school diploma. OH, happy day!

I thanked God that Rob had not joined the Navy, and I thanked God for leading us to him. I concluded that my son needed the experience of working for a stranger, and to hear what someone in business had to say about the necessity of education. Perhaps Rob also needed to feel how strong our love for him was by searching and finding him and bringing him home. I was happy to have him home again.

SUNSHINE AND A TEACHER'S DISMAY

Debbie and some of her friends were running across the street with the green light, on the way to school one bright sunny morning, when one of Debbie's friends knocked on my door and breathlessly said, "Mrs. Miller! Your daughter has been hit by a car, down by the Light!" I was shocked because Debbie is always careful about crossing streets. I wasn't even dressed yet, so when I arrived on the scene the ambulance had already left for the hospital. I was informed that a teacher, turning the corner had driven into my daughter and that, with tears in her eyes, she exclaimed, "The sun was in my eyes! I didn't see her!" Can you imagine how she must have felt; a teacher hitting one of her students? A witness offered, "Her head hit the bumper and I could hear it." After I arrived at the hospital I found Debbie on a bed in the hallway crying, waiting for care. "Hi honey, where were you hit?" I asked. "My head hurts so bad!" she sobbed while holding the back of her head. I asked a very busy nurse for an icepack. With my hand over the icepack directing God's energy into Debbie's head the pain let up. Finally an X-Ray was taken which showed a fracture near the base of the skull where the car bumper struck her head as she fell. "Thank goodness!" I exclaimed to my husband. "What do you mean, "Thank Goodness!" our daughter has a fractured skull, and you say, "Thank Goodness"? What do you mean?" "Well, I thought there might be a concussion," I explained, "but a fracture is actually better because the pressure from swelling is allowed to escape due to the split, therefore causing less pressure on the brain." With a sigh of relief, he said, "OH, Ok, I understand." Her right arm and leg were bruised also. I stayed with my daughter until she was dismissed from the hospital that day. I continued to enclose her with God's Healing Light while she was recovering. I felt that having a Home Office is a blessing, because I am so close in case of emergency.

IT ISN'T HYPNOSIS

My friend, Sara said, "I'd like for you to go with me to a Special Meeting that has something to do with your mind, and give your opinion". I was very skeptical, especially when it comes to my mind, because I want to keep control of what goes into my brain. Jack, the instructor had quite a sense of humor and put us all at ease right away and began to explain that no one is going to control anyone's mind in this class. "What we will learn to do," Jack explained, "is to control our own minds, by the power of concentration and our own self will." Well now, this sounds very interesting; my power of concentration isn't all that great some of the time. After looking at pictures of anatomy, and practicing concentrating on one thing, we took turns at scanning each other's arms and then told Jack what we saw, if anything; he would tell us if we were right. When I "saw" a screw in this guy's elbow, I thought I was imagining it, because I really wanted to see something physically abnormal. Ha, ha, it was abnormal all right! He said, "I had a fall about a year ago, and the screw is holding my elbow together." Then all the others took turns; some could see the screw and others could not. I was so impressed that I invited Jack to have dinner with us before the nightly session. Jack explained what else we would learn; Bob was so interested saying, "I'll join the class also." We met every week for six weeks, learning more and more about "seeing" what is inside of us. Those classes really helped me in my Practice. Some of my patients didn't write the whole truth on their History Records; now I was able to 'see' inside of them and I knew more about their bodies; thus I was able to give them better care. This experience has helped me to develop my clairvoyance and to give me the courage to trust this ability not only as I examined my patients, but also as I interacted socially with others.

VIRGINIA BEACH

For over eighteen years we vacationed at Virginia Beach during the last two weeks of August. There's a wealth of knowledge in the Association For Research And Enlightenment (A.R.E.) Library that is available to anyone who is interested in Edgar Cayce and what all he has done to help humanity. All of Edgar Cayce's Readings were documented (there were thousands), and commentaries were added. During many of those eighteen years some of our friends and their children joined us on the Golden Beach of the Atlantic Ocean, swimming and body surfing and just enjoying each other's friendship. (Actually, my youngest daughter, Terri (Theresa) learned to swim there.) Since I am fair-skinned and didn't want to get sunburned, I spent less time on the beach or in the ocean than anyone else. After lunch each day I would say, "You all go have fun on the beach! I'm going to Edgar Cayce's Library; see you later." After about an hour I joined the fun on the beach. One day I said to my friends and family, "I might be in the library for over an hour today." I had brought with me some notes of my patient's problems, other than spinal problems so that I could research Cayce's Readings and Commentaries for psoriasis and other skin conditions, intestinal bloating, unusual head pain, and other conditions. I feel the need to constantly educate myself so that I can give better care to my patients. In many cases Edgar Cayce would mention which vertebrae were misaligned. Suddenly I looked at my watch and I called out, "I've been here three hours!" Oooops! I'm supposed to be quiet in a library! I had been so fascinated with the Readings that time stood still! As I approached the beach, "Here she comes!" I heard someone call out. "We thought that you got stuck in all of those books and we'd have to come and pull you out," laughed our friend, Sam. Since I would be at Virginia Beach anyway I took advantage of what the A.R.E. Library had to offer, so that I could offer my patients more suggestions that could be beneficial for their health.

The next day as I looked out of the window of the hotel, I exclaimed, "Hey! There's Rob; he just now drove into the parking lot; and now he's limping, he can hardly walk! I wonder what happened!" He limped into my loving arms, and then sat on the bed explaining, "My friend and I were at the beach (in Michigan) walking across some shale when I slipped and some shale went in-between my toes. I thought I pulled it out." Rob continued, "At work my foot was hurting really bad, so I went to the Nurse there and she thought she had cleaned the rest of it out, but it really hurts, and is red and swollen; so I came here, Mom; I knew that you would know what to do." The only thing that came to mind was a Castor Oil pack. I sent the family out for the necessary products, then wrapped Rob's foot with the caster oil pack, tied a plastic bag on his foot to protect the bedding and said, "Now you can sleep; you've been up all night, driving 12 hours to get here. We're going to the beach. See you later!" Later in the day, the swelling had subsided as well as the pain. I thought it best that he not go to the beach, but he insisted, so off my happy son went to enjoy diving the waves of the ocean! Pain-free the next day he left to drive back to work in Michigan. A couple days later he phoned to say that his foot was all healed up.

Bob and I enjoyed our bike rides on the boardwalk with our friends, riding along the ocean and stopping for a nut topped vanilla ice-cream cone along the way. One day I stopped in to the Health Store that carried some of Edgar Cayce's health formulas and other items such as gems and stones. Suddenly my eyes were drawn to a group of quartz crystals; "Oh!" I thought, "The happy energy of that group crystal would certainly lighten up the energy in my office!" Each crystal point seemed to emit light. The more I looked at that crystal, the more excited I became. As I shopped around the store I was constantly drawn to that same crystal; finally I said to it, "You're coming home with me."

In reviewing my vacation time with family and friends; enjoying companionship with my family and friends playing in the ocean, as well as camaraderie with our friends while eating 'all-you-can-eat' shrimp, I am blessed. I realized how understanding all of them were about my sun sensitivity, and the fact that I need to constantly educate myself so that I can give better care to my patients. I feel that all of this resulted in a closer bond with one another.

The Association for Research and Enlightenment (A.R.E.) has a Camp for kids, in the mountains of Virginia, which is a very special place for friendship, companionship, learning to cook vegetables fresh from the earth, and learning how to meditate which could help to develop one's Psychic ability. One day the idea of a Camp came up in conversation with one of my patients who said, "That's a wonderful idea! I think my daughter would love it there!" My daughter and his daughter had psychic ability; they needed to be around more like-minded kids without their parents around. Off to the A.R.E. camp in the mountains they went by Bus, for ten days, neither one had been away from their parents for very long as young teenagers. Debbie and Linn came home laughing with many stories to tell.

After Debbie was home she said to me, "I'm going to show you how to bake bread, a special kind of whole grain bread." I had never baked bread, the closest I came to it was when I was a teenager in the 4H Club; I baked biscuits that turned out to be hard as a rock! So off Debbie and I went to the store to find preservative free ingredients. After we got home Debbie called, "Mom, come here in the kitchen to see how this is supposed to be done." She was very confident in teaching me just how and when all of the ingredients were to be mixed in. I was quite impressed. When the bread came out of the oven, I said, "Debbie, that looks wonderful and smells delicious!" As I was getting the bread knife out of the drawer, I was remembering when my Mother baked bread and we sliced it as soon as it came out of the oven, and ate it with the butter melting into it. Debbie explained, "Now we have to wait till the bread cools first before putting butter or anything else on it and eating it." Oh my, I wasn't ready for that as she explained, "If you eat the bread when it's still hot it won't digest properly; it just lays there in the stomach and might give you a tummy ache". To wait for the bread to cool took a lot of self-control on Debbie's part. Later, as I sank my teeth into her bread, I exclaimed, "This is delicious, Debbie!" My family and I enjoyed that delicious whole grain bread with our dinner, especially with all the love that Debbie had baked into it! I came to the conclusion that Children's Camps are a good way for them to learn things that the others are also experiencing, in different environments and situations. It gives them a sense of accomplishment and boosts their self-esteem, especially when they can show parents something that the parent knows nothing about. I feel that Debbie and I had a closer connection after that day of baking.

FIFTIETH WEDDING ANNIVERSARY

Not many couples live long enough, or stay together enough years to celebrate their 50th Wedding Anniversary. My parents, Arthur and Alice, along with the help of their daughter, Marjorie were going to celebrate their 50th in their church Social Hall. Their very best friends had been invited. We were all excited to go to Texas where it's warm in November! What to wear, what and how much to pack, and trying to keep the number of suitcases to a minimum, since we were flying, took a lot of planning. (Other years when we drove we could take everything that we wanted.) We arrived a few days early so that I could help with the arrangements, and I said, "What can I do to help?" but everything was under control. My sister's daughter, Johanna was a couple years younger than Debbie, and I thought that they and Terri would have a great time together.

Finally, The Day arrived and Mother was dressed prettier than I had ever seen her, in her silver and gold dress that fit her perfectly, the dress set off her beautiful blond hair; she looked like an angel. I said, "Mother, I like your dress, it's really pretty! Your hair is so pretty." She seemed to be so happy. My Dad looked really nice in his white shirt and gray suit. I turned to Dad and said, "You look super today!" A delicious lunch was served by the women of the Church's Ladies Aid Society; followed with cake and ice cream. Mother had fun opening the gifts; most of them were trimmed in gold. I went over to hear what Mother and Marjorie were laughing about; they didn't see me coming from behind them. Mother was saying, "Aileen really likes my dress." "Wouldn't she have a fit if she knew where your dress came from?" remarked Marjorie. I stopped short, feeling a chill. Marjorie went on, "Wonder what she would say if she knew that it came out of the alley." Mother said, "And all it took was a little adjusting at the waist; you saved me from going shopping and spending money on a dress that I might wear only once." I turned around and eased away, nearly crying, so they wouldn't know that I had heard their conversation. I was confused and shocked as to why they had those thoughts. Later that evening, when Dad and I were alone, Dad said, "I know you heard Mother and Marjorie talk about Mother's dress." "Yes," looking puzzled, I asked, "What was all that about?" Dad told me that the neighbor across the alley from Marjorie's apartment is always throwing things out in the alley; new towels, a new set of sheets and even clothes that still had the price tags on them. (I already knew that.) "So," Dad went on, "one day Marjorie found that dress in a box with the price tag still on it, brought it to Mother; well you know the rest." "But," I asked, "Why were they making fun of me? If it's new, and still in the box and clean, what difference?" "Well, they think that you wouldn't touch it with a ten foot pole, if it was in the alley," he offered. I wondered if Marjorie would ever tell me the truth.

A few years ago Marjorie showed me some towels that she had picked up in the alley behind her apartment. I said to her, "Why would you want anything from a dirty alley?" to which she replied, "The lady across the way throws out good things, mostly new, I pick them up, wash them and use them. Come on back there with me and I'll show you." When we went into the ally I was surprised and said, "This is the cleanest ally that I've ever seen; most of the alleys that I've seen up north are so dirty that you wouldn't want anything from them. What a difference!" Apparently Marjorie had nurtured the negative thoughts through the previous years that I had about alleys, therefore she didn't want me to know about Mother's dress. Anyway, her remark was so unexpected that it shocked me. That night I re-assessed the day and was pleasantly impressed that my Dad thought to explain to me the reason for Marjorie's remarks; and I remembered that she seemed to avoid talking to me. I feel that apparently Marjorie thought that I thought that I was too good to pick up anything from an alley, and I wondered if others have the same opinion of me. I decided to accept her attitude and not let it interfere with our relationship or my positive attitude. From then on I tried not to make any remarks about what she did or didn't do.

JAPAN

Bob's active membership in the Lion's Club, earned him the vote to be President. The Club supplies eye glasses to those in need and also trains Leader Dogs for the blind so they can be more independent. This year was also the 52nd anniversary of the International Lion's Club, to be held in Japan! Wow, we've wanted to see Japan for a long time! Bob's Motto is "Togetherness", and he held quite a successful fund-raiser to buy glasses for the children. Another "Togetherness" would be for the club to attend the 52nd anniversary of the International Lion's Club Convention to be held in Japan. WOW! We've always wanted to see Japan! Bob was so excited and said, "Shall we go?" I answered, "Yes! That would be so much fun!" Our members and their wives and members from other cities nearly filled the plane. I was served many different kinds of food, drinks and snacks. I tasted many kinds of seafood for the first time and prepared in many different ways; some delicious and some, well, not so much. When I was given a blue blanket, pillows and warm slippers for the overnight flight and then offered hot tea, I felt like Royalty. During the day everyone joined in with songs from all over the world; what fun! The Convention was a lot of fun as well as being quite educational while listening to many different speakers. Our secretary had many Lions Club pins from previous years for us to trade with other Clubs. It was exciting and fun to cover our yellow vests with pins from all over the world. During a special ceremony the International Lions Clubs presented a very tall Clock Tower to the people of Japan. The elevators in the hotel were so busy that we took the stairs from one floor to the next four hospitality rooms to meet our friends. My feet were so sore, wearing those high heels, that I soaked them every night; I didn't care, I was having so much fun talking with so many women from so many states and countries.

The Bullet Train from Tokyo to Kyoto was so modern and well organized, giving everyone only a minute to board; all automatic, going up to 100 miles an hour; that was pretty fast in 1969! What a thrill! Rachel and I were quite an attraction with our blond hair, and taller than most of the Japanese women. My Bob and friend, Marie went through exhibits and attractions pretty fast; Marie's husband, Emerson and I liked to study them and were together most of the time, which really confused some of our group. Who belongs to whom? There were elephant and dragon statues everywhere. Brilliant, floating Restaurants served fresh seafood day and night. The Gold Buddha, the Gold Temples and the Emerald Temple in Thailand are magnificent. There was so much more to see, but it was time to board the plane back home.

Traveling with so many different personalities, idiosyncrasies, time changes, and schedule changes really tested my patience at times and I learned to be more flexible. There was a lot of walking on the extra tours that we took; I noticed that some of the members had some difficulty keeping up, so I came to the conclusion that it's much better to travel while you're young enough to really enjoy the trip.

MY TWENTY-FIFTH WEDDING ANNIVERSARY

"Honey, what are we going to do on our Anniversary?" I asked Bob. No matter that you tell friends, "Please, no gifts!" they bring gifts anyway. The twenty-fifth is silver; I love silver, but not the polishing. Whenever I can use silver, I never think about it needing polishing until I want to use it, then it's too late to polish. I said "We know that our friends want to help us celebrate, and are probably expecting a party. What do we do?" Bob suggested, "Let's go to the Bahamas." I called our friend and neighbor, Marie, "Would you and the family like to go to the Bahamas with us, instead of having a party for our twenty fifth?" "Oh, that sounds like a wonderful idea! Yes! I'll tell Em, (her husband)." Then I called another close friend, Connie and her husband, Ken and invited them. They were delighted! At night the guys went to the casino while we gals entertained the kids. When the guys finally came back to the Hotel, Bob was all excited. "Guess what honey, look," as he tossed the money onto the bed, "I think I've won enough to pay for our entire trip! Em and I had so much fun with the other guys at the craps table"! The next day while shopping I saw this beautiful pendant in the jewelry store window; in we went and I came out with a beautiful gold Nefertiti pendant! I was so excited to have her! I had always admired her and Akhenaton for what they tried to promote, the teaching that there is only one God, and not to worship the statues. The next evening I went to the jewelry store and selected a blue sapphire ring for Bob's birthday, which is right after Christmas.

I seem to be a people pleaser but this time I decided to put my husband and me first, by doing what we really wanted to do for our Anniversary. This resulted in a fun time for us, our children and our very best friends, as well.

MY CHRISTMAS SURPRISE

Getting ready for Christmas was always fun celebrating together with the family. Presents were under the tree and I just had to see whose name was on that big box. To "Aileen from Bob", the tag said. I could hardly wait to open that box on Christmas Eve! When I did, I could hardly believe my eyes! A ¾ length gray/beige fur coat! I nearly fainted, I was so happy! I was always cold in the Michigan winters, and no wool coat ever kept me warm. That fur coat was so toasty warm I didn't mind going out in the freezing cold or snowy weather. I was elated! It was so beautiful that I wore it only to church and on Saturday night. Bob said, "Honey, I got you that coat to wear to keep you warm; yes, even wear it to the grocery store." I felt like I was a 'show-off' because in those days it was prestigious to wear fur, not like today, how you're looked down upon because of animal cruelty; but I soon became accustomed to wearing it everywhere. I understood that my husband's love for me was very strong.

MUSICALITY

All three of my children sang in the Church Junior Choir; I was so proud of them! Now they want to play a musical instrument, so I said, "Learn to play the piano first and get your basics; then if you still want to play something else I'll get it for you." Terri played the flute in the School Band and Debbie played the clarinet and the bass fiddle in the School Bands. I was so proud of them wanting to continue to enjoy their musical talents! My Mother and her Mother played the piano and my Father loved to dance, so I felt blessed that my children had rhythm in their bones and they were expressing it. Debbie formed her own Band in our basement playing the drums; others played other instruments and she had a singer. My patients loved hearing their music, except one Saturday a patient held her head as she walked in to be adjusted. I rushed to the basement door and flicked the light switch off and on. Debbie called up to me, "What Mom?" "My patient has a migraine," I called down, "please wait, and when she leaves I will flick the switch off and on again." "OK, Mom", she replied. That was the beginning of my "light switch" signal. By observing other families, I noticed that when music is incorporated within the family structure, there is more happiness and peace.

WISDOM TEETH

Debbie said, "Mother, my jaws hurt all the time", and that night she was crying from the pain. I took her to our Dentist, who said, "All of her wisdom teeth are coming in at the same time and there is not enough space in her jaws for them; they are crowding her other teeth." No wonder that her jaws ached! Solution? "Have them surgically removed; one at a time, or two on one side, or all four at the same time," our Dentist gave choices. "It's your mouth, Debbie, it's your decision; tell me soon, so I can make the appointment," I said. I felt that she didn't want to prolong the agony. After dinner she made the decision, "I think I'd rather have them all out at the same time. If I have them removed on the right side, I'll still have the pain on the left side, and then they'll have to come out anyway." "Debbie," I said, "I'll make you comfortable in our adjustable bed, with your head elevated with ice packs on both sides of your face." "Oh. I get to stay in your room?" she said with a big smile. "Yes and you can watch TV!" I added. Having a Home Office I could check on her in-between patients. When the icepacks were off her face I would place my hands on her face to direct healing energies into her jaws. The Dentist was surprised at how fast she healed. Debbie said, "I'm so glad that I made the decision to have them all removed at the same time! I wouldn't want to go through that again, even with your special hands, Mom." I let Debbie make the important decision about her teeth because I felt that it would help to build her self-confidence. I also realized again, the convenience of a Home Office.

4TH OF JULY SURPRISE

Picnic baskets and extra clothes were packed in the back of our Ford Station Wagon, ready for fun with our children Debbie and Terri (Theresa). Our friends, Em and Marie with their children Douglas, Pamela and Nancy would follow us in their station wagon. Rob and Sherry wanted to go with us, but she was due to have their baby anytime so they decided to stay home. On the way to the State Park we stopped at a gas station to call Rob to find out how Sherry was doing. Rob said, "Sherry's in labor in the hospital!" Now we were in a quandary; we were halfway to the Park; do we go back home or go on? Rob said, "You go on, have fun, you can't do anything here anyway." After eating our picnic lunch Bob called the hospital and Rob excitedly answered, "We have a baby girl!!! Sherry's OK! You can hardly see her hair, it's so light." Now we could stop worrying and enjoy the day. My 1st Grandchild, Candace was born on the 4th of July, and she is still a firecracker!

A few years later as I was taking care of a patient, my son called from the hospital and said, "You have a grandson now; we're naming him Robert Nathan. Sherry is doing fine."

DEBBIE'S WEDDING

Debbie had been talking about becoming a Chiropractic Assistant, when out of the blue she said, "I think I'd rather go to Beauty School." That was a surprise and I asked, "Why, what changed your mind?" She sort of shrugged her shoulders. She loved Beauty School and one of the first things she did after graduating, was to talk me into letting her cut my hair; I liked it and I haven't had long hair since.

Oh, Oh, just as I thought, Debbie's in love with that tall, dark, handsome guy who she's been dating, and now she's talking of getting married. Her God-Mother gave her a shower, and her sister and bribes-maids gave her a shower; she's floating on a cloud. The beautiful wedding was officiated by The Rev. Dr. B.H. Crewe. Debbie was a beautiful lady and an even more beautiful bride. What fun I had talking with everyone at the Reception!

I came to the conclusion that it was best to let my daughter choose her profession and love it, rather than to insist that she learn something else and perhaps not be happy. I miss my oldest daughter's happy Presence around the house, but where love abounds, everyone is happy

DEBBIE HAS A BABY

Bob and I had just returned from Florida when Debbie was on the phone the next morning, "I think my baby's coming, and Paul has gone to work; I can't get in touch with him!" I tried to be calm when I said, "OK, get your bag ready and I'll be over to take you to the hospital."(They lived across the street.) She insisted, "But I want Paul to take me!" I said, "We better go now, or you might have the baby in the car!" We raced up the highway with my horn blaring, ran red lights and then she was into a wheelchair and into a delivery room. Finally Paul arrived, smoking one cigarette after another because he was a very nervous Coach. Only The

Coach was allowed into the birthing room, so I couldn't be helpful. Finally around 6:00 P.M. (I think), an exhausted Debbie gave birth to my 3rd. grandchild, Eric Michael.

SURPRISE AT THE RACE TRACK

My birthday is coming up; what will the family think of doing this year? Bob had a grin on his face when he asked me, "How would you like going to the horse races this year, the ones with the jockey on the horse?" "Horse races?" I nearly jumped up and down because we had not been to the races in a long time. The most exciting time we had was a few years ago when our youngest daughter was too young to bet on the horses. Her Dad said, "Terri, I know that you are too young to place a bet, but look at the program and pick a name and tell me which one you would bet on." She said, "I don't know anything about race horses; how would I know?" He said, "Just tell me which one you would bet on. Hurry! Before they close the betting windows!" After looking at the program, suddenly she gave him a name and number "Four"; he and all the rest of the family and our friends excitedly ran to the windows to place their bets. The parade of horses with their jockeys came out onto the track. Just then someone yelled, "There he IS! Oh! No! His right front leg is all bandaged up." We were all laughing, and I said, "I wouldn't bet on that one." My daughter looked sad, but joined in our exuberance of urging her horse to win. "Come on! Come on! Come on!" we shouted, jumping up and down and swinging our arms. "Come on, come on Four! You can do it!" He was so far behind; the finish line was getting closer! Suddenly he came around the others and off he ran! "Come on, hurry up, come on, you can do it!" Oh, the horses are so close to the finish line! Will he make it? So close, so close! "YAY!" We all shouted! "Terri, your horse won the race!!! Whew! He was a long-shot and he won!!!" Terri was as excited as though she had actually placed the bet! I don't remember how much my husband won on that horse, but he paid the dinner check for everyone and had some money left over. I was as excited as everyone else was and we talked about Terri's horse all the way home.

A few days later, Bob came home from work and said to Terri, "Come on Terri, we are going shopping." As they drove down the driveway I called out, "Shopping? Shopping for what?" "Just you never mind, that's our secret, isn't it, Terri?" Bob answered. Terri just laughed as away they went. Dinner was almost ready when the two of them came laughing through the door. Terri held up her hand and said, "Look what Daddy bought for me," as she showed me a beautiful ring. Bob said, "I wanted to give her something really nice because she had picked the horse that gave everyone some extra cash; and if it hadn't been for her choice, your birthday party would have cost me a lot of money." I didn't quite understand until later when Bob said that Terri had told him a while back that she always wanted a ring; she had never said anything to me, or if she did, or even hinted, I wasn't listening. I was really happy about the outcome of the race; everyone with us profited as well as having fun. I learned that I should not only hear, but to actually listen to what my children are saying when they are talking to me.

CAMP SILVER BELLE AND VIRGINIA BEACH

"School is out; where shall we take the children this summer?" I asked Bob. For some reason we never thought of going north on our vacations, always south and gravitated towards the water, the beach in Virginia. We had extra time this summer, so we decided to stop in Pennsylvania and visit Camp Silver Belle, a Spiritualist Hotel, and learn more about communication with the so-called dead. (The story about Camp Silver Belle is one that you can research on your own). I could feel the Spirits there as we walked through the Hotel, and were told about all the classes and Mediums giving Readings. Bob and I had 'Readings' from well-known Mediums of that time: Rev. Riley, son of Ethel Post Parrish, a lady who I don't recall her name, and Rev. F. Reed Brown. They all gave me some amazing information, including names of deceased relatives, past things that they could not have known, and future that did come true. My daughter, Debbie was quite psychic, so she would know if they were fakes.

We stopped in Maryland and I ate the most delicious She-Crab soup; I'd never eaten anything like it. As we crossed the Chesapeake Bay Bridge we saw some sharks through the clear, clear water; what a treat for the kids as well as us, since we had never seen sharks before this! Virginia Beach!

Aaahhh! The ocean! Not many people know about the gold in the sand there, which I learned from reading books in the Association For Research And Enlightenment Library. My son loved to surfboard there with two of his friends, who usually came to vacation at Virginia Beach at the same time as we did.

It was a blessing to me that we had spent time at Camp Silver Belle; I believe that my awareness increased as I focused in. Due to that increased awareness I spent less time analyzing my patient's X-Rays. I think that it's just as important to take time to explore interesting places on the way to your destination as the destination itself; I believe that it broadens ones perspective of the world.

ACUPUNCTURE

I'm always going to classes and seminars, educating myself about helping people. Acupuncture is becoming more popular, and is a way of balancing the autonomic nervous system along with chiropractic adjustments, especially if there has been surgery to cut out an organ. I've studied needle acupuncture under Acupuncture Masters from Japan and China for the last few years, and a well-known Master Acupuncturist taught us the Ryodoraku Method. I really like this method because there are no needles involved. This method locates the precise acupuncture point with a probe. Another probe gives the treatment according to the prior test of basic points. According to the law, at that time, chiropractors were not to pierce the skin, therefore, this is a safe method of acupuncture treatment. I obtained excellent results in conjunction with chiropractic adjustments; very exciting! I learned that acupuncture is a good adjunct to any healing method.

EXCELLENT MEDIUMSHIP

Rev. Warren Smith of Pennsylvania came to Michigan to talk to our church congregation and to give "Readings" in the evening. The women prepared a delicious dinner for anyone who attended the evening service. He did 'Blind-fold Billet Reading". When he came to me he said, "Say, "It's a beautiful Day", and then he gave me some information concerning my question. He called my Spirit Guide and my Indian Guide by name and said, "They are here with you". Everyone has an Indian Guide, and many others who help to guide us on our earthly journey. If the information would be of a personal nature, he would ask the person to see him after the service. Rev. Smith was amazing!

Jacqui was local and gave excellent readings also. Whenever it rained, the roof leaked over the table where we sat, so we always took something that we thought that she would need. She told me, "You should slow down a bit." She taught a class in how to see Auras and to interpret them. I learned so much from her! As the year progressed I felt very tired all the time; I agreed with Jacqui, I was fitting too much into my daily schedule. Finally I decided to make an appointment with Rev. Virginia Leach Falls in Indiana to find out what she could pick up about my health. (I'd had Readings from her in the years past and she was very accurate, so I trusted her.) Rev. Falls came right to the point. She said, "There is something with your blood: I feel that it is not right. Go to your doctor and ask for some blood tests." (Mediums are not supposed to give medical diagnosis, but she came as close to it as she was allowed to.) I made an appointment the very next day for blood tests. My blood tests showed that I was hypoglycemic and have a hypothyroid. The recommendation was for me to go on a hypoglycemic diet plan, take thyroid medication, close my office and rest until my system was regulated, or at least not take any new patients. I chose not to take any new patients, but that did not work. How can I refuse to accept a relative of one of my patients or a close friend?

I was becoming more and more exhausted, so late in September I decided to take time off and stay with my parents in Florida. I didn't want to leave my patients without Chiropractic care and even though my husband (also a Chiropractor) had not Practiced for a few years, I asked him to fill in for me for a couple of weeks, which he gladly did. All I wanted to do was sleep, and sleep I did; after breakfast, after lunch and ready to sleep after dinner. I didn't even help Mother prepare the meals. No, I was not depressed, just tired. A beautiful Mockingbird sat in the crabapple tree outside of my bedroom window and I looked forward to hearing his lovely melody every afternoon while I napped. Weeks went by. Bob flew down to visit me/us for my birthday in October, and we had a wonderful visit enjoying my Mother's cooking and humor. A few weeks later he called and said, "When are you coming home?" I didn't really have an answer, so off the top of my head I said, "When you get another phone line in the house; the kids need to be able to use the phone in the evenings." (I thought it might take a week or so to get the phone line in.) Three days later Bob called and said," The phone line is in; are you coming home?" I told him that I was still weak and so tired, but would let him know soon. I felt my Master Healer working on me every day and I began walking around the yard and feeling stronger and getting lots of sun without my heart pounding, and also helping around the house. Mother was so wonderful in helping me regain my health. Mother was going to have a big turkey with all the trimmings, but I thought it best to be home for Thanksgiving with my family. It was a sad "Goodbye" to my Mother; she enjoyed having me there. It was a happy "Hello" to my family, and good to be home.

I am so fortunate to be able to trust the advice of some excellent Mediums; otherwise I might have waited too long to get help. Upon reflecting how much my Mother enjoyed having me in her home and preparing my meals, I realized that not all daughters have a thoughtful and loving Mother. I am so grateful. I also realized how much I had missed my family while regaining my health. After returning home I noticed how much I missed that beautiful mocking bird's sweet, calming melody.

HELPING A FELLOW COLLEAGUE

"Hello, Dr. Brown, it's good to hear your voice!" as I answered the phone. "Hello, Dr. Miller, I've called to ask a favor of you. Due to my motorcycle accident I have two fractured legs. I don't really want to close my office, so would you take care of my patients two days a week for a few weeks?" This request took me by surprise, but after a minute I said, "I'll be glad to help you out, Dr. Brown; what days would you like for me to take?" Dr. Brown sounded very happy, and after a bit of discussion he said, "Great! I'll call Dr. Frazer to help two other days". Those were fun days since his patients were very cooperative. A few patients wanted to transfer to me, so

I explained to them that it was unethical for me to take his patients; that I was doing him a favor by continuing their care while he was incapacitated, and for them to continue with him when he is able to be back in his office.

I learned that taking care of a colleague's patients without prior knowledge can be fun, yet rather a stressful experience due to a different office flow, and his handwritten notes were difficult to read. I gained a better understanding of the various situations that a temporary doctor has to contend with. I had had many previous conversations with Dr. Brown, therefore he could trust that my conduct would be ethical and that I would be true to his expectations.

MEXICO, LAS VEGAS, PHOENIX, DALLAS

A spiritual message came through Rev. F. Reed Brown who said that my Mother-in-law, Rose would be all right, because we were concerned about the cancer on her nose. I went with her and learned so much about different cancers at the Mexico Cancer Clinic, as other patients shared their cancer stories. A woman had cancer of the lung, which is considered to be fatal, but if she followed the special regimen she would be nearly pain-free without strong pain pills and have a longer life. My Mother-in-law had a tiny amount of skin removed from her nose and a specialized treatment on the nose, which killed the remaining cancer cells. My being with her gave her a sense of security that she needed, especially in a foreign country. We had a really good time together; she has a remarkable sense of humor when she's not all stressed out.

Rose had never been to Las Vegas so we stopped there on our way home. Neither of us was very interested in gambling; we just played the slot machines in a few of the Casinos. We walked up and down the streets, ate in beautiful restaurants, and walked in and out of those beautiful Casinos until our legs could hardly hold us up; it was amazing how much energy Rose had after having been in the Cancer Clinic for treatment!

Phoenix was a bit cooler than Las Vegas. Long time friends there were so happy to see us and prepared a delicious turkey dinner ending with wild strawberry shortcake. Next day we visited my doctor friend's Alternative Medicine Clinic where he had been researching the castor-oil packs that Edgar Cayce recommended for so many ill people and had remarkable results. I had learned about the packs while attending classes in Virginia Beach, and had been using them for a few years and recommending them to many of my friends and patients. One of my patients had a tumor surgically removed from in-between his toes which had healed, but every time he ran on the track at the high school, that area hurt so much that he could hardly walk afterward. I taught him how to apply the castor oil packs and to repeat the procedure five times. After a couple weeks, he was able to run pain-free.

Our next stop was Dallas to visit my sister, Marjorie; she worked as a Registered Nurse in the Premature Baby Department in a Hospital and practically ran that department as she was a perfectionist and probably drove the other nurses half out of their wits. Marjorie worked till 11:15 P.M. so I prepared dinner for her. One night I just happened to be on the landing as she was coming up the stairs to the second floor. I nearly cried as I saw her pulling herself up the stairs by the banister. She was so tired that her legs couldn't lift her feet up each step after riding the streetcar and then walk 1 1/2 blocks home. She claimed that she couldn't afford a taxi. Later I learned that she was helping another person financially.

I realized how hard my sister worked and did without necessities in order to help someone else. No matter who I see or where I go, I always learn something new about health, or living conditions in other countries, and even about family, which keeps me humble.

DAD'S GED CERTIFICATE

My Dad was a very social person, belonging to three Veteran's organizations, a member of the Men's Club at church, had taken Creative Writing classes at the high school, had written quite a nice story about horse farms in Florida in the local magazine, and would come home very enthused about the day's happenings. Mother didn't seem to enjoy his enthusiasm by making any complimentary remarks. Mother, on the other hand was very much a homebody ever since moving from Texas to Florida. She had joined the Ladies Aid Society at church but didn't quite fit in. She told me, "They talk about their new dress, or car, or gossip about their husbands or someone else's husband or wife, or surgical operations they've had or will have soon; nothing of any real significance to others, like how to crochet fancy patterns, or how to refinish an old chair, or how to grow bigger potatoes, or make apple pie more tasty." So, she said, "I quit going. I have more important things to think about." Both Mother and Dad realized that education was very important, and helped make it possible for my sister to become a Registered Nurse, and that I became a Doctor of Chiropractic. Dad proudly showed me his GED Certificate, obtained at the age of 82! Dad said, "I've always wanted to be able to say that I at least graduated from the eighth grade, and now I have!" "That's wonderful, Pop, I'm proud of you!" as I gave him a big hug! Mother just looked at him, shrugged her shoulders and said, "Who is going to hire you at your age?" He apparently thought that remark didn't require an answer. I came to the conclusion that married people have a responsibility to nurture each other in their individual interests which helps to promote communication, respect and love in a marriage.

1980-1990

ETHERIC HEALING, SNOW & CHEESECAKE

While leaving Bob at Dr. Doreen's home in Florida, she and I flew to Virginia to see Dr. Al who had been having very good results with his patients using Aura Etheric Healing for sinus conditions, urination problems and esophageal reflux. (My understanding is that this is a method of using Universal Intelligence directed to the person's Aura to correct the condition.) I asked, "Dr. Al, will you work on my inguinal hernia? I don't want to have surgery." He laughed and replied, "If you don't want surgery, I'll do the best that I can." Dr. Doreen asked for his expertise also. Dr. Al suggested, "It would be best if you stay overnight here in our home, give your bodies a chance to recuperate from the etheric surgery, and leave tomorrow." We took his suggestions and when we came into the kitchen for breakfast, Al's wife, Ell said, "Good, morning! Have you looked outside?" "No, not yet," I said, as I pulled back the curtains. I called, "Oh, Doreen, look here!" "Why, what's out there?" as she looked out the window, and with a look of total surprise she said, "Oh, I haven't seen snow since I left Michigan two years ago! Isn't it beautiful? Look how high it is piled." Then I said, "Snow? It's not supposed to snow in Virginia!" Al said, "The radio announced that the freak snowstorm had closed the airport and all of the roads until further notice." "Now, how are we to get home? Even the buses won't be moving!" Doreen exclaimed in a very concerned voice. We were a bit frantic there for a few minutes. Ell said, "I volunteered to bring a cheesecake to the Chiropractors' meeting in a couple of weeks and I've never made one before. I have several recipes; shall we experiment?" Oh, it looked so good coming out of the oven we could hardly wait for it to cool.

After it had cooled, Ell called from the kitchen, "Come let's eat cheesecake!" Oh, no! The cake had fallen to half its height. I said, "What went wrong?" Doreen laughingly added, "We didn't dance any jigs to shake the house to make it fall." (Being Welsh, she loved to dance). Ell looked in her pantry and said, "I have more cheese to make another cheesecake, let's try another recipe!" Doreen cut the top off the firm bottom part of the first cheesecake, and the top tasted really good. Suddenly Ell said, "Would you look at this recipe? It says at the very bottom, 'be sure to leave the cheesecake in the oven after you've turned off the oven, for at least 1/2 hour before removing it from the oven'. Oh MY! Well, let's hope this next one turns out right!" Would you believe it? It came out in pieces! Ell said, "Well, let's make another one, as she took some cottage cheese from the refrigerator!" We were all laughing so hard that Al had to come into the kitchen to see what was so funny.

Al's fireplace is actually an iron stove, and it was necessary to put wood into it very frequently. The system was to send heat through pipes into other rooms of the house, but it was so cold that the system couldn't keep up. Every time the door opened the smoke came out into the room; the fan and withdrawal system were supposed to keep the air clear, but that did not happen and I ended up with sinusitis and laryngitis. Doreen and I cannot sleep together because we are so restless, so I said, "I don't mind sleeping on the porch couch." Ell divided up all of her blankets among us; she wasn't prepared for a sudden cold snowstorm! I slept in my leather jacket, slacks and socks on my feet trying to stay warm.

Fortunately Al and Ell were prepared with food staples, but they didn't have fresh fruit and vegetables. Next afternoon the sun had warmed the snow enough that the snow could be shoveled away from the back door just enough to be able to open it. Al called to see if the local grocery store was open for business; yes, since the owner and wife live upstairs. Al bundled up with boots and warm clothes and trudged thru the thick snow, coming back with an armload of food for all of us. Juicing fresh fruits and veggies is more nutritious than cooked veggies, so Al showed us how he combines certain veggies to be the most compatible for our digestive systems. I had fun, as well as learning a lot about proper nutrition! What about the third cheesecake? We couldn't wait for dinner, so we tasted the third cheesecake; yummm! "Ella," I said enthusiastically, "this is the best cheesecake, so I suggest that you use the recipe for this cheesecake to take to your Chiropractic meeting; this is so delicious!"

"Al," I said, "my inguinal hernia no longer needs the support, and the pain is gone. What a relief!" Doreen said that she felt so much better and with more energy. The Etheric Healing was a success. "Ell and Al", I said, "I realize that you have gone above and beyond your responsibility of healing, and you have been so gracious with your hospitality; thanks again for everything!" I love you both! Next day the airport was open and we could get back to Florida. Bob was so glad to see us, and I said, "It is so good to be where it is so nice and warm again!"

It seemed at first that the freak snowstorm delay was a negative, but as it turned out, it allowed us to better understand each other, and to learn more about nutrition and baking, all in the name of fun and love. I noticed that the delay allowed my body to regain its health much faster without the stress of immediate travel back to Florida. I also learned that it's a good idea to take more clothes on a trip than what you think will be needed.

POT ROAST AND GLASS

After we were home again in Michigan, my daughter, Debbie phoned and said, "How about coming out to our house for dinner tomorrow?" Well, I had just bought a really nice looking beef roast, so I said, "That would be super! I'll bring the roast already to eat, and you fix whatever else you would like, how does that sound?" She laughed and said, "Who could refuse that?" So, the next day Bob and I started out to Debbie's house, with the pot roast in a pot on the floor of the truck between my feet, suddenly I yelled, "LOOK!!!" At that very moment a car hit us broadside on the driver's side shoving us across the right-hand lane onto the grass in the median of the cross-street highway, even as Bob's foot immediately hit the brake! It was a miracle that we missed the signposts on the highway! Our glasses flew off our noses into the back seat! Our heads hit the doors! My right shoulder slammed into the door! The lid flew off the pot roast and glass from the windshield and door shot into the pot roast and ruined it! All that happened so fast we didn't have time to think! We were so dazed at first that we couldn't think. People gathered 'round the car, police came with sirens screaming, and a fire-truck came blaring down the street. Someone ushered me into a nearby restaurant to sit and gain my composure, as my neck began to hurt. (Before I put the pot roast in the car I had a feeling that I should put it into a paper bag, and I thought, "Oh, they'll just make fun of me and say, "just like Grandma Rose"!") Debbie met me in the restaurant with ice packs (Bob had called her). "Oh, Debbie! Thank you! Those ice packs sure do feel good on my neck and shoulder!" as I hugged her. We finally did have dinner at her house; it wasn't pot roast, but the hamburgers were delicious! My neck was too painful, even though wearing an ice pack, for me to drive those 45 miles to the Chiropractor and back; so I said, "Honey, do you mind driving me to Ann Arbor to see my chiropractor? I know that your neck hurts too, but who else will drive me at this time of the day?" So Bob drove me to Dr. Grostic's office for new X-Rays and the specific type of cervical adjustment that corrects the subluxations that were produced by the sudden abnormal flexion of the neck during the auto accident. The next day I took X-Rays of Bob's neck and adjusted his vertebrae. He was so happy to get his neck adjusted! He said, "Wow, what a difference those adjustments make! The tension is already gone and my neck already feels better! I think I can even think better!" We both laughed at that remark. That's not the first time that my neck has been injured, so I'm thankful that I have an excellent chiropractor that corrects the subluxations. I was also reminded to always follow my inner feelings.

As I reflected back on the past two days, I realized how kind and helpful people could be in time of emergency. I still have no idea who helped me across the traffic to the restaurant, or who the waitress was who offered me a cup of coffee or glass of water. I know that God gave me the strength yet peace and calmness, for me to be able to sleep those first few nights.

GUIDES AND GUIDANCE

Isabelle Pettibone was the Facilitator of our Guides and Guidance Meditation meetings at our house. She said, "Tonight we're going to find out who our Spirit Guides are". When it was my turn to tell what I had experienced during meditation, I said, "I didn't see much of anything, all I saw was a huge blue eagle sitting on the fireplace mantel." Mrs. Pettibone started laughing and said, "How much clearer do you want it? Your guide is the Indian, Blue Eagle!" We all began laughing and I felt so silly. Isabelle said, "Blue Eagle, your faithful Indian, has always been with you from the beginning, helping to guide you through life's experiences."

CHESTER'S HOLE IN THE HEAD

The phone rang and it was Grandma Rose, "Chester (her gentleman friend) has been having dizzy spells and falling, and I'm afraid for him to climb the stairs at his house and at my house, could he stay with you until we find out what is the problem? You don't have any stairs to climb," she explained. "Well, I wonder what could be wrong; sure he can stay here for a while," Bob replied. I asked Chester, "Have you ever had dizzy spells before this?" "No, never, I don't understand this," he replied. "How long have you been having these dizzy spells?" I pursued. Chester thought for a few minutes and said, "Well, come to think of it, I don't remember being dizzy before I was hit over the head." "Hit over the head? Where? When were you hit on the head? How did that happen?" I exclaimed! "Well, I had just bought some groceries and was walking home when out of another store some boys attacked me. I tried fighting them off but one of them hit me on the head knocking me down. I was dazed for a minute and when I came to my senses there were a couple of people standing by my side and asking if I was all right. They said, "We saw what happened when we stepped out of the grocery store, and when the boys saw us, they ran with your bag of groceries." "I'll call the police and maybe you should go to the hospital," volunteered the lady. I said, "No, I'll be all right. I'll put some ice on my head when I get home." I asked Chester, "Do you have headaches and he said, "No, just a sore head," and laughed. I asked him to stay home when all of us were out of the house, just in case he would fall. He did have some dizzy spells and if he had not been close enough to a door or table to catch onto, he would have fallen. "Chester", I suggested, "you really should have a doctor check your head, an X-Ray or something; we'll take you, and find out why you're having these spells." No, he just wouldn't let us take him to a doctor. One day he fell and couldn't get up. He's over six feet tall and a good strong build, so we had to leave him on the floor and called the EMS. The EMS Technicians checked him over and got him standing, but he couldn't hold his balance and sat down. The guys tried to get him to agree to go to the hospital, but he absolutely refused to go. Of course they cannot take him unless he agrees, even when we agree that he should go.

Bob and I had planned quite a while ago, to spend some time in Florida after Christmas. "Now, what do we do, we've already made reservations," I said to our family. Our daughter, Debbie said, "Chester can stay at my house while you are in Florida." I took a deep sigh of relief and said, "That's a great idea, Debbie! Thanks!" While Chester was at Debbie's house he was falling more frequently. Someone convinced Chester to go to the Veteran's hospital; he's a veteran, so why not go? His head was scanned and a blood clot was pressing on his brain. "A blood clot? No wonder he was dizzy and falling," I exclaimed, "What can they do about a blood clot on the brain? Will he be paralyzed somewhere instead of being dizzy? That would be even worse." The doctors at the hospital had a neat method that was fairly new at that time, and they used it on Chester. They bored a hole in his skull right over the clot and suctioned it out. As soon as he was able to stand after the surgery, he was no longer dizzy and of course had no more falls. He wanted to stay in the hospital; he had such good treatment, LOL! He did move back home. What a relief for Chester to be normal again; climbing the stairs, visiting the library and doing whatever he desired to do with no problems.

After a few years, Chester decided to move in with his sister in Minnesota; he probably was in his late 80's, possibly even 90. He continued to eat healthfully, and take his daily walks in the park at the same time each day, regardless of the weather. This one day he didn't return when expected, so his sister went looking for him and found him sitting under a tree resting; he was resting all right, forever. What a wonderful way to go!

WEDDING BELLS & LAS VEGAS

Bob and I were guests at Lloyd and Marie's Wedding, and as we were leaving I asked, "Where are you going on your honeymoon? Oh, I forgot. No one is supposed to know where the bride and groom will be after the wedding." Lloyd and Marie began to laugh and said, "We want you two to go to Las Vegas with us!" "Las Vegas? Are you serious? That's your honeymoon and you want us to go with you for a whole week?" I could hardly believe my ears! Well, we had so much fun traveling around the city, and visiting The Hoover Dam, as well as walking from one casino to another trying out their food, slot machines and the crap tables. Bob was pretty lucky at craps when I left him alone, so after a while I went to his table and picked up a handful of chips and cashed them in (I knew that Bob had his initial investment safely in his pocket.) Of course I knew that prices were high in casino dress shops, but I didn't have much time to shop for clothes at home, so I took advantage of the situation; after all, it wasn't our money! Marie had a good eye for style, and helped me decide on a soft yellow dress that had tan vines climbing around it, which I just loved. We had fun shopping for the kids also. As we came toward the crap table again, Bob said, "Here honey, would you like to roll the dice for a while? I'll show you how the game is played." I thought that would be fun, and soon, every time that I rolled the dice I came up a winner, so most of the people at our table began betting on me. We were laughing and having so much fun winning, that the manager came over to our table and said, "We have to close this table; move on to another one; the dealer's time on this one is up." "What?" one of the gamblers complained, "I thought that was illegal!" Bob said to me, "Come on. Let's leave." We collected all our chips, turned them in and left the casino to go to another one. I asked Bob, "Why did he close the table?" Lloyd was laughing and said, "Honey, we were breaking the bank! Did you notice that everyone was betting on you because you kept rolling the winning numbers?" "Yes", said Bob, "that table was losing money. They probably were hoping that we would go to another table; your luck would change and they would start getting some of their money back, but we fooled them!"

As I assessed our trip to Las Vegas, I realized how much love our friends have for us by wanting us to share their fun trip. I am not a gambler, but when I was having so much fun throwing those dice with Bob, I understood how a person could become a gambling addict. It takes a lot of self-control to walk away from a table when you're winning.

CAN ONE PERSON BE IN TWO PLACES AT ONCE?

How I wish that could be a possibility! The very same day that my minister, mentor and friend The Reverend Dr. B.H. Crewe passed away, I received another long distance phone call; I was a bit nervous as my sister said, "Our Dad passed away this afternoon in the hospital!" Bob and I had been to Florida to visit him very recently, so this was a total surprise. "What happened?" I asked. My sister took a deep breath and replied, "He was taken to the hospital a few days ago; I went to see him; he could barely breathe and could hardly talk, and seemed very weak, but everything was under control. I was surprised when the hospital nurse called to say that he just stopped breathing soon after I left the hospital." "Of course," I said, "I will fly down to help you make arrangements for Dad's funeral."

OH, OH! I remember! I gave my word that I would give Dr. Crewe's Eulogy. How I hated to make that phone call to Dr. Crewe's daughter, however, she was very understanding and very sorry to hear that my Dad had passed away the same day. Terri flew to Florida to be with me, and the rest of the family. I felt her empathy and I thought that it was so thoughtful of her and very much appreciated.

The Mason's Chaplain gave the Mason's Final Farewell to Dad at the Funeral Home and the Service was well attended by Dad's American Legion and Veterans of Foreign Wars friends as well as those from Dad's Church. The Church Guild was so thoughtful as to supply a lovely luncheon for all of us, which I really appreciated.

My Dad, in prior conversations had mentioned that he would like to be buried in a Veteran's cemetery. Dad was a World War 1 Army Veteran, and was liked very much by his buddies in the local American Legion Post and the Veterans of Foreign Wars Post; they took over and made all the arrangements for Dad to be buried in Bay Pines Military Cemetery, St. Petersburg, Florida with a 21-gun salute. After the United States flag was folded it was given to my Mother; the gunmen and all those present filed past to shake her hand in respect. It was quite an impressive ceremony and good closure. Our Dad had lived a very full and interesting ninety-two years. Mother and Dad had been divorced just before their sixtieth wedding anniversary, so I wondered what was going through my Mother's mind. The ride back home was very solemn and quiet.

I had so wanted to attend Dr. Crewe's funeral, but family comes first; I didn't even have time to write Dr. Crewe's Eulogy and send it to his daughter. Even though my Dad had not been active in the Masonic Lodge in later years, I appreciated the fact that the Lodge was represented and that The Final Farewell was given. The local Veterans took quite a load off my sister's and my shoulders by orchestrating Dad's burial, and now I know how valuable it is to be active in church and civic organizations; they are your support system when needed.

BACK TO WORK?

As soon as we returned home one of my chiropractic associates told me that he had decided to leave the Chiropractic Clinic and build his Practice in a new location. I told him, "While I was away I was thinking of retiring," He asked me if I would relocate with him rather than to retire. Oh, What a temptation that was! My husband, Bob and I talked about this offer and he encouraged me to relocate with Dr. Young for at least one year. I was happy that Bob had encouraged me. "OK, I will join you," I replied to Dr. Young, "I will give you at least one year, if that is acceptable to you?" Well, Dr. Young was delighted! Dr. Young and I didn't sign any legal or binding contract, but trusted each other to be upstanding and decent with regards to our Practice. We had a very amicable relationship, taking care of each other's patients when the other needed to be out-of-town, or absent from the office for any reason. A year or so later our joint decision to accept Dr. Weil, an intern from Palmer Chiropractic College, supported the trust, respect and compatibility that we had for each other and the work that we have done together. After a year, Dr. Weil moved to Canada to start his own Practice. As it worked out, I stayed another ten years there with Dr. Young. I enjoyed taking care of patients again; I guess I was not ready to really retire. Looking back, I never regretted joining Dr. Young, and our chiropractic practice together was a huge success.

Respect in my marriage, voiced as encouragement to pursue my joy in life and in my professional practice, was the glue that bound a chiropractic practice to succeed. As I walk the path of life, I have come to realize that respect is a vital quality one can bestow to another; and it is my fervent hope that those whom I love realize that one simple truth about me and by my example, hold the quality of "respect" dear in their lives as well.

FUNERALS

My friend, Isabel is in the hospital. What a dear lady! She's given me much spiritual advice through the years. Isabel was sitting up in her bed and welcomed me, "Well, Hello Aileen! I'm so glad that you came today!" She didn't appear to be ill at all, yet as she spoke there was a bit of difficulty in her breathing. "Hello, Isabel, you look quite chipper today!" I remarked. Soon she said, "I won't be here much longer." I was surprised at that remark and said, "What makes you think that?" She smiled and said, "Oh well, I know because I've been seeing my relatives (she named her Mother and an Aunt) and some of my friends who are not on earth anymore." I had never heard of anything like that before, so I just listened. She went on, "They come and go." Pointing to the dresser where I was standing, she said, "There's an opening right there; there are lots of people there who say that they will be here when I leave my body when it's time to go. They can't all be in that opening at the same time, so I see different ones at different times." "Are you sure that they are for you?" I was a bit doubtful. "Do you know all of them?" I continued. "Oh yes, I know every one of them! I have taught Medium-ship to some of them, some I have told about Edgar Cayce, some have gone to our Meditation classes, and some went to the same church that you and I go to; yes, I know them all, except sometimes one will appear very hazy so I'm not sure until she tells me who she is." I had moved to the side of the dresser while Isabel was speaking, and as I stood there contemplating on all that she had said, I could feel the Presence of an entity almost touching me. I felt goose bumps all over me. Apparently Isabel could see or sense this and she said, "You feel them too, don't you?" This was such a new experience that I just wanted to stay in that moment.

During the times that I visited Isabel in the hospital, I had the same experience while she told me who all were there. She was very happy and actually had a glow around her. Was I imagining the glow, or was I becoming more in tune to the Spirit side of life? Isabel was certainly well known here on earth by the attendance at the funeral. I was aware of the spirit relatives and friends near the casket, and wondered if anyone there could see or feel what I was feeling. I felt sad that she's leaving us, although happy that she will be with her friends and relatives on the other side of life. My dear friends Nell and Esther passed away on the very same day. Both of these dear ladies had given me direction also through their connection to the Spirit side of life, and for their examples of being genuine and trustworthy, for which I am eternally grateful. I have learned that by becoming more aware and "listening" to my gut feelings, sensitivity to the Spirit World can be developed.

BOB'S SURPRISE! SURPRISE!

No birthday party for Bob this December, the weather was snowy and icy and I didn't want anyone to go out in such stormy weather! I said, "Maybe we should have your party in July with our grand-daughter whose birthday is on the 4th!" We both laughed at such an idea, but it WAS an idea! Bob's Mother, my kids and I wanted to give Bob a combination 60th Birthday party and Retirement party and wanted it to be a surprise. Bob owns a Window and Door Company, so of course we wanted to invite the employees who worked there. "How can we do this without him becoming suspicious?" Candace, our son Bob's daughter, pondered, "The restaurant across the street has the most delicious pizza, and every one loves their pizza; let's have it there!" Debbie offered excitedly! "Oh, that's a great idea!" exclaimed our daughter, Terri, "There are always so many cars there that he won't notice that all of us are there too!" Everyone agreed. Bob's Mother said, "Then it's settled. All we have to do is ask the manager what days are open for a large gathering, and set the time. Bob can come on over there after work, and the employees can follow; and I hope that he won't suspect anything." THE day came with great anticipation! I told Bob that I had a last minute errand to run and that I would meet him at the restaurant at 6:00 PM. The only glitch was that he knew that I didn't particularly care for pizza, "So why are we meeting there?" he asked. I hesitated for a moment, then answered, "Well, it's close to home and your office, and if either one of us is late, the other can start with the pasta salad, OK?" He agreed. We waited; minutes seemed like hours. "Here he comes!" someone shouted in a whisper. Candace couldn't wait; she dashed up the aisle to greet him and keep him looking at her until they arrived at the table and then all of us yelled, "SURPRISE! SURPRISE!! Bob was so surprised that he could hardly speak! Someone made a banner that said, "HAPPY BIRTHDAY!" Someone else made a banner that said, "HAPPY RETIREMENT! There were balloons and streamers and horns and love, celebrating him! Everyone had a fun time that we will always remember. It takes a lot of preplanning for a surprise to be a success; when I saw the happy, pleased expression on my husband's face, I realized that it was well worth the effort that I and everyone else had put into the celebration!

HOUSE ON LAKE ST. CLAIR

It had been raining so much that the St. Clair Lake water level had risen a few feet above normal and gone up over the sea wall, and some of the homes had water in them or up to their back door. Bob and I had often talked about how nice it would be to live on the water. Bob said, "Honey, let's take a ride out to the lake. This is a perfect time to investigate where the water level is." "That's a great idea, Bob!" as I grabbed my purse and ready to go. We had made a list of a few areas of where we thought that we would like to live. Oh No! Every one of those had water higher than we thought would be safe, so we continued to look farther up the coast. After much deliberation on the prospect of buying a house on the water, we decided that perhaps the best thing to do would be to rent a house on the water for a year, and then decide if we really wanted to live that close to the water. We looked in the paper for "House For Rent". The idea of renting was certainly new to us because the only houses that we had ever lived in after moving out of Bob's parents house when we first moved to Michigan, were the houses that Bob had built. "Are you sure that you want to rent?" I asked Bob. "These won't be new houses, you know," I added. "Yes, Honey, it will be for only a year and then we can make a decision on what we think is the best thing to do," sighed Bob. "Bob!" I called out excitedly, "Look here! A French-style house has an apartment for rent; and it's right on the lake!" "Hmmm, I wonder what that would be like; old and musty? The rent is pretty high, so it can't be too bad," Bob muttered thoughtfully. Next day we drove out to see that it was off the highway and had a beautiful view up and down the lakeside; what a beautiful house! The owners were a lovely couple that love to travel and are living in their motorhome. "We love the apartment," Bob told the owner, "the rent is a bit high; we'll let you know." The owner didn't want to come down on the rent. We didn't look at any other apartments because we fell in love with this one, and location. On the way home I said to Bob, "I wonder if I talked to his wife and told her that we don't need the third bedroom, if she will lower the rent; do you think she will go for the idea?" Bob laughed and said, "Well, it's worth a try." I called, "Marian, we really won't be using the third bedroom; how about if you keep one of them to store some of your things in? We won't mind you coming and going when you need to go into that room." Marian thought for a minute and agreed that that is a good idea. "So," I went on, "then you could lower the rent for us, OK?" She began to laugh and said, "All right, it's a deal!" As we were moving in, Gunder said, "Hey, Bob, you know that you have the use of the garage for your two cars, don't you?" "WOW!" I exclaimed! "There are already two cars in the attached garage and we get to use the other two spaces!" When winter came I found out that the garage was heated. What a deal and a dream come true!

One day when I came home from shopping I saw my husband in front of the house laying brick between the patio and the seawall. "Do you think that is a good idea?" I asked him, "Does Gunder know that you are doing that?" "Gunder hasn't been here to finish the job that he started, so I thought I would lay the bricks that are stacked along the seawall, and see if he notices what I've done," he retorted. (Ever since Bob has owned the Window/Door Company, he hasn't had much opportunity to do any masonry work, and I knew that he missed it.)

About a week later, Gunder and Marian came to cut the grass and do a little shrubbery trimming. Gunder was complaining that he hadn't finished the brick job, because he had injured his knee and couldn't kneel on it. Gunder said, "I don't know who I can get to finish this job and do it to satisfy me."

You see, Gunder is a temperamental artist and a perfectionist, therefore very difficult to please. Bob said, "I'm a bricklayer by trade; I'll finish it for you if you're not in any hurry." Gunder laughed and said, "Oh, I don't know; show me some of your work first." At those words, Bob stepped off the patio and said, "You're standing on some of it." "What? What? Where? What do you mean?" as he looked down and around his feet. Bob said, "Look at your pile of bricks over there; didn't you have more than those last week?" Gunder was really confused and looked again at where he was standing. He looked a bit unhappy. Bob said, "Gunder, I challenge you to tell me where you left off and I started." Gunder bent over and walked over the area where he thought he had stopped, pointed and then shook his head, doing this several times, and couldn't find the demarcation line. Stroking his chin, Gunder said, "Nobody has ever finished any of my work! I'll have to think this over, Bob." I said to Bob, "I bet that he can't find where he stopped and you started." Early next morning, Bob looked out over the lake and saw Gunder examining the brickwork. Bob began laughing and said to me, "Honey, do you know where Gunder is? He's looking over my work again; wonder what he's thinking. I think I'll take a cup of coffee out to him." "Well, good morning Bob! You have me stumped! You can finish the job," laughed Gunder. It didn't take Bob long to finish the bricklaying. It made me so happy to see how happy Bob was while laying those bricks! I remarked to Bob, "I love this house! When I come home from the office to this home on the water, I feel so peaceful! I even sleep better!" The huge mulberry tree in the big back yard gave us so many mulberries that we enjoyed them on our cereal, on our pancakes, in smoothies, on ice cream, you name it; so delicious! While living in that house on the lake that Bob also loved, I realized that he received the luxury of the Peace and Quiet that he so needed during his last couple years on this earth, which I didn't know at the time was not far off.

"REMEMBER WHAT I JUST TOLD YOU"

Bob had much difficulty in breathing. As a child he had asthma, which Chiropractic care healed, although leaving a weakness in the lungs. As I came home from the office to give him a kiss, he said, "Come here, sit here, I want to tell you something." Bob was very serious, and I wondered what's up? He proceeded to tell me exactly what he wanted done when he passes away. Many years ago we had talked about who, what and where for both of us, so I laughingly said, "Do you think you are going to die tomorrow?" "Honey," he said, "just listen to me and remember what I just told you." He was using an inhaler by now and was on oxygen every few hours to help him to breathe. Of course the fact that he would not quit smoking and continued to drink alcohol, added to his misery. Ever since the window company was going bankrupt, he drank more; apparently alcohol helped to dull the mental anguish. For two nights our son came to the house and gave his Dad a hot mustard footbath after massaging his feet; he had read that mustard would help draw toxins out of the body and help to ease the breathing. I was so proud of him!

Bob couldn't sleep and wanted more and more Vodka with his Pepsi, all through the night. I asked him, "What is the matter? Why can't you sleep?" He smelled terrible! I tried to sleep in another room, but he would come in and want me to just hold him. About the time I thought he was asleep, I would slide out of bed and go back to the other room away from that awful odor. I would just get settled and he would come in to bed. Earlier he had said, "I don't want aspirin, I need Vodka!" OH, that awful odor! The next night I asked him again, "What is the matter? Talk to me." Finally he said, "I'm in pain all over. I ache from the top of my head to the bottoms of my feet! Get me some more Vodka! The next day and next night were the same with Bob in so much pain. I didn't know what else to do, so finally, in the early morning I said, "Let's get you to the hospital; maybe there is something that they can give you to stop the pain. Bob finally agreed, so at 5:00 A.M. he was admitted to the hospital. By the time I parked the car he was already in a room, and I was told that I would need to wait a few minutes before going in to be with him because he had had a seizure and they had to calm him down. "A seizure? What kind of seizure, what happened?" I was really distraught! I couldn't find out any more than that. Later the doctor said, "He had to be heavily sedated. His blood is full of alcohol." Then he added, "He's on oxygen, and we'll make him as comfortable as we can.

As difficult as it was, I called my children and close friends. Bobs' best friend from the Navy, Ken and his wife, Connie came from Pennsylvania to stay with me; they've been friends forever. They visited him during all the visiting hours. As the "grapevine" grew, many visitors came. Many tests were performed; the brain showed atrophy; he had cirrhosis of the liver and his lungs were hardly functioning. His voice became very weak and I put my ear close to his mouth so I could hear him say, "Get me out of here!" I was so sad; I wanted so much to help him, but there was nothing that I could do except pray. "Honey," I said, "I can't get you out of here, you're hooked up to so many things to help you breath!" He had already pulled some of the tubes away when he wanted to go to the bathroom, not realizing that he was connected to a catheter. I continued seeing my Patients in-between hospital visiting hours so that my mind could be clearer; even then it was difficult to keep my mind focused on my patients, and not get stuck on my husband's condition; my stomach churned when I thought about him. He could not write, and nodded or shook his head to answer questions put to him.

Bob's last wish as I put my ear against his mouth, I thought he said, "Get me a Pepsi!" I said, "Ken, see if you can make out what he said," and he put his ear to Bob's mouth. Ken laughed and said, "I think he said, "Get me a Pepsi." I laughed and said, "That's what I thought he said," as Bob was nodding his head slightly. Some times it seems like it takes forever to get anything from a nurse because they are so busy, and as far as they are concerned, getting a Pepsi is not a priority; but I tried that route anyway and Ken went down to the canteen. Bob didn't care much for soft drinks other than Vernor's Ginger Ale (especially a float) and Pepsi Cola. Pepsi was his favorite, which he drank everyday, so if at all possible, Ken and I would make sure that Bob would get his Pepsi. Ken and I came into the room laughing, about the same time, with Bob's Pepsi. Bob was very weak, but he managed a little smile and was able to drink some of the Pepsi. Imagine! "Get me a Pepsi!" was Bob's last wish while he could still talk.

A Neurologist examined Bob; poor nerve function. The lungs were suctioned, hoping to improve breathing, but blood came up every time. I called my Mother and my Sister, bringing them up-to-date on what's happening with Bob. I knew that they could not come from Florida to see him, but they needed to know about his condition.

After a few days the doctor made an appointment with me and I asked my husband's best friend, Ken and wife and Terri to come with me to hear what the doctor would tell me; I wanted them to verify everything, because I felt that I wasn't thinking clearly. I had a feeling that the information would not be good. The doctor went over everything that we already knew and then said, "Mrs. Miller, your husband's body is shutting down; he's not going to live." Inside me I already knew that, but to hear that verdict from the doctor, it had a whole new meaning. It was a shock to hear it from the doctor. As Terri and I went into the waiting room we held each other tightly as I cried, "Oh Terri!" (We understood each other.) We had no Kleenex and none in the waiting room, good old toilet tissue to the rescue! The next day the nurse asked, "Do you want life support for your husband?" What a question at this time! Bob and I had talked about life support in the past and agreed that we didn't want it when there was no hope for improvement. After we had talked with the doctor one of the children asked their Dad if he wanted to live and he nodded his head, "Yes." Now what do we do? OK, his wishes, more O2 and a feeding tube even though I felt that to be against Spirit's wishes. Now he's in ICU! A spinal puncture proved to be clear; the TB test was clear. Bob hemorrhaged four times next day and the doctor didn't know why, so a Gastricoscopy showed that a vein had ruptured, so then it was cauterized, and a pint of blood was given. I'm wondering, "Does he really want to go through all this pain?" I couldn't ask him because he was less responsive.

Would you believe that Bob's Mother had not been to see her own son? I had said several times, "Mom, I'll pick you up on the way to the hospital to see Bob." She always refused and finally Terri convinced her and brought her in a wheel chair, but she would not touch her own son, or talk to him, just looked at him. Two days later one of our other children wheeled their grandmother in to see him again; she's alert but doesn't seem to realize how ill her son is. Was she in denial? Two days later she visited him, and finally touched his feet, but still didn't talk to him. After she left I was alone with Bob and told him, "It's OK honey to leave your body and pass on into the Spirit World; it's OK, but I will miss you. You can be free of pain and all responsibilities. I love you and always will love you." His friends and my children told him the same thing as they came to visit him. As I left Bob

I said, "No kisses because I have a bad cold and sinus." Now wasn't that silly of me? What difference? He was dying anyway! He formed his lips with a kiss anyway. Oh, how I regret that opportunity! I just couldn't get out of bed the next day; my head hurt from sinus infection and I hurt all over; lying there feeling guilty about not being able to be with Bob. I began praying, praying for his release, he had suffered so much! Fortunately for me, or rather fortunately for Bob, his friends and children were with him, so he was not alone while I was home. During the night Bob had been put on a blood pressure machine to keep his blood flowing, even though he wasn't supposed to be on one; my oldest daughter was so upset and was trying to get them to take it away. The procedure is that once it's started it cannot be removed until the time runs out, which will be at 1:00 P.M. next day. Ken called me and said, "Bob stopped breathing at 1:27 this afternoon. "I'll pick you up and take you to the hospital to sign some papers." Oh, I did not want to go! I just wanted to stay in bed and breathe a "Thank You, God!" for taking his Spirit, his Soul to another Plane, a better place to rest, and be pain-free. My understanding is that before we are born, we have decided what our plan is, how we may best be of service, and how we will leave the earth at the appointed time. A few years after we're born, we don't remember all that and there are detours, but the general plan is followed.

Friends were so thoughtful, bringing food and compassion and understanding to our children, me and to Bob's Mother. Friends and relatives came from out-of-town to stay with me; some stayed with Bob's Mother in her apartment so that she would not be alone. I respected Bob and followed his request that he had made earlier, when he said to me, "Listen to me and remember what I just told you".

Bob's Celebration Of Life Service was about to begin, and as I looked back over my shoulder I saw so many of our friends, and my eyes welled up with tears as I saw that the church that Bob had helped construct (St. Gabriel's Episcopal) was filled to overflowing. Our oldest daughter, Debbie and Bob's best friend, Ken gave the Eulogies. I was so proud of Debbie, the rather emotional one who I thought would never get up in front of so many people to tell her story. I could feel his Presence during the ceremony.

Bob's body was donated to the Research Department at Palmer College of Chiropractic; flowers and pictures of him were in front of the church altar.

My daughters, Debbie and Terri, and Bob's Mother took turns staying overnight with me, and helped address Thank You cards, which was a big help. Friends also stayed overnight with me. Then a snow storm came that brought nine and a half inches of snow that fell in 24 hours, which was the most in five years; what a surprise! It gave us something else to think about for a while. I feel that it is an honor to follow wishes that a person has given prior to their passing. It is also honoring that person when telling your thoughts to family and friends at a Memorial Service or Funeral.

Three months after my husband passed away I attended a Séance Class by dear friends Rev. Reed Brown and Rev. Smith at the Masonic Temple in Detroit. At the Séance there, Bob appeared in Spirit holding out his arms and said, "I found my way. I'm all right! Not to worry; I'll get in touch. I'm all right." Then a dear friend, Esther who has been in Spirit for quite a few years, came forward and said, "He's all right honey, he's all right!" I was so happy to receive those messages; I knew they were authentic because Esther had given me true messages when she was on the earth and I had true messages from Rev. Reed in past years. Yes, since then I have received messages directly from Bob; he tells me what he's doing "up there", and gives our children and me guidance whenever he thinks that we need it. How does he get in touch with me? That's a secret for now.

My children loved that house on the lake so much so that my son, Bob (we call him 'Bob' now, since his Dad, Bob has passed on) and his fiancé, Dana were married there in June, on the very bricks that his father had laid, with the beautiful blue lake in the background. Bob's bride, Dana was so beautifully radiant in her beautiful white gown, and Bob looked taller and even more handsome as they stood under the trellis that Terri had trimmed with roses. Of course she and Debbie were there. Bob's children, Candace and Robert (Bobby) liked Dana, so were very happy that they were getting married. (Robert (Bobby) later married Melissa Totoraitis, the parents of Nathan and Ryan). (Candace later married Ray Fradi, the parents of Joseph). Dana's two daughters,

Dana ll and Kelly were joyful as they witnessed their Mother's wedding. (Dana ll later married Ron Boggia, the parents of Taylor and Joshua. Kelly later married Thaddeus Marcola, the parents of McKayla, Thadeus and Ethan.) Our neighbors, and relatives from Florida joined in on the celebration. Bob and Dana are as happy today as the day that they married. I am so happy that Bob and Dana decided to be married at this house that my husband, Bob and I loved.

UPSTAIRS DILEMMA

My Bob's Mother Rose's heart problems put her in the hospital. Of course she didn't want to die in the hospital, so when she was able to go home we brought her home, but now there is a problem. Mom Rose lived on the second floor and she was too weak to climb those stairs. Finally we had enough help from strong men to get her up those stairs. She couldn't live alone, so when I was taking care of patients at the Clinic I had a nurse come in to help, which worked just fine; Mom had someone to talk to and not be alone.

During this time I moved from the Lake house, which was being sold, to live in Mom's apartment building. Mom was delighted that I moved in and would be coming in and out to see how she is, and share meals with her; she misses her one and only child so very much of course. At night, on my way home from the office, I often stopped at the Big Boy Restaurant to pick up her favorite strawberry shortcake, or a strawberry sundae. We had special time together in the evenings, which I really enjoyed.

EGYPT? OR NOT?

As was pre-arranged nearly a year ago, when Mom was taking care of her self and shopping, etc., I planned to go to Egypt with a church group; everything was already paid for. Mom's health began to fail and I wondered if she would live much longer. "Now, what do I do?" I asked my children, "I think I should cancel the trip." and they said, "No! You go ahead and go; there are three of us to watch over Grandma. You've been looking forward to this trip and you will enjoy it with Rev. Reed's group; just go and don't worry about a thing." They loved their Grandma so I knew that they would make sure that there would always be someone with her. I did not tell Mom/Grandma that I was going overseas because I thought that she might have a heart attack right then and there. You see, she always discouraged vacations ever since her husband passed away unless she could go with us. One thing that she did understand was that Chiropractic License Renewal Seminars were very necessary, and she never complained about me going to them. So I just told her, "I'm going to a long Chiropractic Seminar in New York and stay a few extra days." (I was planning to explain everything upon my return.) I wrote everything down with phone numbers, so that if anything happened while I was gone, the children had all the information right there on my desk. The children said, "We'll keep her entertained while you're gone so that the time will not drag for her."

So off I flew with my group to Egypt, and upon landing in Cairo we were driven by bus to a really elegant Hotel. One of the first places that most everyone investigates is the bathroom, right? I was so surprised to see that it was blue and white ceramic tiled and had a telephone beside the toilet! Another surprise was that when I turned on the faucet in the sink, the water came out brown. I don't think that I will be taking a shower.

After a delicious buffet dinner we enjoyed a belly-dancer show; I had never been to one, so I really enjoyed this special treat. We visited the Coptic Christian Church and many others. St. Sargius Church pulpit is made of marble and fifteen pillars hold it up. Each pillar is different from the other and so intricately made. The Temples, with all their carvings of their Gods and Rulers were magnificent! I brought home a sandstone bust of Queen Hatshepsut, who I understand, was the only female ruler of Egypt; after she had ruled for seven years, she was given the Title of King of Egypt. Also, I brought home a statue of King Akhenaten, who believed that there is only one God, and promoted Peace. I had the opportunity of riding a camel from the bus (about one of our city blocks) to the third pyramid. What an experience, but you know what? I'd rather ride a camel than a horse; it's sort of a sideways around movement that is very pleasant. Well, I don't know how it would feel, if he would be running. LOL. My bus partner was so much fun; she had never been away from her home state, and she was enjoying every minute of her trip with comical remarks and laughs. We were supposed to board the same bus and have the same seat partner, so I was so thankful that my partner had such good energy; she was a joy to be with!

The Reverend F. Reed Brown, who helped conduct our group, received special permission to visit the pyramids at night and have a meditation ceremony alongside the Great Pyramid. After the ceremony I put my hands against the side of the Great Pyramid; what I felt was startling! I felt and heard the most beautiful heavenly singing! As I removed my hands from the pyramid, the music stopped and when I replaced them the music began again. Could it be my imagination? There were houses in the distance, but no radio was playing; I faintly heard some barking dogs. I placed my hands again on the pyramid and heard different, but heavenly music. On another night we were having a meditation and prayer session between the paws of the Sphinx Pyramid; as I looked up I saw my husband's Spirit sitting on one of the paws, smiling at me. I knew he was there, because I felt his energy, and to prove it further, he had a special way of sitting. When we visited the Papyrus Factory, I couldn't resist purchasing a papyrus with a symbol of peace and my name in Egyptian in gold within a cartouche; I had it framed upon returning home and placed it in my office; I really love it. On the way to Aswan we passed what looked like a forest of tall date palms; I didn't realize that so many of our dates came from Egypt. I loved the trip to Egypt, learning about its ancient history and learning about how they lived then and now, and how friendly they are regardless of the turmoil that they have experienced through the years.

It was time to return home to the United States and all of my children met me at the airport, which was also my birthday; I was so happy to be home after two weeks in a foreign country; hugs and kisses all around. Then I asked, "And how is Grandma? (my mother-in-law, Rose)." They looked at each other, then one of them said, "Well, we guess she's all right, now." Rather puzzled I started to say, "Why?" and then I knew; she had passed away. "Don't worry, Mom, we took care of everything," they sort of all said together.

In years past I had made the remark, "I never seem to remember when people pass away, it's just something that doesn't stay in my memory bank very long." Mom was going to make sure that I would remember her Spirit birthday; she would leave the earth plane on MY birthday! Yes, I surely do remember HER day! Mom's Celebration Of Life Service was held at the same Church as my husband's. I was so happy that my son and oldest daughter participated. Her body was also donated to the Research Department of Palmer College of Chiropractic. One amazing thing that the students will find, is that she had all but two of her own teeth; I don't know of anyone else who still has that many teeth at the age of 93! WOW!

THE "I AM" TEACHING

A few years ago Isabel, my friend and Spiritual Medium introduced me to the concept of the "I AM Teaching". What is that? How is it so different from the traditional Orthodox religions? The only way to find out is to go to a meeting or two, right? Oh, No! The church is not anywhere close; it's on the other side of town. It would take at least an hour or more to get there, and I'm not sure about the safety of that area. Oh well! If I want to know what this I AM Teaching is all about I must go. "There it is!" On the front of the building was a huge portrayal of a Spiritual figure all lit up in color. The parking lot was patrolled, so I felt safe going into the building. After signing my name in the Visitor Book, a lovely lady ushered me into the room where I could hear beautiful organ music. I felt as though I was walking on air as I found a seat among a hundred or more people. I felt so light, the air so fresh. I've never felt like this before! After a few words of welcome and announcements, a lovely lady stepped onto the podium and was introduced as Mrs. Ballard. She gave a beautiful dissertation on "Your Spiritual Self". On the Screen were Mantras that we repeated, all about your Master Teacher and you.

Many Discourses had been given to her husband, Guy W. Ballard in 1930 through St. Germain, an Ascended Master. Mr. and Mrs. Ballard knew how important the information was from Master St. Germain; that they opened the "I Am Center" for any and all to come and learn. I learned that it's not a Religion; it's a way of living. One of the Decrees that was given to us began, "I AM the Mighty Presence of pure energy," which I say every day. Another is, "I command my I AM Presence to bring harmony and happiness into my world." I felt so joyful that I went to classes there for many weeks. Patience was not one of my virtues, but I began to feel more patient and calm. The I Am Teaching is ingrained into my whole being. I always had an inferiority complex; by learning what St. Germain was teaching I began to realize that each of us has our own strengths and abilities to excel in, and now I feel good about myself.

NEVER TRIMMED A CHRISTMAS TREE?

Dr. Jean joined our staff at Chiropractic Physicians; it was good to have another female doctor with us. One day I mentioned that I was going to decorate my Christmas tree over the weekend. "Do you decorate your tree early, or wait until Christmas Eve?" I asked her. She hesitated for a moment and then said, "I've never decorated a Christmas tree." "Why? Did your parents always decorate it?" I inquired. She hesitated again, "Well, we never had much money, so never had a tree." I was shocked! I really didn't know much about her. "Oh, my goodness! Would you like to help me trim my tree?" I asked. "OH, could I?" she exclaimed excitedly. I had the tree set up by the window and all the decorations out of storage when my colleague arrived. I explained that the electric lights go on first, and then the rest. I have some very beautiful and very old bulbs that really intrigued her. "How can you keep them for so many years and not break them?" she asked. "Oh, I wish I had more of them, I've given some very unusual ones to my children and some have been broken through the years," I explained. I put out some nuts, chips and fruit to snack on in-be-tween laughs and trimming. I had no idea how much it would mean to her when I asked her to help trim my Christmas tree. Watching her enjoyment in trimming my Christmas tree was a real treat! Actually it was a treat for both of us.

1970- My husband Bob at his favorite place, the beach

1978- Bob's Mother, Rose Miller (Weber-maiden name), having her favorite food of ice cream

2017- My daughter-in-law Dana and my son Robert Miller in Seattle at the Top Of The Needle.

2017- My granddaughter Candace with her husband Ray Fradi and their son Joseph in Michigan.

2016- My grandson Bobby and wife Melissa with their sons, Ryan and Nathan in Michigan at Christmas time.

2016- Baby Blake Wolk and his parents, Taylor and Jordan; Robert Miller, Ron and Dana Boggia, Dana Miller and Joshua Boggia gathering at Christmas in MI.

2016- Dana Miller's daughter Kelly and husband Ted with their children, Thadeus, Ethan, and McKayla during family Christmas time.

2008- I am with Derek O'Neill at a healing seminar in Ireland. He translates ancient wisdom into modern day teachings.

2013- My mentee Lazaro and I at his High School Graduation in Tavernier, FL. I mentored him for 5 years in the "Take Stock In Children" program.

1999- My daughter Terri and her husband Roger are having fun playing with a dolphin in Grassy Key, FL.

1994- In my office standing beside my atlas vertebrae adjusting instrument in Warren, MI.

My fabulous 90th birthday party orchestrated by my daughter Terri in the Florida Keys.

My exciting camel ride to pyramids in Egypt.

1906- My Grandparents, George and Ida Michael, daughter and son, Alice and Louis

1972- My Mother and Father, Alice and Arthur Dettmer at their farm in Texas

2016- My niece, Johanna Lott in her lab at work in Texas

1991- My Sister Marjorie and our Mother Alice Dettmer taken in Bellview, FL, where they lived together

1964- Our family of five. My daughters Debbie and Terri; our son, Robby and my husband Robert (Bob)

1991-2000

UNUSUAL EXPERIENCE IN A FUNERAL HOME

My friend, Marie asked, "Will you go with me to view my Aunt at the funeral home?" I had planned to go to the Funeral the next day, but since she asked me to go with her now I said, "Sure, Marie, I'll keep you company." It was a lovely funeral home and the room was filled with flowers; her Aunt's dress was a beautiful soft rose color with a white lace collar. I paid my respects and said a prayer as fast as I could and said to Marie, "I'll meet you outside, take your time." When Marie came outside she said, "Why did you leave so suddenly?" and almost in the same breath, she said, "I'm getting a headache. I never felt like this before in any funeral home." I explained, "Marie, you know what kind of person your Aunt was, so faultfinding, complaining about any one she knew, so negative. That energy is still with her body; it was so heavy that I had to leave. I couldn't let her negative energy pull me down. It takes a lot of spiritual energy to build it back up; that's why you have a headache." "Hmmm," she contemplated, "I never heard that before, but it does make a lot of sense." I suggested, "Take a couple of deep breaths and think of your house by the lake." Afterward she said, "My headache is gone! That's amazing!" I had forgotten to bless myself before entering the funeral home, however I did remember to leave as soon as possible so that my energy would not be depleted. I felt that it was important for me to explain the "heavy, negative energy" feeling, so that she could explain it to others who might have the same feeling.

ARIZONA BOUND

Jean and Buster are "Empty Nesters" since their three children are on their own. (I've known Jean since she was eight years old.) They invited me to their new home in Arizona and I said, "I'd be delighted to visit you!" Jean replied, "We'll pick you up at the airport." I could smell her chicken dinner as we walked in the door of their house. After dinner Jean said, "Would you like to visit my step-mother, Dorothy? She lives in her own apartment near here." I replied, "I'd love to see her; I didn't realize that she lived so close by." The next day when Jean and I visited her, the first thing that Dorothy said was, "Why, Aileen, you look just the same as the last time that I saw you," (which was at least ten years ago when she was in Michigan.) We both laughed and I said, "Why Dorothy, you haven't changed a bit either." (Jean's Mother had passed away many years ago.) Dorothy was a really good wife for Jean's Dad and had the same good humor that he had. We talked about old times and then she said, "It looks like you have narrow feet, just like I have." I said, "Yes, and isn't it difficult to find shoes that fit; most shoe stores don't carry narrow widths." Dorothy laughed and said, "The only shoes that I can wear are Selby shoes. What size do you wear? Your feet look about the same size as mine." I told her my size and then she said, "I don't want you to think I'm presumptuous, but here's the thing; ever since I broke my foot, I can't wear the same size shoes, and some of mine are practically new, you are welcome to them if they fit." She stepped from the bedroom with several of the most beautiful shoes; tan and white, a red pair, a navy blue pair and a white pair, saying, "Here they are, try them on, I hope they fit you." After trying all of them on I said, "Dorothy, I can't believe that all except one pair fit me so nicely! Thank you for having such narrow feet! I really appreciate these!" I was pleased that Jean's stepmother felt comfortable enough with me to offer her shoes to me and wouldn't take any payment. Two other friends live in Arizona, and Jean let me use her car to visit them. I felt very grateful that Jean trusted me with her car, especially since she had never driven with me. Of course I had to get up early in order to drive Jean to school; teachers can't take days off whenever they want them. She had a Chiropractor's appointment the next day so I looked forward to meeting him and checking out his adjusting technique; I was pleased. Next day I drove to another city to visit Esther, former patient, her sister and her nephew. My patient exclaimed, "I'm just amazed that you would fly alone all the way from Michigan to Arizona! You look great!" She didn't look so great, so I said, "It's so good to see you all. Are you keeping up with your Chiropractic spinal care?" "Well, no, I had a fall and couldn't find a Chiropractor nearby, so I'm getting along with medication that my sister's doctor gave me." I couldn't believe my ears; she had been such a good patient while she lived in Michigan, and was so healthy. I explained, "You know, Esther, medication is only a temporary fix; you really need to go to a Chiropractor so he or she can open up all those nerve channels so your body can heal." "I know, I'll see what I can do, and who can take me," she agreed. As I left I saw some of the food on the counter; all junk food and/or starchy food, food that she did not eat when she lived in Michigan. I had a feeling that things would not be any different after I left than before I arrived. I was disappointed that Esther didn't think that her health was important enough to insist that she eat food that was beneficial to her health, and to receive Chiropractic care. Jean had developed into a charming, gracious lady and I felt very welcome in their home. All in all, the visit in Arizona was delightful and a joy.

A SURPRISE IN GEORGIA

My youngest daughter, Terri drove me to the airport so that I could attend the Chiropractic Orthogonal Seminar in Georgia and learn if there was anything new concerning the specific non-force technique of adjusting the atlas/axis vertebrae. "Hi Roy! It's good to see you again!" as we hugged each other. "Well, Ahleen, (in his southern drawl.) Ah was hoping that you would be here for this session. Lots of your friends are here!" It was a happy time getting re-acquainted with colleagues who I've known and studied with for many years. Just before adjourning for lunch, Dr. Roy Sweat said, "Ahleen, please come up front for a moment." He then presented me with a plaque that read, "Atlas Orthogonal Humanitarian Award"; I was so surprised that I hardly knew what to say! I am so honored!

OUT WEST

"Hello? Charles? How are you?" as I heard his voice on the phone from Virginia, I immediately wondered if something was wrong with my friend, Vickie. "I'm fine, Aileen, and yes everyone here is just fine" he went on, "Hanna is putting on a Peaceful Retreat Seminar in Colorado; were you thinking of going?" "Well, what a coincidence," I answered, "I was reading the brochure and thinking that I would really like to see how she makes those Herbal Formulas, and learn more about them." Charles sounded excited and asked me, "Would you like to drive out to Denver with me; can you take that much time away from your Practice?" (If I went alone, I would fly and then rent a car.) His idea sounded very enticing, but I said, "Let me think about it and I'll let you know." What would my family and friends think about me driving out there with a man? After all, we've known each other for a long time; we are friends, not romantically inclined. I know his lady friend who has her own business, and doesn't want to leave it for 3-4 weeks. Finally I called him, "Charles, I've decided to go. Could we take some extra time and sightsee? I've never been that far north and west." Charles was elated! He said, "I'll do some more research about what to see and when we should leave." "Charles," I interrupted, "I have some dear friends in Wisconsin, somewhat on our way, that we could stop to visit. Shall I call and tell them our plans?" "That sounds great!" exclaimed Charles. My friends wanted us to stay a couple days so that they could show us some of the sights. "Have you seen "The House On The Rock"?" Bud asked us; "It's known all over the World." "I had seen pictures, but to actually see it would be a real treat," I volunteered. This house really IS built on and IN a huge rock; I'd call it a huge boulder! Inside the house were so many beautiful pictures, statues, paintings, exquisite crystal chandeliers, many different musical instruments and artifacts from all over the world too numerous to mention! He certainly had a unique way of protecting his possessions; no one could ever get into his house! I thought that it might be damp in the huge rock, but the owner had a very effective air transfer system that made it very comfortable.

"Have you heard of the Wall Drug Store in South Dakota? It's the World's most famous drug store!" volunteered Charles, "in a unique town that has all kinds of free attractions." Wall Drug Store became famous for providing free ice water to tourists when towns were few and far between and before air-conditioned cars were in existence. The Badlands of South Dakota may be bad, but the mountains and rocks are certainly beautiful! We toured Gold Mines, watching how raw gold from the ground ends up as jewelry; fascinating! The Wastewater Treatment Plant there uses bacteria to "eat" the contaminants in mine water. At that time, it was the only plant of its kind in the world.

Near Mt. Rushmore is the beautiful Rushmore Cave, which shows beautiful floral Stalactites, Stalagmites and Columns. Of course we wouldn't miss Mt. Rushmore with the carvings of our Presidents: Washington, Jefferson, Lincoln and Roosevelt. As we watched the traditional Indian Dances nearby Crazy Horse Mountain, which is only seventeen miles from Mt. Rushmore, we were fortunate to actually observe the dynamiting necessary to carve Indian Crazy Horse out of the mountain. (Crazy Horse is one of Charles's Guides.) We could see the dust from the explosion before we heard the explosion of the dynamite. Oh, yes! Awesome! We picked armloads of sage along the highway in Wyoming. I was laughing and said, "Charles, we'll need a trailer if we pick anymore!"

At last, the Hanna's Peaceful Retreat!! Since we arrived late every bed was taken in the Dormitory, so we were sent to a private home where there were four other guests in the basement, each of us having our own fold-up bed; not at all what I had expected. Charles ended up sleeping in the back of his Van and coming inside to shower, etc. Everyone was quite congenial so it was a happy situation.

When Charles and I arrived at Hanna's Peaceful Retreat Seminar, I noticed that Hanna's home, dormitory, classrooms and factory were on the same property. "Come, everyone," called Hanna, "I will give you a tour of my herbal facility, and some of my herb fields; all of my herbal formulas are organic." She believed that the power of prayer increases the energy of the product, therefore she prayed over each and every product that left her facility. (I had been recommending many of her products to my patients, especially to those whose eating habits were much to be desired. Good food helps the healing process of the body). Hanna had a very strong accent and so it was difficult for me to understand everything that she said, as she taught us about her products and what they should be used for. Fortunately one of her assistants, and then a man from Sweden with less of an accent, helped explain some of her instructions. We took notes like crazy, and hoped that we could read them.

During the lunch break one of the students asked Charles, "Have you ever been to this special Art Studio in Denver where this artist paints on glass? I know how interested you are in art." This sounded intriguing, so Charles said, "Let's go see what this is all about." "Charles!" I exclaimed, "Look at these paintings! Have you ever seen anything like them?" The Artist explained how he painted the Universe as he saw it in his dreams the night before. He painted on the underside of the glass that he was holding, and fired it more than once during the painting process, which gave it an entirely different perspective. I thought that these paintings were so beautifully different that I brought many of them home as gifts.

The next day some of the students asked Hanna what formulas would be good for certain ailments. To substantiate her answer, she took from her pocket a pendulum and proceeded to answer the question by how the pendulum swung. She then instructed us on how to use a pendulum. It seemed to be so accurate that I decided to use a pendulum in my Practice, as well as to be able to help family and friends in making their decisions. As Hanna's Peaceful Retreat Seminar ended, she invited us to her church. The service was very upbeat and spiritual, which sent us on our way home in a very uplifting, happy mood.

On the way home we stopped at an Indian Store that exhibited beautiful handmade pottery. "Charles, do you think these vases would make good gifts to my friends and relatives?" I asked. Charles laughingly said, "You know how much I love Indian everything, so of course I will say, "of course." Charles collects paintings and spent so much time in this particular Art Store that I sat outside in the warm sun to wait for him. We drove past acres and acres of onion fields like I had never imagined! We arrived home in Michigan late in the evening, tired, but happy. I was anxious to get back to my patients the next day. Charles stayed for a few days to rest up, before continuing on to his home in Virginia.

I realized that I took quite a chance by traveling for a month with someone who I've never traveled with before, at least not any distance; however after meditating about it, I felt confident that I could trust him and his driving ability. I had a lot of wholesome fun visiting places that I would never have seen if I had flown to Denver. The Seminar was more than I had expected; learning about Hanna's Nutritional Supplements, and how to properly use a pendulum was invaluable. All that I experienced on the entire trip was extremely educational as well as being fun, and I am very glad that I went with Charles.

CHINA FOR FOUR WEEKS

"Hello, Aileen? This is Bea, I'm thinking of going to China, and I would like for you to go with me." "China?" I said on the phone. Bea continued, "This is a Research group for the Study of Traditional Chinese Life Science. Dr. Frue, the Director lives in Oregon, but he has spent five years in China with the Chi Gong Masters." Bea is a close friend and I know that she would be a really good companion. I love to travel and soon I found myself flying to the West Coast and on to China with Bea. Upon arriving in China, we were escorted to a Health Center and served hot tea. Hot tea? It felt like 110 degrees outside, and we were served hot tea! Our luggage was still on the truck, so I could not retrieve cooler clothing. I rolled up my lined polyester pant legs and rolled up my sleeves, and enjoyed the ride to the foot of the mountain and then walking up the steps to the Monastery. If they were trying to scare us to death, it was a good try, as we encountered larger than life statues of snarling tigers, pouncing brown monkeys, dragons that were blowing red flames from their mouths, diving brown eagles, and other birds, which lined the tiny stair steps. With sweat trickling down behind my ears and running down my chest, I trudged onward and upward.

On a level area of the mountain there were Vendors selling colorful necklaces, embroidered towels and bags and more. We trudged on and suddenly the view opened up, and there stood a huge statue of Quan Yin dressed in white, with strands of colorful red beads cascading almost down to the hem of her dress. Breathtaking! (She is known as the Goddess of Mercy.) There were Beautiful Fresco paintings on a wall behind Quan Yin depicting the history of the Monastery. I looked around for Bea and found her in her sky blue blouse, in front of the Monastery, sitting in the middle of a six feet wide Yin Yang symbol on a dark green ceramic tile background, meditating. She looked so serenely beautiful!

A boat took us across a lake to a cable car, which took us to a restaurant at the top of a mountain, I said to Bea, "Thank goodness we didn't need to climb that mountain!" In a Nunnery nearby we were blessed. We must ask permission of the person that we wish to take a picture of. Why? It is their belief that when a snapshot is taken, it takes away some of the person's essence (energy). Acupuncturist, Dr. Wang checked my health condition by pulse diagnosis; waving his hand in front of him he said, "NO problem!" That was really great news, since I had been doing a lot of mountain climbing already, at over the age of seventy!

A bus dropped us off at the foot of Mt. Qingcheng where I saw nothing but tall green trees and a dirt path leading upward to the sky. I asked Dr. Frue, "Where is the Retreat Center?" He smiled and said, "It's at the top of the path." Bea and I, along with half of our group, began to trudge up Mt. Qingcheng; huffing and puffing with sweat pouring down our necks and backs, I thought that we would not ever get to the top of that mountain! Mt. Qingcheng is known as one of China's Holy Mountains therefore it was chosen as the perfect location for the Retreat Center. The Retreat Center was still being built, even though it was supposed to have been completed by the time that our group arrived. The view was outstanding, overlooking the green trees dipping from one valley up another mountain and down another valley and up again.

Finally we made it to the top of that mountain and were told that our rooms are on the second floor, furnished with two bamboo mats on the floor. I'm certainly glad that I brought a small foam-filled mat with me; my son-in-law's down sleeping bag was in another location, not anywhere nearby. Breakfast was spicy meat, eggs and rice. After breakfast everyone, and I mean every one there, practiced Chi Gong in the courtyard. Classes were beginning, and as I walked through the door I looked for a chair to sit upon. "Leave your shoes here, and find a (Bamboo) mat, or a pad if there is one left," said one of the students. Two Chinese interpreters spoke before we heard the talk in English on the history of Mt. Qincheng. Lunch was served family style, with plenty of spicy food and rice again. One of the cooks stood by my shoulder to make sure that I ate plenty of rice; it apparently balances the spicy food and kills the parasites.

"Bea," I said, "I think that the Outhouse is on the other side of the courtyard." It is built of bricks with brown tile floors, with a three feet high decorative tile partition that separates five holes in the floor. (We had been told to bring our own toilet paper.) I never was good at squatting, and this really stretched my endurance. LOL.

A group of us were on our way to a Monastery situated on another mountain. At one point we climbed into a swinging basket for two, and down the zip-line we went above the treetops and the valleys and streams, waving "Hello" to those coming toward us on another zip-line. "Bea, I've never been on a zip-line, have you?" I laughed. She was laughing and said, "No, isn't this fun?" There were four men waiting for us with two chair-carriage apparatuses each tied to four poles. Bea sat in one chair and I sat in the other. One man in front lifted the two poles onto his shoulders and another man lifted the two poles behind me and proceeded with me sitting in this chair-basket, between the poles, on a very narrow path down this mountain toward the Monastery. This path was so steep and so treacherous that I closed my eyes, but then I would be missing all of the beautiful flowers that were blooming along the way, so I tried not to look down very often. I could see snow covered mountains in the distance, which took my mind away from the danger of falling down this mountain. It was a rough ride, but Bea and I laughed as we looked at the beautiful trees, mountains and flowers all the way, as we were jostled from one side to the other.

Arriving at the Monastery I was amazed at the beautiful but very ornate carvings on the entry door. In the center of the Monastery there was a square courtyard; on two sides were the kitchen, dining area and workrooms. On another side is where we (the group) kept our clothes, etc. which was under and on top of the bed, which was a bamboo mat on a wood foundation about two and a half feet above the floor. A mosquito/bug net covered an area of approximately the size of a full size bed. The women occupied the front of the room with the beds end-to end, three on each side of the room, and the men occupied the back of the room. There was one 25-watt light bulb to light the entire room at night. Bea and I were across the narrow aisle-way from each other, using our flashlights so we could see what we were doing at night. "Bea," I called over to her, "My flashlight went dead." And it wasn't long before hers went dead also. Some of the women didn't bring a flashlight, so we couldn't borrow one for even a few minutes. There were no stores up in the mountains to buy batteries or another flashlight, so we had to get everything organized while it was still daylight.

One afternoon I was standing in front of our rooms on the covered walkway that surrounds the courtyard, when it began to thunder, lightening and rain. Master Zang appeared looking up at the sky, and every time there was a bolt of lightening, he shook himself. I asked Dr. Frue, "Do you know why Master Zang shakes himself every time there's a bolt of lightening?" He laughed and said, "There's energy in that bolt, and he absorbs as much of that energy as he can." "Oh," I said, "Bea, let's absorb some of this energy too", and there we were, standing at the edge of the walkway, laughing and shaking ourselves! You know, I did have more energy after that.

Upon returning to the Research Center, we needed a bath. Water was limited; we each were allotted a dishpan full of water and a quart thermos of water to use. Bea said, "The guys over there said that there is a family over thru a forest of trees and up a steep path that has hot water and a shower; everyone takes turns." I don't remember how much it cost, but we really needed a shower. It was dark and we stayed on the path by feeling the bushes, and trying to see the girls ahead of us who had flashlights. (Remember? Our flashlights were dead.)

There were two men and three women stoking the fire under the washtubs, so we had to wait. No one spoke English! Finally, a woman motioned for me to follow her behind a makeshift wood and cotton-sheeting wall where there was a light bulb hanging by a rope and a showerhead hanging by a rope. She motioned for me to remove my clothes as she put them on a bench. I waited for her to leave, then I motioned for her to leave, but she insisted on staying, while she soaped a washcloth and started to wash my back. That was OK, but then she insisted on washing my entire body, drying it and then helped me to put my clothes on. Imagine! Getting service like that up in the mountains of China!

A side-trip is on the agenda, so we rode buses to the Chengdu Hospital. I was in awe at the beautiful countryside; passing large white lily ponds and very steep, narrow waterfalls cascading straight down to plunge into a foaming pond. We stopped at the Embroidery Institute and were given lessons on how to embroider so beautifully; small children were learning the art also. Upon arriving at the Chengdu Hospital we were given a tour. Every profession is included in that hospital; we watched professionals give acupuncture treatments; some of our group received acupuncture treatments while we were there. Some received massages; some had analysis for the use of herbs. Some received Chiropractic spinal adjustments. It is my opinion that it would be an advantage to everyone if hospitals in the States would include all professions, with co-operation among all of them. Then we were introduced to their cafeteria and kitchen, which were spotless. I was asked to plan a meal and to prepare it, which was fun, yet a stressful experience since I could use only the ingredients that were in that kitchen, and I didn't know what half of them were!

As Bea and I were walking to the Educational Building to attend a class, I stumbled on a slight raise in the sidewalk, and down I went on my face with my glasses flying. Some students came running out of the classroom to help me up, and saw that blood was running from above my right eye. Dr. Frue ran to his room and brought back a powdered herb and said, "Mix some spit with this and put it over your eyebrow, and lie down in the reception room for a while." The result is that there is barely a noticeable scar where the skin was broken. The next day I said to Bea, "I must find out why I fell right here. I have a feeling that I lived here in a previous life." Upon meditating, I 'saw' that I had been a very mean Taskmaster, yelling at the men and using a whip to make them row the boat faster down the river that was there at that time. At another time on this trip, I stumbled over a twelve-inch board that was across a doorway and fell on my face again, but no broken skin. I meditated on that one also, and 'saw' that I was a very mean headstrong man again, in another lifetime, and threw a young boy down a stairway because he was so sassy. Wow! I didn't know that I could be so mean! Forgiveness was in order, which I did later in my prayer and meditation time. I am so thankful to have been so aware that I could receive such a wonderful gift from Spirit.

Bea and I were outside of the Educational Building the next day getting a breath of fresh air, when she motioned, "I wonder what that man is doing on his hands and knees." There were many different kinds of writing tools and a bottle of black ink along side him as he was writing on a long, narrow strip of thick, white paper. He spoke enough English to tell us that he was writing a message for another lady. I said, "Bea, these are really nice, and won't take up much space rolled up in our luggage, let's get one." Bea asked the man, "Will you make one for each of us?" The man stood up and said, "I made all of the tools that I use for drawing the letters on this paper." After he finished our prints, I said, "This is beautiful: thank you so very much!" and then I asked, "What do those three words say? "Essence, Chi, Spirit," was the answer. He continued, "Essence is the body or nature, Chi is the mind, and Spirit is life." As I looked more closely at my painting, I saw that he had painted cute little singing blue birds on top of some of the letters! What a novel idea! He was a true artist! I handed him my new camera and asked him if he would sign it for me. He seemed excited, and on my camera he wrote in gold: "Keep all the memories of China forever."

On another day when Bea and I were hanging our clothes to dry on the lines outside of the Campus Building, we noticed another man on his hands and knees in the Campus Courtyard. "Hmmm, I wonder what's going on over there; let's go see," I suggested. Under this man's hands was approximately a five foot long, two feet wide sheet of black paper; on it was a sheet of white paper about three and a half feet long. With the side of his hand dipped in black ink, he drew the Chinese interpretation of a dragon. There was writing along both sides of the tail of the dragon, but I could not understand what he said they meant. He showed us tigers and monkeys, indicating that he would draw any animal that you wanted. A man nearby came to us and said, "This man calls himself the "Barefoot Wandering Spirit." I asked, "Where does he keep all of his paint, paper and everything?" The man interpreted and said, "He says, "My office? The world." I came away with a painting of a dragon and Bea, a tiger, very beautifully done! I realized that these Artists portrayed themselves as being very proud of their profession in spite of the fact that they had no office room/building.

Some of the streets that we walked along were lined with Vendors selling any and everything that you could think of, even bowls of vegetable soup hot off the fire. I took a picture of a man cleaning the wax out of a fellow traveler's ears right in the middle of the sidewalk. Is that a bicycle parking lot? It looked like thousands of bicycles all lined up very orderly in one place. There were very few cars in the streets.

Buses drove us back to the Research Center and as I looked over the brick wall of the Chengdu Research Center I was amazed to see acres and acres of beautiful maize that was in tassel. One of the women in our group said, "I just found out that there is a well and a spring quite a distance from here, where we can bathe and wash our clothes." "Are you kidding?" I said. "Let's go there tomorrow after class." I could hardly wait to tell Bea! Vendors were selling corn, squash, grapes, watermelon, apples and unknown vegetables on the way to the well. We took our dishpan, soap and clean clothes to the spring; brrrr, what cold water for bathing, but it was clean! I noticed a house in the far distance, on the other side of the valley; I was hoping that they didn't have binoculars!

Nearly every one had diarrhea, except the gentleman about my age, another lady and me. Since water was scarce, those who bought produce, like grapes from the Vendors, didn't wash them. I asked one of the men in the room next to our room, "Have you eaten as much rice as the women in the kitchen tell you to?" He frowned and said, "I hate rice!" I said, "I'm getting my fill of it, but I'm forcing it down! Apparently the rice is a neutralizer for all the spices they put in the food, and so that we don't have parasites or have diarrhea." My opinion was that even those who ate rice had diarrhea because they didn't wash the grapes and other fruit; I stayed with watermelon.

One hundred guests had been invited to the Dedication and Opening Ceremony of the Qingcheng Retreat and Research Center; however, more and more people came anyway, until they were sleeping in the Courtyard, in the hallways and outside of the facility. The last count was over five hundred people; many came from hundreds of miles away, (most of them walked) just to be a part of the opening celebration of the Retreat and Research Center. To move from one place to another we had to step over bags of clothes and people; you can imagine how long it took me to go to the toilet facility at night, and standing in line to wait my turn?

The Retreat and Research Center Opening Day of Celebration has arrived and our entire group was getting all prettied up for the occasion. It was so hot; I had no idea that it could be so hot up in the mountains! Dr. Frue, our Director was up on stage with all of the other dignitaries of the Province. The rest of our group had reserved seating right up front. There were many speeches; some were translated and some were not. Appreciation was shown for the building of the Mt. Qingcheng Retreat and Research Center, with song and dance given by several young women performers in colorful traditional Chinese dress; (I could almost touch them as they swirled past me.) It was very emotional and beautiful! There were cameras everywhere. There were people everywhere, even sitting on top of the surrounding wall.

The day following the Ceremony our group was transported by bus from Mt. Qingcheng to Shanghai. One of the bus drivers told us that we absolutely must visit the Underground Mall, so of course that is the first place that we went. The Underground Mall was so extensive that I think it would take days in which to explore it. You could probably furnish a house, a person or an office with any kind of an accessory, plus there was a grocery store, a pharmacy, and a bicycle shop; new and used, but no cars. LOL. I finally sat down with Bev to people-watch, which was a show in itself. Some people were dressed in American attire looking very eccentric, others looked like they worked in an office, or on a dump truck; others wore traditional Chinese attire.

That night I was so glad to finally be in a modern hotel in Shanghi, after sleeping on bamboo mats! Those beds were so comfortable! In the morning I was wondering what our meals would be like. As we sat at the table in the hotel dining room, Chinese waitresses dressed on black with white aprons, served very delicious food, even though I didn't know what most of it was. It was served in courses, family style on a very large black onyx turntable on a white tablecloth, to accommodate about twelve to fourteen people at each round table. The plates, cups and saucers and rice dishes were white china decorated with blue flowers. A watermelon filled with fruit and carved with Chinese sayings all around it was brought to the table; so beautiful! Most of the second day was spent waiting in the long lines at the airport. My endurance was tested again, which was stronger than at the beginning of this trip! Oh, YES!

What fun the zip-line was! I could see that the zip-line was an ingenious method of travel from one mountain to another that would otherwise have been inaccessible; I concluded that it also supplied a means of income for the locals. I admired the Barefoot Wanderer and the other painter for promoting their talent, which they enjoyed, and at the same time it supported them in a free and easy manner of happy living. When Bev invited me to join her on this Research Venture I had no idea how much I would learn about China and the people there; how many health benefits are in herbs; that I would also learn about a couple of my past lives. I am so happy that I accepted her invitation; I feel very blessed!

SHOULD DOGS OR CATS SLEEP NEAR YOUR HEAD?

My son's best friend called and said, "My wife is to have surgery behind her right eye." "What? Why surgery?" I inquired. "Well, she's been having severe headaches; you know, she's had headaches for years, and been so tired, but the headaches have been getting much worse, and unbearable pain which seemed to be in her eye. She had all kinds of eye tests and there's nothing wrong with her eyes, so she went to a Neurologist, had X-Rays and an MRI or CT Scan or something, and the doctors found this tumor behind her eye." "Wow! That's pretty serious," I exclaimed. "We've been praying real hard that she won't loose her eyesight," he offered. "We'll pray for her also! Don't worry, she'll be all right," I said sincerely. I got to thinking, "Why would a tumor grow behind her eye?" Later in the day I remembered something that was said during an earlier visit. We happened to be talking about how dogs love to sleep in bed with their owners. I remember my friend laughing and saying, "My dog sleeps practically on my head; she wiggles herself between my head and the headboard every night." Her husband said, "Yes, she (dog) doesn't pay any attention to me, she's always on top of my wife's head." At that time we just laughed and I thought no more about it. Now that I'm giving it more thought; the Crown Chakra is the top of the head; that's where Universal Energy comes into the body supplying our strength and energy. Could it be that the dog has been receiving energy that my friend should have been receiving all these years? The surgery was successful and now she has good eyesight and we were all very thankful. After she was home I visited her, and told her about my theory concerning the Crown Chakra. "Well," my friend replied, "I'll try to get my dog to sleep somewhere else in the bed from now on, it's certainly worth a try! I certainly don't want anymore tumors!" Months went by and when I talked to her on the phone she said, "You know, I have more energy than I've had for years! That must be the reason that I've always been so tired, my dog sleeping on my head." I laughed and asked her, "Where does she sleep now?" The reply was, "We both had to retrain her, and we finally got her to sleep between us at our legs and now she keeps our feet warm." We both laughed and she said, "I'm so glad that I took your advice!" Circumstances like this keep me inspired to inform others of things that can improve their health.

HAWAII

"Hawaii? You're inviting me to go with you to Hawaii? Bob is no longer alive, and I don't know if I should go," I hesitatingly answered Ken. "It's our 25th wedding anniversary, and we want you to go with us anyway, why not?" countered Connie. So Ken planned the entire trip for us to see four of the islands in February, which is a very cold month in Michigan, and February is a very good time to go to Hawaii. After the long plane ride and the door opened, I heard, "Aloha! Aloha!" Everyone received beautiful fresh orchid leis; mine was blue, yellow and pink and I felt like Royalty! To the hotel we rode for an elegant breakfast buffet. "Connie," I remarked, "These tree ripened bananas, and fresh pineapple from the fields just melt in my mouth; I've never tasted anything so delicious! I never liked papaya, but these are really delicious!" There were many other fruits such as, kiwi, grapes, oranges, grapefruit, plums and other fruits. Eggs were prepared several different ways, bacon, ham, cheeses, sweet rolls, toast, milk and coffee; I'm sure that I left out something.

That evening we enjoyed a scrumptious Luau, and the next day we visited orchid gardens, and poinsettias and azaleas that were over six feet tall, and Macadamia trees. The largest Banyan tree that I had ever seen was planted in 1873 at Lahaina, Maui and shades an area of three quarters of an acre! Imagine! Connie is scared silly of birds, so I was wondering what she would do at the Bird Show. "Come on Connie, that bird won't hurt you! Stand a little closer, just a little more, Connie, just a little more, so I can get the bird and you in the picture," Believe it or not, I got her to stand within two feet of this huge parrot!

We flew to Pearl Harbor, Oahu to see the U.S.S. Arizona Memorial, which was quite impressive. The Arizona is under a shelter and we couldn't get very close to it. The Memorial Wall has the names of all the men and says "To The Memory Of The Gallant Men Here Entombed And Their Shipmates Who Gave Their Lives In Action On December 7,1941 On The U.S.S. Arizona". The Punchbowl Crater outside of Honolulu is where our Pearl Harbor Service Men of WW ll, were buried. At the end of a long path the Lady statue at the top of the steps is holding an Olive Branch, which represents Peace for those who were not found.

Waterfall, waterfalls, waterfalls! I couldn't believe how many I saw on every Island. "Ken", I called from the backseat of the car, "there's a waterfall alongside the road up ahead, let's stop and get a drink from it." Connie said, "We don't have any cups." "We'll use our hands for cups," I laughed. Oh that water was so cool and tasty! I was surprised that most of the beaches are rocks; one beautiful sandy beach was at the hotel on Maui. I had no idea of what a pineapple looks like while growing in a field, well, we saw acres and acres of pineapples growing near Kahului; it takes 18 months for one crop to be ready to pick. What a sight! We stood on the southernmost point of the Big Island of Hawaii, and it IS a Point. Barren, rocky land stands high above the Pacific Ocean where a lookout platform has been erected. The waves below us were pounding up on the cliffs showing us just how powerful water can be; then the waves turned into a white, foamy, frothy substance that made me wonder; how could water be so powerful?

The Kilauea Volcano was erupting and we drove as close to it as we could get; I said to Ken, "How can we see it more closely?" "In a plane!" Ken said. (Connie is afraid to fly in a small plane even though Ken is part owner of one.) Ken said, "Aileen, Connie, how would you like to fly over that volcano?" I said "I would love to, wouldn't you, Connie?" Connie took a couple steps back and said, "NO, No, do you really want to go up in that little plane, Aileen? Well, OK, you go ahead and tell me all about it when you come back." I was becoming excited and asked Ken," How much would it cost, and for how long?" He said, "It really doesn't matter, does it? When will we get a chance like this again? It isn't every day that a volcano decides to erupt, and here we are when it happens." We were about to get into the plane when Ken asked me, "You won't get sick, will you?" I told him, "When I was a teenager my cousin treated me to a ride in a small plane, and I really loved it, so I assure you, I'll be all right." The pilot was very accommodating and friendly by flying around the perimeter of the volcano so we could see how large the volcano is, then he flew higher up so we could see the lava spewing out through a hole near the top of the volcano, then he said, "Now I'm going to fly over the top of the volcano and you can see right down on the top of it." Ken said, "Look how that red-hot lava undulates as it boils up to the top, and when you think it will spew out of the top, it shoots out of the hole." It was so fascinating to watch the red-orange lava as it undulates up near the top and then out of the hole. "OH, Look, Ken! See how that red-hot lava is still boiling hot as it runs toward the sea! It looks like fire!" It had run over one of the roads nearby, cooked the landscape and destroyed a house in its path as it continued on to the ocean. "Listen Ken! Hear that hot lava crackle when it hits the sea? It's really loud!" The Pilot offered more information, "See, over there that black sand? The lava is what makes that black sand. The Hawaiians make many things out of that black sand, statue images of King Kilauea, ash trays, dolphins, lamps and many other things which also helps the economy." He flew over the volcano several times as we admired the beauty of the erupting Kilauea Volcano and I wondered if it would suddenly shoot up toward the sky!

We visited the Haleakala Crater on Maui, 7 1/2 miles long, 2 1/2 miles wide and 3,000 feet deep. We had to see it to believe it was so huge. It had erupted in 1790. Our last day on the Islands was spent enjoying the beach in front of the hotel in Kauai celebrating Ken and Connie's 25th Wedding Anniversary. Ken presented Connie and I with beautiful corsages before dining on a fabulous meal served so elegantly that I felt like royalty!

As I reflect upon that exciting, interesting trip, I realize how much love there is between my friends and me, by inviting me to share their joy in celebrating their 25th Wedding Anniversary. I'm not sure if a scheduled, guided tour would have been as thorough and as interesting as the one that Ken planned for us, which I thoroughly enjoyed. I had so much fun with Ken and Connie, especially drinking from a roadside waterfall and watching from the air an erupting volcano. I feel that it has been an honor enjoying this trip with my friends.

TERRI'S AND ROGER'S WEDDING

My youngest daughter, Terri and her fiancé, Roger decided to get married on a Yacht out in the ocean!"(Roger doesn't like to get dressed up, and on the yacht he can wear shorts. LOL.) "That's a great idea," I exclaimed. I was so excited as she was explaining all the details. Her brother, Bob said that he didn't know if he and Dana could make it, "Summer time is the busiest time of the year for me, you know,"(being a Builder). That made Terri very sad. When we arrived at the Yacht, the Skipper and Mate welcomed us aboard. Bob and Dana's surprise arrival had to be coordinated with the time that the bride and groom would be down below getting dressed for the ceremony. When Terri came up the stairway, the first person that she saw was her brother! With tears in her eyes, and almost falling backwards on the stairs she yelled, "BOB! You're here!!!" hugging and kissing him and Dana!

The wedding was lovely at the bow of the Yacht, with Terri's brother, Bob as Best Man and Terri's sister, Debbie as Maid of Honor. I blessed the rings, and the Captain performed the lovely Wedding Ceremony. On the plane Terri had brought a special cake and cookies, from her special bakery in Michigan; yes, they were still in perfect condition and so delicious!

After the ceremony, Terri said, "Let's everybody go swimming and snorkeling!" I said, "Go ahead, I don't swim, and I've never snorkeled, I'll just watch." "Don't worry," said the Captain, "I'll put a life jacket on you, and when you get into the water, just hold on to that line. I'll keep a close watch on you." Terri said, "I'll show you how to snorkel." I really wanted to do this, so I conquered my fear and trusted the Captain and my daughter's experience in the water. "Oh, my!" I exclaimed, "I can hardly believe how beautiful the fish and everything is down there!" I was so fascinated that later they could hardly get me out of the water! Dear friends, Sam and Rachel joined us in the evening at the outdoor freshly caught fish fry reception at a hotel. Everyone had so much fun! Looking back at my daughter's wedding and noticing how much fun everyone was having, I concluded that a non-traditional wedding can be as much fun as any other wedding.

ISRAEL

Cousin MaryLee phoned one day and excitedly asked, "Would you like to go to Israel with our church group? I know that you've been to Egypt, but this trip is to Israel, and it would be fun to have you with us." "Oh, I'd love to, MaryLee, I will have to let you know." So I'm thinking, "When will I have a chance like this, with a group that I know, and will be safe traveling with?" Putting the budget aside, I called MaryLee and said, "Good news, MaryLee! I've decided to go with you. When will I have another chance to spend that much time with you, and see the sights at the same time? I know that it will be fun, too." She excitedly said, "I'll call the Pastor of the church right away and tell him that you will be going with us!"

In Tabgha, beside the Sea of Galilee we visited the Church of the Primacy of St. Peter where Christ preached to the multitudes and multiplied the fishes and the loaves of bread. Our group boarded boats that sailed out onto the Sea of Galilee for prayer and meditation on Sunday morning. I thought that it was a very uplifting experience! We visited Church of Gethsemane, (which is called The Church of All Nations), the Church of Pater Nostra, The Church of The Holy Sepulchre, and the Holy Nativity. I noticed that most of the churches that we visited had very beautifully designed colorful tile floors. I learned that Megiddo was a very important city because it controlled the trade routes between Egypt and Mesopotamia, and the Phoenician cities with Jerusalem. I saw that the huge public grain silos in Megiddo were built in the ground rather on top of the ground as we do in America; it's claimed that grain keeps better in the ground. I waded in the Dead Sea, which is really a lake, and it felt different, rather thick.

The only Golf Club in Israel is in Caesarea. I'm smiling because in the States there are Golf Clubs/Courses everywhere! The huge Amphitheater is also in Caesarea and had perfect acoustics. I asked MaryLee, "Why can't we build something like that in the states?" She didn't have an answer. I dipped my hands in the Jordan River at the place where Jesus was supposed to have been baptized; I thought that the water felt soft. New settlements/buildings were built near the Mt. of Olives, for 25,000 Russians to live in. I wondered what all the fighting was about? Thousands of people come to the Wailing Wall to pray and leave notes of their wishes in-between the stones. On the streets are Vendors with their wagons loaded with round or long loaves of bread and they offered me a piece of bread with finely ground thyme; I liked thyme so much that I brought some home and have used it ever since in making soups and in baking.

We traveled to the Garden Tomb amongst the olive trees and held communion there. We saw where the huge round rock was rolled away from the opening to the tomb, which was in a huge boulder in the side of the hill. The trench was quite deep.

Back in the city we met a man who has seven wives and eighteen children who were all elegantly dressed with much jewelry. I wondered how he made a living for that family! On our way to Cairo on the Egyptian border by bus, several Police cars stopped us at noon and one of the officers said, "Here are your box lunches." Why? We were informed that we were too close to the West Bank where there was fighting, so it was too dangerous to get off the bus!

On our flight back to the United States everyone was talking about how happy they are that they took the trip, even though they are tired. I was thinking how thoughtful my cousin was to invite me to go with her group to Israel since we live in different states. I enjoyed being with them; we had a lot of fun!

MOTHER! EAT YOUR BREAKFAST!

Sometime in 1990 when I visited my Mother in Florida, I noticed that she had lost some weight and seemed to have lost interest in life ever since my Dad (her husband) had divorced her just before their 60th wedding anniversary. As I was leaving to return to Michigan we kissed Goodbye and I said, "I'll see you in about six months." Mother smiled as she said, "Make it three months." I shook my head and said, "I don't know if I can come back that soon, but I'll try."

"Mother! Come eat your breakfast; your coffee is getting cold," called my sister from the Florida kitchen. (Marjorie related this information to me.) Marjorie said that she heard no movement from the bedroom, so she called again, "Mother, are you sick? Don't you want your breakfast?" Again no answer, so Marjorie went into the bedroom and saw that Mother was still in bed and said, "Mother! Get out of bed!" Mother very weakly said, "I can't move," whereupon Marjorie tried to help her to sit up but she was too stiff. Marjorie called EMS and the doctors and nurses were astonished that such a healthy looking woman could be so ill. After many tests the doctor explained, "She has a blood infection, but why she can not move is a question that we are unable to answer. All the above took place exactly three months after my visit. I wonder if she had had a premonition. As soon as I could get a flight to Florida I visited Mother in the hospital; she was no longer stiff. Mother seemed quite chipper as I walked into the room, greeting me with, "Hello, daughter! How long will you stay this time?" As the days passed, her memory passed also, and it surprised me that she recognized her cousin, Loren, who she hadn't seen in a long time. As I entered the dining room the next week I called, "Happy Birthday Mother!" On her table was a vase of colorful flowers and in front of her was a beautiful pink and blue decorated cake! I told the Staff how grateful I was that they had remembered her birthday. 90 years old already, and she doesn't look her age after having worked on the farm most of her life, and then helping in their Rose Fields in her 80's! Mother's health continued to decline and sometimes she knew me and sometimes not. My daughter, Debbie and I drove home to Michigan together. Upon entering the house, the first thing I did was to check the answering machine messages, "Hello Aileen, this is the Nursing Home. I'm so sorry to leave this message, but your Mother passed away just this morning. I've already called the Funeral Home. Call me as soon as you get this message." (Mother passed away the day before my birthday.) I took a deep breath. My dear friend, Connie offered to go with me in her new Lincoln. The Nursing Home had taken care of everything, so all I had to do was sign some papers. The day of the funeral began with heavy fog, progressing to drizzle then pour down rain; I mean in buckets! After the Service we went to the restaurant where I had made arrangements for everyone who was brave enough to weather the weather, to enjoy a buffet lunch. It was of great comfort to me that my dear friend Connie was with Marjorie and me, to give us consolation during this time of sadness. Mother's faith in God and prayer were very strong, and she did not suffer physical pain, therefore I was content in her passing. She was 94.

CHIROPRACTIC CENTENNIAL, DAVENPORT, IOWA

What a great celebration this will be! I planned to go, but it would be so much more fun to take the trip with someone, but with whom? The phone rang. "Hello Dr. Miller, this is Dr. Allene. Are you going to the Palmer Centennial in August?" "Yes, Allene, I am planning to go; this will be my 50-year Anniversary of being in Practice! Are you going?" I asked. I was getting so excited that I could hardly wait for her answer. She said, "I've already looked into Bed and Breakfast facilities; I'll send you some pictures and see what you think about which one we would like, rather than to live in a hotel for a week." That sounded just perfect and she had done the 'leg-work' already. "Great! We can share the driving, gas and other expenses," I volunteered. "I'll do all the driving because I get nervous when someone else drives," she insisted. We agreed on the B & B not far from where I began my Chiropractic Practice in Rock Island, Illinois after graduating from Palmer College. "Just one thing, Allene, if you don't mind," I said, "There's a cousin just outside of Chicago who I'd like to stop and see on our way home from the Centennial. I haven't seen him for many years. We'll just stop for a couple hours so we can be home on schedule, OK?" I could hear her breathe a sigh of relief as she said, "Of course we can do that; it will give us a nice break."

As we drove up to the Victorian Inn I felt that we had made the right choice! It was truly Victorian outside and inside! Pictures, clocks, many dolls, lamps, china, crystal pitchers, wedding gowns in every room; even an antique grand piano in the corner of the living room. Breakfast and dinner were served family-style with other guests at a long table with an embroidered white tablecloth. A crystal vase with fresh flowers and crystal candlesticks adorned the center of the table. The food was served on special china plates, cups and saucers with blue flowers; beautifully embossed silverware and etched crystal glasses. Breakfast began with assorted fruits, a choice of eggs to your liking with bacon, or cereal or both, muffins, toast, assorted homemade jams and jellies, honey, butter, coffee and tea, milk or rice milk. Dinners began with fruit juice and there were always several vegetables, two salads and meat or fish; I was happy that there was no pork (except the bacon for breakfast). The owner of the establishment served us a very unusual delicious dessert, which she made fresh each night.

The Centennial Convention was held in the River Convention Center in Davenport, Iowa and right at the front entrance was displayed Dr. B. J. Palmer's yellow Cadillac car. So many people and so many Vendors and so many classes to attend; it was difficult to make choices. My favorite Philosophy Instructor, Dr. Galen Price gave an informative talk on what else but Philosophy and The Science of Chiropractic. (Of course I had my picture taken with him). Amongst thousands of attendees, I thought it a stroke of luck to meet up with friends, such as the Activator Developer; the Developer of the Atlas Orthogonal Technique which is a refinement of the Grostic Technic, the Technic that I use; Dr. Parker, Founder and President of the Parker Chiropractic College; President of the Sherman Chiropractic College; the N.U.C.C.A. Instructor, and others. It was fun browsing through the B. J. Palmer Archives, looking at the many skulls and spines and bones and much more, and to see how the design of the adjusting tables has evolved through those 100 years. In 1995 I wondered how there could be any other improvements, and yet each year there are many more improvements to make it more efficient for the Chiropractor and more comfortable for the patient, while receiving practically non-force adjustments of the spine.

The highlight (for me) was special recognition by the "50 Year Club" in the Palmer Mansion at which Dr. B.J. Palmer's daughter, Dr. Agnes Palmer pinned a beautiful corsage of yellow roses on each one of us, and the President of Palmer College, Dr. Strang presented the Palmer Crest Pin and Crest Fountain pen and 50 year Service Medallion to us. (Twenty years earlier I had been presented with a 30 year Humanitarian Award plaque.) Pictures were taken, which included my dear friend, Dr. Theresa Gray who came from Wisconsin, Drs. Marvin Frederick, Jean Koffel and Jaqueline Elmer; Dr. Aline Merkel was not able to attend. Drs. W. Derifield, S. Fredericks, McGinnis and Radell, who had been honored in previous years watched from the sidelines; also joining us at the luncheon were Drs. Esther and Arthur Mork who had been in Practice for over 60 years; Theresa's husband, Dr. Merlin Gray, and others attended.

On our way back home to Michigan we stopped at my cousin, Floyd's home. My cousin, with his 3 fluffy, brown dogs welcomed us in the driveway. "Hi, Aileen, it's so thoughtful of you to stop by here, and so good to see you," remarked Floyd. "Come on in", called his wife, Helen from the kitchen door. Their home was lovely, and we had a few laughs bringing each other up-to-date, which ended all too soon, so that we could get home the same day; well, almost, at 1:00 A.M. the next day.

I had wondered about traveling with my colleague, Dr. Allene because our personalities are so different. Since she had already researched the various

Bed & Breakfast's showed me that she's very responsible. Her desire to do all the driving suited me just fine, and she didn't hesitate at my desire to visit my cousin on the way back home. It was fun visiting my Alma Mater. Upon reflection of the very enjoyable trip, my wishes of attending the 100th Anniversary of Chiropractic were fulfilled, and more. I am blessed!

I give much of my success as a Doctor of Chiropractic, to the Specific Adjusting Technique that I used since 1947, especially the Grostic Technique. Dr. B. J. Palmer, President of the Palmer School of Chiropractic (now named the Palmer College of Chiropractic) developed the "Whole In One" method of adjusting the cervical (neck) vertebrae, and my Mother was one of the first recipients. I was very impressed that he was continuing to improve upon the very technique that he had first discovered. Later, when I was enrolled in the Palmer College, I was most interested in the Art and Science of Chiropractic and my goal was to administer the most effective adjustment.

During one of my Post Graduate Seminars I attended a lecture given by Dr. John F. Grostic and was so impressed by the improvements that he had made concerning X-Ray analysis and the adjusting technique of the Cervical spine, that I attended many of his classes and used his new non-force technique, which was named the Grostic Technique. After Dr. Grostic's passing, Dr. Gregory, his assistant teacher, began teaching the classes, of which I attended. Dr. Gregory named the group NUCCA (National Upper Cervical Chiropractic Association). Later most of the students who lived in the southern states, broke away and when I heard that a few of my Grostic classmates had improved upon the Grostic Technique, I had to find out what it was, so I began attending their classes of which was named Orthospinology; I am always learning and improving.

As time went on, other classmates, mainly Dr. Roy Sweat, changed the Orthospinology Technique a bit and invented, or helped to invent an instrument designed specifically for adjusting the atlas vertebrae. Of course I attended many of Dr. Sweat's classes so that I could also improve. Through Dr. Sweat's perseverance, an adjusting table was designed and manufactured to accommodate that instrument. Yes, more improvements and even better patient results. There probably will be even more refinements of the non-force adjusting technique in the future. I am so very thankful that God directed me to attend Dr. Grostic's lecture so many years ago, that kept me on that path of expertise, and that He and my family supported me all the way.

HEALING CIRCLE EXPERIENCES

For the last few years we've met in Joyce and Harold's home since Harold was in a wheelchair, unable to walk or dress himself. Harold enjoyed being in the Circle with us, so Joy maneuvered Harold from his bed onto the harness "Lift" and swung him around to release him onto the wheelchair so that he could join us in their living room. We (about fifteen of us) would gather around the massage table, join hands, and Joyce would offer a prayer of healing to the Universe and ask for Divine Guidance. Those who desired healing would take turns lying on the massage table; then each of us would scan the body that was on the massage table and send healing energy into the area. During this time I noticed that Harold's facial muscles would relax, and sometimes he would laugh softly; I'm sure that he felt God's energy in that room. On one particular evening one of the participants brought her little grandchild (approximately 4-5 months old) to our Circle. When Grandmother Laura stood beside the massage table this baby leaned over the person on the table, scanned up and down the body very intently with her eyes and then just stare for a few seconds; when she was finished she would stare at another area. When she was finished, she would settle back into her Grandmother's arms, coo, play with her grandmother's hair or necklace, or want down on the floor to play, just as though nothing unusual had taken place. We looked at each other and agreed that this sweet, precious baby was sending healing energy into each one of us as we presented ourselves for healing. I could feel a wave going through my body. This baby was such a pure channel of God's energy; we were always happy when Laura would bring her grandchild to our Healing Circle. Today this person is married, has children of her own and uses her Healing Gift wherever she is called to go.

One of my unusually wonderful experiences was during the time that a worried Mother brought her teenage son to our Healing Circle. She said, "I've taken my son to many doctors to find out why he is so tired all the time, no amount of sleep seems to help; and he's been to Nutritionists to change his food choices; he gets blinding headaches that affect his eyesight and suddenly leave; he's had X-Rays; the doctors say, "There is nothing medically wrong with your son." I don't know what to do, so here we are." Laura said, "We don't diagnose, we don't even touch whomever is on the massage table. If it's meant for him to receive God's Healing energy, it will happen." Turning to the boy, she said, "Do you like school? What is your favorite subject?" I don't remember what he said, but I do remember what he said when she asked him, "Would you really like to be well?" "I sure would!" he exclaimed, It's awful, just hoping the pain will go away, and when it does, I'm too tired to study, or do anything." After the teenager was on the table I concentrated on him, and my attention was drawn to his head, so I began to scan his brain; at first I thought it to be the pineal gland, but as I scanned farther back I saw a dark spot and knew it should not be there. As I focused on that spot, I pointed my finger to that spot, and saw a golden ray of light project from my finger to that dark spot in his head. I moved my finger slightly, which sent the ray around that spot. Without moving my finger I saw the golden ray of light go down through the boy's body and out. I felt elated, and a bit dizzy. In a minute or two he got off the table and said to his Mom, "I feel like my head is not so heavy and it doesn't hurt!" Hesitating a bit he added, "My eyes feel different." A few weeks later the Mother contacted Laura and told her that she was so grateful for having brought her son to our Circle because he has not had a headache since then, and has more energy each day. Due to these healing experiences I am convinced more and more how important it is to call upon God's healing energy anytime and anywhere.

MARJORIE'S BIRTHDAY PARTY

My sister has reached the 3/4 of a century mark this year and I decided to give her a surprise birthday party the following February when I planned to vacation in Florida. One day I called her and during the conversation, I said, "Marjorie, how about giving me all your friend's phone numbers?" I could hear the crunching of the newspaper, so I knew that she had been reading the Daily News, when she asked, "Why do you want their phone numbers?" (She has always been so secretive about her personal life.) "Well, if for some reason you can't get to a phone, or something happens, I think I should have their numbers on hand, don't you think so?" "OK, I have my address book right here, so I can read them off to you," she offered. I was so relieved that she didn't question me further, and I called her friends to say, "I'll be in Florida in February, can you meet us at Baker's Restaurant, on the 1st, at 12 noon? It has easy access and good food." Each friend said, "That's a great idea! October birthday in Feb! I'll mark my calendar."

"Why does it have to rain today, of all days?" I inquired, as I was trying to get the Birthday Banner, balloons and gifts inside the restaurant. I held the umbrella over Marjorie as she was trying not to slip on the wet sidewalk; it's a bit tricky when relying on Sister Kenny Walking Sticks to help give your legs support. Marjorie was almost too excited to eat her lunch; after she finished I said, "Now Marjorie, you can open your gifts." I had never seen Marjorie so emotional! During lively conversations Marjorie spoke up saying, "You don't know how much I am enjoying this! I've never had a birthday party since I went away to Nurse's Training, other than with my immediate family." I was shocked! I couldn't believe what I was hearing! Lena said, "Oh, Marjorie, surely you've had a birthday party before now!" Everyone became so quiet because they couldn't believe it either. "The only party I've ever had," she began, "was a "Going Away" party when I graduated from Louisville General Hospital as a Registered Nurse." "Oh My!" Eva blurted out, "I'm so glad that I came to help you celebrate! I hope you have many more happy birthdays and parties!" I put the birthday cake in front of Marjorie, lit the candles and said, "Now make a wish first, then blow out the candles." As she blew out the candles we all sang, "Happy Birthday to You", and "For She's a Jolly Good Fellow!" There wasn't a dry eye among us. I never knew that none of Marjorie's friends had ever given her a birthday party; I was so happy and grateful that Spirit had led me to give her a party with her friends. I'll always remember that emotional day!

Which reminds me of my first real birthday party. I was working at a big Engine company, saving tuition towards Palmer Chiropractic College. I rode my bicycle home from work and parked it alongside the other employee's bikes. I had worked really hard and was rather tired as I slowly climbed the wood staircase up to my room. My roommate, Loraine met me at the top of the stairs and said, "Come in here for a minute, I want to show you something." I said, "Well, Ok, but I have to wash my hands first." She seemed in a hurry when I came out and rushed me to the dining room. As she opened the door I saw the table surrounded with people; suddenly they all jumped up yelling, "SURPRISE! HAPPY BIRTHDAY AILEEN!!" I was shocked and ran out of the room crying to the bathroom with Loraine on my heels. She anxiously asked, "What's the matter?" Between sobs I said, "I don't like surprises! Why did you do this?" She said, "Are you really mad? You're not, are you?" She finally calmed me down, and with my flushed face we entered the beautifully decorated room with streamers, Happy Birthday balloons and little individual flower plants on the table. All I could say was, "I'm sorry!" I was so embarrassed! Everyone laughed as we played games and I opened little gifts; then we enjoyed cake and ice cream. I will always remember that day, my 18th birthday! I didn't realize until much later how much I meant to Loraine; she wanted to surprise me on my 18th birthday and share it with my/our friends.

"BEAUTIFUL OVER HERE"

Sound asleep, or I thought I was sound asleep, when I heard my name, "Aileen, it's Norman!" just as clear as though he was right in the room with me. Norman was one of the students in Palmer College who introduced my husband and I when Norman was working for a hotel parking service in Davenport, Iowa. "Norman," I mentally answered, "did you just cross over to the other side? What happened?" "Yes," he answered, "and it was so easy; I just floated up and out of my body and looked around, and there I was down there." I was afraid that he would leave if I didn't talk, so I said, "What's it like where you are? Did you see your wife or anyone who you know?" "Oh, every one I ever knew was there when I opened my eyes again, or so it seemed, laughing and clapping. Your Bob was there, with open arms, just wanted you to know. It's so beautiful over here! Beautiful beyond words! So free!" he explained. I wanted to know more, but he had to go as his words were fading. What a surprise; to hear from someone who I had not thought about for a long time! I then realized that there has been a very strong connection between the two of us because of Bob. I was consoled to hear those words from the "other side".

MY ORDINATION

My friend, Emily C. and I left early to drive to Seminary classes in Roanoke, Va., stopping along the way to visit Tamarack, the General Lewis Hotel, Greenbriar, Warm Springs, Natural Bridge and Falls and the Wax Museum. Upon arriving at the United Metaphysical Churches Headquarters we registered and asked which room we would be occupying. The Dormitory had been newly decorated and I was given the best room, with Emily just down the hall. I said, "There are two beds in this large room, and Emily can room with me." The Registrant smiled and said, "Rev. Reed Brown has assigned this room to you alone." My, what a surprise! I asked why and got a shrug of her shoulders, as she walked away smiling.

Most of the classes I had already attended, but it was good to review them, and to renew acquaintances at the same time. It was fun. After one of the evening meals as I was riding in Rev. Reed's car to see the City Star at the top of The Hill, Rev. Reed said, "It's about time that you were Ordained, have you thought about it?" Surprised, I commented, "I've been taking your classes in Michigan, and here, and Camp Chesterfield because I wanted to learn more about the Bible and how it pertains to man today. I've had no intention of being ordained."

Rev. Reed laughed and said, "I'm sure that you have more than enough credits to be ordained." I countered, "I don't know if I want to be a minister." "My dear, you are a minister anyway, with all that you do in your Practice and in your church," he went on, "You might as well have a title to go with it." Next day he said, "I already have all of your records. I'll present them to the Board and let you know what their vote is."

The United Metaphysical Churches Annual Convention was coming up; the local church board had voted me in as a Delegate to the Convention. My friend, Emily and I were preparing for the drive from Michigan to Roanoke, Virginia. The day before leaving for the convention I received a phone call from Rev. Reed. "Hello Reed, how are you?" I could feel the smile on his face as he shouted, "I couldn't be better! BRING YOUR ROBE! The Board voted you in to be Ordained!" "Wow!" I exclaimed,

"Already?" I really was surprised! A good thing that we were planning to drive; my robe could hang in the car and not get all wrinkled in a suitcase. On the way, we took a drive through a beautiful State Forest. Finding a picnic table, we sat to meditate; I heard a little rustle and turning slowly I saw a beautiful, tan colored doe only about fifteen feet away, just standing there. I motioned to Emily; as she slowly turned a little beautiful champagne colored fawn came out of the foliage toward her mother; they hesitated and then disappeared through the foliage on the other side. Meditating with your eyes open is not an easy thing to do, but I didn't want to miss anything else. A Muskrat shuffled through the leaves as a bushy brown squirrel sat up in the tree two feet away gnawing on something. As we decided to leave, four wild turkeys crossed the path only ten feet away as though we were not even there. I felt that I was so lucky to have been there at that time! Look what we would have missed if we had flown! Emily and I were assigned lovely rooms in "The Big House" where we had kitchen privileges and a washer and dryer. How thoughtful! I felt very privileged!

The Ordination Day arrived and I was ready in my navy robe. My local minister, Rev. John presented me at the Alter to The Reverend F. Reed Brown to be Ordained. Three others were ordained with me. Four more people who had been ordained in other churches were accepted into the Ministerial Service of the United Metaphysical Churches. A lovely Reception of Hors d' Oeuvres, ice cream, cake and wine followed the Ordination Ceremony. I was sorry that my family, all living in Michigan could not attend, but I was happy that my friend, Emily had accompanied me on this important trip.

MARJORIE HAS CANCER

Dr. Shelby, a Neurosurgeon who I had met at the Edgar Cayce Foundation, invited me to visit his Clinic in Missouri. He was considering adding Chiropractors to his Staff. While there I received a phone call saying that my sister in Florida, was taken to the hospital. I flew to her side and the doctor informed me, "Marjorie has cancer; I recommend radiation treatments; surgery is not an option." I was shocked! I called her daughter in Texas to tell her the news about her Mother. Hope Lodge, supported by the American Cancer Society and Winn Dixie Grocery Stores, was across the street from the hospital; I was so thankful that we could live there, and that I didn't need to drive back and forth from her home everyday for five weeks. Winn Dixie supplied some of the food for the patients who were staying there; I noticed that they ate mostly starchy and sweet foods like pastries, which are not nutritious for cancer patients. I noticed also that those who were quite mobile just sat and read or watched TV. Those observances bothered me and so I approached the Manager of Hope Lodge, and the outcome of the conversation was that my talk on Exercise was attended enthusiastically, and so was my talk on Nutrition! I felt that I had performed a necessary service.

Following my sister's series of radiation treatments, the doctor recommended a week's rest and then radium treatments to perhaps kill the cancer. I asked, "Marjorie, do you really want to go through with those treatments after all you have been through?" She responded, "What do I have to lose?" I felt that she would not live much longer, so I called her daughter, Johanna, (they had not seen each other in many years). "If you want to see your Mother alive, your visit would be a wonderful birthday gift to her; you don't know how happy she would be to see you!" I was so afraid that she would not come, until I saw her car in the driveway. I was so glad that they had a happy reunion before the radium treatments began! After the radium treatments, which she said, "They were so painful!" Marjorie was settled in the hospital and well taken care of. A doctor from England was going to lecture on Astral Projection, on Transfiguration and Life After Death; I felt very fortunate to be able to attend them between visits to my sister. I was also grateful that I could slip in a visit to Warm Mineral Springs for a bit of rejuvenation! Terri and Debbie came to Florida to visit their Aunt Marjorie, and helped me clean and distribute some of her clothes. At a later time my daughter Debbie visited and had her laughing. I needed to get back to Michigan for a while and said to my sister, "Marjorie, Debbie and I are going back home, and I will try to come back in a week or so." She was very weak, but I thought that she might live a while longer. The first thing upon entering my house was to check my answering machine messages: I heard, "This is the Nurse at the hospital; Marjorie passed away at 6:30 P.M. (the very day that we left), she's at the Funeral Home." When my sister was stricken with Polio on her 21st birthday, my Mother was told that Marjorie would probably not live past her 41st birthday. Having good genes, good food, excellent Chiropractic care, a strong faith in God, the power of prayer and determination my sister proved that her capabilities as a Registered Nurse were needed much longer than 41 years. She was 79. I am very proud of her!

My friend, Connie drove with me to be with me during my sister's funeral. Terri asked me to put the family cameo pin on her Aunt. Friends came in shaking their coats; wouldn't you know it! Pour down rain! The air was heavy as the minister ended the Service.

To relax and uplift our Spirits before our trip back home, Connie and I took a dip in Warm Mineral Springs. It's a good thing that I was relaxed; I drove us through a snowstorm from Tennessee to Michigan! I asked for God's help and received it; therefore I felt calm and peaceful rather than uptight.

TO STAY OR NOT TO STAY

My voice had become very weak and I had heart palpitations/fibrillations all the time, which took much of my energy. (I had been under quite a lot of stress.) I did see a doctor, who gave me some pills, which didn't do a thing for me. Ten days later I was resting in bed during the day feeling very weak, and began meditating. I felt very light, like I could just leave the earth at any moment, if I wanted to. I called upon my Spirit Guides and asked them what I should do; they suggested that I stay with my family and also be available to help others, and to get more rest; I took their advice. From that moment on, except when I was over-tired, I had no more fibrillation of the heart. I decided to rest more frequently, and be more aware of my Spirit Guides and keep an ear open when they needed to tell me something.

I had been having some difficulty in talking. My voice sounded horsey/ raspy, so I went to an Otorhinolaryngologist who told me that since I had strained my voice talking to my nearly deaf Aunt I should take this liquid medicine twice a day for two weeks; when I returned in two weeks he said, "The polyp is gone, but the vocal cords are bowed. The vocal cords should be straight and touching when not talking." How did he know this? He actually took a picture of them and showed them to me. "What do we do about that?" I inquired. The doctor instructed, "Don't talk or even whisper for two weeks." When I told my children that, they just laughed and said, "You? Not talk for two weeks?" I think it was Debbie who laughingly said, "I'd almost put a bet on that!" Believe it or not, I did not speak, but wrote a lot of notes. On the sixth day, the doctor had me say a few words and my voice was normal! "Talk as little as possible and not loud," he said, "or your voice will be back where it was. We need to do some Voice Training to strengthen your vocal cords in the right manner." Voice training was successful; after eight weeks my voice sounded normal again. I realized how important it is to follow the doctor's directions for healing to take place.

INTERESTING VORTEX

A member of our Meditation/Healing group invited the rest of us to her farm for a Potluck Gathering with her daughter and her tiny tot, and her Mother. After filling ourselves with so much delicious food, Laura said, "Let's go for a walk into the wooded area, there's a vortex of energy up there and I'd like to see how many of you can find it." Hmmm, I thought, a vortex? I found the one in Camp Chesterfield; I wonder if I can find this one? Others ahead of me found the vortex quite easily. Laura's beautiful collie dog walked ahead of us; did he lead them to it? Laura's father was a member of the Masonic Lodge for many years and the members would meet there during the summer months. As the older ones passed away, the younger ones said that they preferred to meet in a building all year around, yet the evidence of the pedestals and the stones and tree stumps as chairs were still there among the leaves. The energy was very refreshing so we decided to meditate on the vortex in the Masonic Center. There were twelve of us on our backs, on the Vortex, with our heads together in the center, forming a circle. Laura opened the meditation with a prayer and then we were quiet for quite a long time, listening to the birds singing in the trees above us. Someone began to stir, then another and finally we were all back to the "Now". Laura said, "Does anyone have anything interesting that they would like to share?" The final sharing revealed that "St. Germain surrounded us in purple"; a couple of the group said they "were singing and floating". Laura said, "I felt as though I sat up (in Spirit) in a white robe, and St. Michael touched my third eye with a gold wand, then touched everyone else's third eye and then we all went in different directions." I must have been with her because I felt the same except for the white robe. I felt like I was hardly touching the ground as we went back to the house. I shall remember this experience forever.

2001-2009

MY HIGH SCHOOL REUNION

Sixty years since I graduated from High school? I pondered about how many of my classmates are still alive, or still able to travel. I wondered, "Would I recognize any of my classmates? I'm always embarrassed when I don't remember a name; actually, why should I be embarrassed? Maybe my classmates won't remember my name either. Yes, I think I will go."

There were sixty of us there in the Reunion Hotel of the one hundred and four graduates, and I recognized only seven. After giving the Blessing at the Buffet table, I turned to look for an empty chair and my eye caught Russell's arm waving me over to his table. He's still a really handsome guy, dressed impeccably, about six feet one with snow-white hair and a winsome smile. He flew from California just for the reunion. The food was delicious and so was the conversation, especially when Russell told me, "You didn't know it way back then, but I had a crush on you." I was flattered, I think I even blushed when I responded, "Oh, my, I had no idea! We all went our separate ways after High School." "I was in the Navy and nearly lost my life a few times," he continued, "and I'm still working as an FBI Special Investigator, and the Air Force Special Investigator, which is pretty exciting." He's a Mason of the Masonic Lodge. (My husband was in the Navy and also a Mason.) I felt that I would have had an interesting life with him, but then I wouldn't have had a beautiful marriage with my Bob, or the beautiful, talented children that I have; some other lucky gal caught Russell.

Carl, another classmate and I had some interesting talks also, about religion and meditation, and receiving information from Spirit; we could have talked all night. I approached cousin Lyman, who was in only one of my classes; he was the Mayor of Georgia for a few years. What a difference in attitude since the reunion ten years ago, when he hardly spoke to me! He hugged me before introducing his son, talked about my parents and my sister, and told his son that we are cousins. I asked Lyman, "How did you like being a Mayor?" He laughed and said, "I didn't like it -- too much politics." As I conversed with my friend, Dorothy, I learned that she was a sixty-year Den Mother of the 4-H Club! What a gal!

I reminisced a bit the next day as I drove around the city where I grew up --- the church, the schools and the library. Zaharaco's Ice Cream Parlor was still there with the huge organ that was as high as the ten-foot ceiling. I told Mr. Zaharaco's son how the football team, the cheerleaders, the Marching Band players, and fans would go there for ice cream and hot chocolate after the home games. I also told him how very thankful I was that I had the opportunity to play the clarinet in the "All Girls Band", otherwise I would never have had the opportunity of attending any of the games and afterward listen to the beautiful music of the organ. The son promptly turned it on for me while I enjoyed a hamburger and ice cream; yes, it's more of a lunch counter now. Upon leaving my hometown I realized how fortunate I am to still be alive and renewing friendships with a few former classmates, who I will never see again. I'm so happy that the amazing organ was still being appreciated. I returned home with joy in my heart.

ANOTHER ORDINATION

After the evening church service Rev. Pat said, "I would like for you to be Ordained in this church. You've taken classes here and have participated in the leadership of this church and I feel that you should be Ordained in Divine Dimensions Church." I was surprised that she thought that I should be Ordained again, but I said, "If you feel that it is necessary, I will be Ordained here." She added, "My Ordinates wear white." Hmmm, now I can't even wear the navy blue robe that I wore at my other Ordination. She said, "A friend of mine is a seamstress and made my robe; she does a nice job. I suddenly remembered that Rev. Pat asked me to design and print the bulletin for the Sunday of my Ordination. A week later Rev. Pat said, "You will give the sermon the Sunday of your ordination." That was another surprise! "At my own Ordination?" I asked, "Yes," she said, "that's the procedure." I have to think about that now. "Also," Rev. Pat added, "Who will walk down the aisle with you? What hymns would you like sung? Will you have a special soloist?" Yikes! I didn't know that it was my responsibility to plan my own Ordination! I called my son, Bob, "Rev. Pat says that I should be Ordained in her church, and I'd like for you to walk down the aisle with me." In a surprised voice, he said, "I'd be honored to walk you down the aisle, Mother." "That's great," I responded, "I think that would be pretty neat if both my son and grandson would walk me down the aisle to the alter." So, I called my grandson, (also Bob) and he said, "Sure, Gram, I'll be happy to." I called my two daughters, Debbie and Terri and asked, "Would you like to light the candles on the Alter at the beginning of the Service?" Of course they were delighted to participate. A friend, who is in our meditation group, sang and her husband accompanied her on his keyboard. Many relatives, along with many of my friends enjoyed the Service, and refreshments were served afterward. Everything went well after all of my concern.

A month later at the regular church meeting Rev. Pat asked me to be her assistant Pastor. Now, I know why she was in a hurry for me to be Ordained in her church. However, I said, "Rev. Pat, thank you for the invitation; that would be an honor, but I must decline." Was she ever surprised at my answer! "But, but why?" she asked. "That's quite a responsibility that I don't wish to take on at this time," I answered, "also, there's a possibility that I will be moving to Florida in the not too distant future." Everyone at the meeting was surprised at my answer. Rev. Pat gave me more responsibility than I already had anyway, such as counseling church members, and leading the Christmas Eve service.

In reviewing the Ordination procedure, I thought it was beyond the Ordinand's responsibility to plan her entire Ordination ceremony. This was upsetting to me, but I did not let Rev. Pat know my feelings since she said, "That's the procedure." I was willing to accept more responsibilities; it gave me more experience, which I feel was good for me.

SUNDAY CHURCH SERVICES

I don't know if anyone ever invited my long time friend, Lena to church, because when I told her that I had been invited to speak at the United Metaphysical Church of the Palm Beaches, she right away said, "I would like to go with you." Of course I was very pleased, even though her hearing was not so good. One of the ministers greeted me at the door, and I could see in the lobby that there were three visiting ministers who I knew; the fact that they were there made me a bit nervous because they are very good sermonizers. A good-looking black-haired gentleman was at the piano, and Carolyn, who has a very beautiful melodious voice, sang a solo. (Wish I could remember what hymn she sang.) I led a guided meditation, spoke on Spiritualism and gave messages from Spirit for 10 minutes. Lena said, "I really liked going to church with you, and everyone is so nice." Back at Lena's apartment, as she was getting the dessert plates out of the cupboard, I asked, "Lena, what makes your lemon pie better than anyone else's?" She laughed as she was cutting the pie and said, "Oh, I don't know, maybe it's the extra lemon juice fresh from the lemon?"

A couple of days later Lena and I drove across the state to St. Petersburg to listen to Rev. Don's sermon. (I had studied under Rev. Don at a Seminary in Indiana.) He gave me a message from my Mother, "I'm proud of you! Remember, the Rev. comes before the Dr." At a church in another city, Rev. Norman, who was very well known as a Medium, was having a "Message Only" Service. "Hmmm, I have a feeling that I should go this afternoon", I said to the mirror. Lena and I went to the message service and sure enough, I heard him say the number on my billet, "Bob is here, dancing and clicking his heals and is so happy! There's an Eagle here and he says, "Put your thoughts and desires out into the ethers, you know how to do it." Suddenly I realized how much Lena loved my visits and how much going to church with me meant to her. And as I reflected back, if I had not followed what my feelings told me, I would have missed the happy messages from my husband and my Eagle Spirit Guide.

CRYSTAL & GEM SHOW

Back home again in Michigan, my daughter, Terri and I decided to visit our friend, Wanda who has beautiful large crystals all over her house, such as amethyst, large crystal balls, citrine, ruby, selenite and others, which I have always admired. We were exchanging healing services when Wanda asked, "Would you and Terri like to use my tickets to the Crystal and Gem Show?" "Would we?" we both shouted in unison. The show was on five floors of this building in downtown Detroit; five floors! WOW! I've always wanted a large Amethyst Geode, but they are so expensive, that all I ever did was look. There were tables and tables of amethyst. Every time that I went past this one particular Amethyst I would study it and go on to look at others, but it seemed that this particular one was talking to me; there was a drawing of energy there, so finally I told the salesman to put that one aside while I looked at other gem stones. When would I ever have another chance like this one to purchase crystals and gems at a wholesale price? An opportunity of a lifetime, so I picked up a few more gems, some as gifts also. From around a corner Terri called, "Mom, come look at these stones! Mom, look at this one!" As she handed the piece to me, an energy force, like lightning shot up my arm! In amazement I said, "Whatever this stone is, I must have it. WOW! That is something that I have never, ever felt when touching a gem stone!" Terri was laughing, and said, "I was looking for something for your birthday, guess I won't need to look any farther!" Terri's husband, Roger trimmed the stone, designed a gold dolphin and attached it to the center of the stone and gave it to me as a necklace for my birthday; it is so beautiful! And that was the beginning of Roger using the Larimar Stone in the jewelry that he designed.

TWO NEW HOMES

Terri and I signed closing papers on each of our new homes in the Keys. Lots of work had been done with Debbie's infectious laugh keeping us upbeat. We decided to visit a unique place called Treasure Village, which had a huge red lobster to mark its location. Did I say huge? It's about 15 feet high and 12 feet long or more! A few years ago while on vacation, my daughter-in-law, Dana, and I had made friends with Ana, a cosmetics shop owner there who was giving a reflexology treatment. While we were waiting for a treatment we asked Ana, "Which one of those two chair-massage girls would you recommend?" Ana looked up and said, "Oh, they are both good! One can give a deep tissue massage and the other is more gentle." I had been watching them and said to my daughter-in-law, Dana "I don't want the one with the light brown hair, I'll make my appointment with the blond." Ana looked surprised and said, "Why?" "Well," I answered, "her hair is a mess, and it looks like she is rough." Ana laughed and said, "I guess that's why all the guys ask for her; she's very strong!" Dana said, "I'll take her, I like a deep massage!" I loved my gentle massage and a few weeks later I had another wonderful massage by the blond. The other therapist (the rough one) began to talk to me afterward and made an appointment for me to give her a special type of hands-on healing session, and she asked if we could trade services. Yes, I was going to have a massage by this rough therapist! I went to her home to have a body massage on her massage table. As she opened the door, the first thing that I noticed was that her long hair was pulled back on top of her head very neatly. I said to her, "I know that you have a reputation of giving deep tissue massages, but I prefer a gentle massage." She was laughing and said, "I can give you a gentle massage." There was a definite reason why I was to have a massage by her. While I was being gently massaged, I could feel the healing energy coming from her hands! I was so elated! No wonder that she was so much in demand! She and I have become great friends. I discovered that I should not judge a book by its cover.

SURGERY?

Quite a few years ago I had fallen over a curb while getting out of the car, my right hip hitting the ground quite hard, dusted myself off and went on about my business. Around a year or so after that I fell carrying a For Sale sign down some steps, missed a step and down I went on my right hip again. As time went on I forgot about the falls. "Why does my hip hurt so badly?" I asked the Orthopedist who took X-rays of both hips and showed me the difference between the right and left hip joint. He said, "The ball and socket of your right leg are wearing away; that's why you are in pain." I could see the difference. "Oh, my! Does that mean that I need surgery?" I asked. He said,

"No, not yet." "Well, that's good, but when do you think I will need surgery?" I inquired. The doctor smiled and then frowned when he answered, "You will want to have the surgery when you can't tolerate the pain any longer." I really appreciated the doctor's honesty; he could have said, "Right now", and made some extra money. It wasn't until two years later, living in Florida, when I had so much pain, hurting all the time, even at night, that I knew I needed surgery. I chose an Orthopedist in Tavernier, Florida. Following my hip surgery, my instructions were to lie only on my back, which took a lot of fortitude, since I was not in the habit of lying on my back due to snoring. I don't know if I snored or not, the Nurses wouldn't tell me, hahaha.

Physical Therapy was no fun either at first, but I felt that I would benefit later. Since I needed P.T every day I stayed in the Nursing Home for a month and learned how to go up and down stairs, which was a must since I would be staying with my daughter, Terri for a while; her house had seven steps that I must navigate. I was not to drive or kneel, so after the month in the Nursing Home, my son-in-law, Roger took me to P.T. three times a week. Terri was working full time as a Reflexologist, and I couldn't very well prepare my meals; Roger prepared fruit, eggs and toast for breakfast, and a delicious salad for lunch. What a great guy to do all that for me! Why? He was a meat-potatoes-cookie guy and thought that salad was only for bunnies! LOL. My hip healed completely! I give credit to the expertise of my surgeon, a positive attitude, wonderful help, and all the prayers for my complete recovery.

IRELAND?

Terri came home very excited from a seminar taught by Derek O'Neill, she said, "Mother, we have to go to Ireland!" With a startled voice I asked, "Ireland? Why do we have to go to Ireland"? She was so excited about this teacher from Ireland who was teaching "More Truth Will Set You Free" workshops, and she had been initiated into the Rising Star Healing Modality already. "The class is in Dublin, Ireland next year," she continued, "so we have time to prepare for it. Derek is a fantastic teacher, you will love him." I was quiet, thinking about the recent hip surgery. "Wouldn't you like to go?" she asked. "Well, I hope that my leg will be strong enough by then to take the trip," I replied. Enthusiastically she said, "Oh, you'll be fine; you'll be in a wheelchair so you won't have to walk very far, and I'll take care of the luggage." And that she did; at the airports, at the hotel and she even pushed me on a stony path in beautiful Powers Court Park. My daughter was amazing! The weeklong workshop was very educational and taught in a different method of easy understanding; maybe that is the Irish way. What we think is what we are; if we don't like how things are going, then change the way we think about them. Derek teaches that LOVE is the answer to every question. Derek asked people to talk about themselves in front of the entire class, and then they received a healing, a unique method of healing. We witnessed several different healings, and experienced two different types of healing: The Rising Star and Prema Birthing. I wanted to be able to give both types of healing at home in the States, but I had to be initiated first. I asked my daughter, "Do you know anyone here, other than Derek who is qualified?" (He's too busy with his workshop.) After a moment she said, "Katlin is here and maybe she will initiate you while we are in Dublin." Terri thought a minute and said, "I think I know where she might be; I'll try to find her." I was on 'pins and needles' while waiting for any information. So, after nine in the evening I was initiated by Katlin into the Rising Star procedure! What a thrill that was! I felt as though I was light as air!

To give our minds a break from the workshops, we toured by bus the beautiful, flowering countryside, and to see some old buildings where soldiers hid while protecting the homeland. Also, we visited a beautiful old church, Hill of Tara, New Grange, Knowth Mounds, Wicklow Mountains and more. Another day we had to wait for a herd of sheep to pass by before we could continue on to the beautiful Powers Court Building to taste their delicious cuisine, and walk the lovely gardens and smell the huge roses of all colors, and other beautiful flowers. That's where Terri pushed my wheelchair over a rocky path so that we could rest on a hill overlooking the beautiful gardens. (She was certainly ready for a rest.) Our workshops were finalized by attending a fantastic banquet and delightful stage show that I really enjoyed, the night before flying back home to the U.S.A. I had taken Terri's advice and was thrilled at all of the knowledge I received and the beauty that I beheld by going to Ireland. I loved the fact that Terri wanted to share all of this with me.

NEW YORK CITY

When Derek facilitated a "More Truth Will Set You Free" workshop in New York City, Terri and I along with my daughter-in-law, Dana attended. The workshops were very educational and fun; Derek has quite a sense of humor, and it was fun to renew friendships with the people who I had met in Ireland. I learned that the more truths I revealed about myself to myself, the less judgmental of everything I became, and more tolerant of the idiosyncrasies of others.

We had previously reserved a Bed & Breakfast for a couple extra nights so that we could experience and enjoy the city, such as the Statue of Liberty, Ellis Island, Guggenheim of modern art, taking a horse and carriage ride through Central Park, and seeing water fountains shooting up from the concrete. "What are those men and women doing?" I asked Terri as I watched them pushing carts full of rags along the sidewalks. Terri laughed and said, "They're selling "knock-offs" under those rags." "And what are "knock-offs", pray tell?" I questioned her. "They are expensive purses, such as Prada and Coach at huge mark down prices, and those people are still making a profit", she explained as she was looking through one of the cart's piles of purses and billfolds. My opinion is that they were seconds; anyway I bought a couple of purses as gifts. We took a long bicycle-carriage ride to the famous Tavern-On-The-Green Restaurant. As we walked in I remarked, "How beautiful!" Shining gold and crystal chandeliers, gold decorated doors and chairs and beautiful flower arrangements in gold vases everywhere! I don't remember what I ate for lunch, just that it was delicious, maybe because men waiters in tuxedos served the food, ha! We rode in about eleven cabs with Cabbies from nine different countries; some of them said that they learned to speak English by being a Cabbie. At night we roamed Times Square and met up with a Michigan friend quite by accident, and listened to bands playing on the street and people watched. Due to attending Derek's Workshop, I was able to see and experience many things in New York City, and I was so surprised at how safe I felt on the streets of the big city of New York!

DEBBIE'S SAD NEWS & HAPPY ENDING

Debbie's been having abdominal pain more frequently lately and she's spending more time in Florida with us for which I'm glad. Terri took her to Dolphin Research Center with special toys to play with the dolphins. Terri said, "Mom, she was so happy there, I wish that we could have stayed there all day!" Debbie's pancreatic cancer was progressing and her days were numbered. Terri suggested that the last fun thing for Debbie would be for all of us to go on a Cruise. I said, "That's a great idea; making it a family thing could lift her spirits." Even though Debbie had some very ill days, she enjoyed the pool, played in the ocean and enjoyed the beach; she was so glad to be with her family. It did my heart good to see how much she enjoyed the Cruise.

Debbie and her boyfriend were planning to return to Michigan as soon as the ship anchored, but we convinced her to stay in Florida where most of her family was and enjoy the sun. A condo overlooking the Gulf of Mexico was available from a friend, and when she saw how ill Debbie was, she said, "Just fix a few things here and Debbie can stay as long as needed." What a friend! Later on the Fire Department took Debbie to Dolphin Cove who let her be with their dolphins, as their gift to her. You could see the pure delight on her face!

Just before Christmas my Debbie passed away, with the family, her boyfriend and Hospice members around her. When she took her last breath, the last words she heard was, "I love you" from her boyfriend. Later we sailed out to sea on a lovely white yacht listening to "100,000 Angels" CD by the beautiful Tami, and let Debbie's ashes fly away into the wind and water in the area in which she spent much of her time whenever she visited Florida.

My family purchased a new stone Memorial Bench in memory of Debbie with her name and date of her demise etched in it, and placed it on the dock of Summer Sea Condominium where she often sat to relax to watch the Manatees and whatever else was interesting along the Gulf.

It was a difficult and emotional experience watching my husband die, but watching my daughter die was worse. (Daughters aren't supposed to die before Mothers.) Debbie's deterioration was over a much longer period of time, and watching her suffer for months and months was much more emotional and traumatic for me. I resigned myself to the fact that when our allotted time on earth had been fulfilled, we leave it regardless of age.

MY LONG TIME FRIEND, MARIE

My friend, Susan and I were returning to Michigan after visiting my Aunt in Seymour, Indiana, and stopped to go to church in Chesterfield when my cellphone rang. "Hello Mrs. Miller, my Mother is in a coma in the hospital; she hasn't responded since Saturday, please come to the hospital!" "Oh, my!" I exclaimed, "I'm in Indiana right now." "She is in the hospital off Jefferson," he explained. "Yes, I'll leave right away and get there as soon as I can; don't worry," I said. I hurriedly told Susan what we had to do. (The last time that I had talked to Marie, as I was leaving her house she said, "I might as well be dead, I don't feel that well anymore." "Oh, Marie," as I hugged her, "you have children and wonderful grandchildren. You have a lot to live for and to tell your grandchildren all the things that you've experienced." I tried to console her before leaving. (Her two husbands had already passed away.) She said, "Oh, I don't know, maybe you're right." I had a hopeless feeling as I left her; maybe I should have stayed longer, but I had to get home.) When I arrived at the hospital, Marie's son, Doug met me at the entrance and told me that his Mother had asked him to take her to the bank and other places to take care of a few things. But then she packed a small bag and said, "Now, take me to the hospital." "Why Mom, are you sick?" I asked. "Just take me there," she replied. He continued, "She entered herself in, wouldn't eat and has been there ever since."

I don't remember who else was in the room, other than Marie and Doug when I approached the bed, and took her hand in mine. I said, "Hello Marie, I came back from my Aunt in Indiana to see you," while putting my other hand on her head I kept talking to her. She opened one eye slightly, moved a corner of her mouth ever so slightly, and squeezed my hand. I knew for sure that she recognized me. I heard murmuring from those present, and her son said, "That's the first that she's done anything; she hasn't recognized anybody!" The next day a close friend and the family were at Marie's bedside, except her granddaughter who was on her way from California; the minister prayed and I led with her favorite Psalm, the 23rd Psalm. (That's the one that she asked us to say over her husband, Lloyd when he was ready to pass away.) I was told that around 10:30 pm. the granddaughter arrived to say Goodbye to her Grandma. Apparently Marie was waiting for her, because at 1:30 the next morning her Spirit left her body. (Marie's children and my children grew up together; our families were like one.) I realized that Marie's son needed guidance and he felt that I would know what to do. I sensed that my being there and giving some direction to all those present helped to console everyone in the room, and the atmosphere became calm and peaceful.

Nine of my friends have made their transitions all in around two years. Even Terri's big brown Chesapeake Bay Retriever dog, Ruger had to be euthanized. Ruger understood everything you said to him. I said, "Ruger, you've had a good, loving and fun life and now it is time to be rid of all your pain." No dog has meant as much to me as that beautiful, intelligent Ruger.

ANOTHER TRAGEDY

Motorcycle happiness or -----? My daughter, Terri's husband, Roger has ridden a motorcycle since he was a teenager and had many accidents, but got right back on and continued to ride with the wind blowing through his dark beard and long, dark hair. He said, "It's so exhilarating." I almost fainted when I saw my daughter on his motorcycle wearing the usual black jacket, pants and boots! She thought that she was re-assuring me when she said, "He's the only one I will ride with; he's really cautious!"

A few years later, as I was on my way to the grocery store my cellphone rang; "Hello Terri." An urgent voice said, "Meet me at the hospital, Roger's been in an accident!" When we arrived at the hospital Emergency room, "I'm Roger's wife, how is he? Where is he?" asked my daughter. In a very calm voice the response was, "Roger who?" "Roger Drouin! He was just brought in here; he was in a motorcycle accident! I just got a phone call that he was taken to the hospital!" was Terri's tearful, excited voice. "No one was brought in here, was this just recent?" We didn't know what to think by this time. "Just a minute while I make a call," responded the admittance nurse. We were on pins and needles, not knowing what to think, this being the only hospital in the Upper Keys. Finally the nurse said, "He's been airlifted to Jackson Memorial Trauma Center in Miami." Miami! Terri sent him healing energies while I drove. More stress! With all the one-way streets we went round and round before we found the Trauma center.

X-Rays had been taken and tests were still going on. Roger seldom wore a helmet while riding his motorcycle because it was not mandatory in Florida; oddly enough, his head and arms were the only places that had not been either severely bruised or fractured. Imagine that! A turning van had run into him while riding his motorcycle. Roger was conscious and talked, but due to the tremendous pain that he was enduring, he was put into a temporary coma and was put on a Turntable, something like when a chicken is put on a rotisserie, so that he would not develop any blood clots or bedsores; his legs were held in traction. There were tubes everywhere. Terri rented an apartment nearby the hospital so that she could be with him most of the time, even though he wasn't aware of her presence, or was he? After Roger was out of the coma, he was so happy when his daughter and granddaughter came to visit from Michigan!

When Roger was able to be at home and felt stronger he just had to be with the dolphins, so Terri drove him to Island Dolphin Care; his friend there helped get him into the water so he could be with the dolphins; just being in the water with the dolphins aided his recovering process. We prayed a lot and sent healing energies for his recovery; it seemed that every time he was gaining strength, he needed another surgery, which was a setback. There was a period of time when we thought that Roger was gaining full recovery. He and Terri wanted another Chesapeake dog to keep their other dog company, and Roger still wanted a hunting dog. One night Terri had a dream of a dog with a white diamond on its chest and while looking on the Internet Terri said "Look, Roger, here are some purebred Chesapeake puppies; one of them has a diamond on its chest." Roger said, "Was that the Chessie that you dreamed of? Roger took mental note of this and when the puppies were ready to be weaned from its Mother and he was well enough to fly to Michigan, he picked up the puppy even though it had hind leg issues, and brought it home. Terri was working full time, so he had the full responsibility of the puppy; he was so looking forward to hunting with this dog they named "Bo".

Four years of treatment in and out of the hospital, a Comprehensive Care Center and a Physical Rehabilitation Center; there was much pain, surgeries and stress for Roger, and much stress for the family. Terri showed how strong she could be; always encouraging Roger and being with him as much as was possible. She was a true example of what love really is! During one of Roger's weakest hospital stays, he had a dream; he said, "I was floating around "up there" and it felt so good, but my Spirit dog, Sand-dog visited me and said, "GO BACK"," so apparently there was still a purpose for his life. It wasn't long and he was back in the hospital for more surgery and was resuscitated several times. Roger's daughter, Holly and her daughter flew in from Michigan to be with him. My daughter, Debbie's Spirit came to me and said, "We will help Roger across; his Mom is here also. We're here to help Terri also. Everything will be fine." There was nothing more that could be done for Roger, and he passed away at the age of only 58.

The Rev. RJ officiated a lovely Celebration of Life Service on January 24, 2010 at A Dive Center on the "Point" beside the water. While I was giving the Eulogy, someone said, "OH! LOOK!! Dolphins!!" pointing to the water. Two Dolphins were swimming alongside us next to the rocks. There was quite a commotion in the Congregation, as everyone was amazed that the dolphins would show up at that particular moment!! It's like they were saying, "Here we are Roger, honoring you for all that you have done for us!" Some thought that Roger's Spirit was there with them; I sensed that he was.

God gave me as well as Terri much strength during those years of Roger's surgeries in and out of the hospital and rehab centers. I encouraged Terri and Roger as much as I could; it was difficult when I knew that he wouldn't live, but I was determined to give encouragement and hope; I didn't know for sure what could happen. Since Roger's passing he has brought messages to his wife several times, which is confirmation that we do live after so-called death.

MY MINISTER'S REQUEST

The Minister of Coral Isles Church had been asking the newer attendees to give a talk about themselves on Sunday mornings. By doing this, everyone would get to know each of us better; which I thought was a good idea until it came my turn. I was quite nervous; so many things had happened in my life thus far; which ones should I include in my talk of twenty minutes? Among other things, I mentioned having taught the "A Search For God" class while living in Michigan, and after the service many were asking about prayer and meditation. This caught the minister's attention and soon she asked me, "Would you be willing to teach the class here at the church? Thursday night once a month is open at this time." I was a bit surprised at her request because "A Search For God" is more on the metaphysical teaching, rather than orthodox religion. "A Search For God" Book l and ll, were compiled by Edgar Cayce and the students of his Study/Meditation Group, in Virginia Beach, Virginia. Simply speaking --- in Prayer we speak to God, in Meditation God speaks to us. When He speaks to us, all we need to do is to be quiet, and listen. From a small church congregation, I was surprised that there were eighteen people present at my first class, and most of them continued thru Book ll studies. I realized that everyone needs Spiritual Attunement regardless of where they live. Having taught the classes in Michigan and teaching them again in Florida was both rewarding and fulfilling, especially since I was no longer in Chiropractic Practice or a Minister in a church.

UNUSUAL SIGHT IN THE SKY

On the twenty second of December 2007 (exactly 2 years after Debbie passed on) I was in the swimming pool area of the Condo Complex, and suddenly I looked up into the sky, and what I saw was amazing! Around the sun was a six-pointed star; under the star was a triangle; from the triangle was a spike going toward people rather than to the earth. I did not have an insight as to what that meant. I'm still wondering. Could it have been telling me that the Rising Star Healing is, or will be used throughout the Universe?

LADY LINDA

Lovely lady Linda O'Neil, Derek's wife! She was in the hospital with a brain hemorrhage and severe pain! I read that the family saw her Spirit leave out thru the window and up along a white beam of LIGHT; she looked back and then went on. That very night in my sleep I saw her, Linda, surrounded by Sai Baba, Angels and other loved ones. Early the next morning my daughter, Debbie came to me in Spirit to tell me about Linda's passing. Ten days or so later, at a Teleconference, two friends told about the brilliant White Light in Linda's room as she was passing away. She was holding a new Symbol as she left. I noticed that everyone who gave a report about Linda's Spirit, saw the same thing. What a wonderful experience --- watching a Spirit ascend from a body; it made me hold my breath in Awe!

BABY MIELI

When my phone rang, it was my dear friend, Jessica, "Hello, Aileen, Would you like to come over tomorrow afternoon to see my new baby girl?" "OH, of course I would! I'm anxious to see your little bundle of joy. Sarah Schweitzer, my friend from Michigan is here, may I bring her?" Jessica said, "Of course you may, I'd love to meet her." Jessica has a boy, JP around three years old, now she has a girl. I was so overjoyed to hold and bless this little bundle of joy named Mieli; she's so perfect! As I gave Mieli a special quartz crystal, I warned Jessica, "I feel that she is very intelligent and energetic and will want to do what she wants to do, when she wants to do it; be prepared to keep her busy." We all laughed, and she said, "Thanks for the warning!" As she grew, Jessica found that advice to be very true, and Jessica said, "She's also very intuitive". When I sensed those feelings about Mieli, I felt that I should forewarn the Mother so that she could mentally prepare herself as her daughter grew up. I felt that it was a real treat and an honor to bless my friend's newborn baby.

SURPRISE BIRTHDAY PARTY

As I was enjoying Terri's back yard with so many beautiful flowers she said, "Mom, our friend, Donnagaye has invited you to her house in Key Largo for refreshments on the 29th." "Oh, how nice of her!" I responded. "Her friend from Canada is visiting and would like for you to meet him; he's very intuitive!" she continued. When we arrived at her house there were quite a few cars there, but I thought nothing of it because another part of the house is rented, and the cars could belong to those people. As our friend greeted Terri and me at the door, I could see more people sitting in the living room, and I began to feel excitement welling up within me. "Happy Birthday Aileen!" rang into the air. I was so surprised and amazed! Terri surprised me by inviting my closest friends and 23 of them were there!

Our friend, Donnagaye performed an "Elder Indian Ceremony" by playing her drum and singing an Indian Song. Another friend played the crystal bowls and performed a healing ritual for me. Another friend played the Didgeridoo and gave me a healing, moving the Didgeridoo all along my spine. I was wondering why the white wool covered stool was sitting in the middle of the living room, and then Donnagaye asked me to sit on it. She then put a lovely orchid shawl around me, and told me how much I have impacted her life. Each person then knelt before me, gave me a gift, and proceeded to tell me how much I have meant to them. This experience was so emotional and humbling that I hardly knew what to say! I am honored that my daughter wanted me to have such a very beautiful ceremony on my 85th birthday! I love her very much.

As I was reflecting on the evening of joy, I began to realize how many of my friends also truly love me and how much influence I've had on their lives. I am determined to continue to be of service.

CHRISTMAS EVE SERVICE IN MIAMI

The Unity Church in Miami had the reputation of having a friendly, yet dynamic speaker and a very melodious choir, so Terri asked me, "Shall we go to the Christmas Eve Service at the Unity Church in Miami this year?" "Yes, that's a great idea!" I answered. (Bob and Dana always spend the Christmas Holidays in Michigan with their children and grandchildren.)

After a light dinner, Terri and I went to Miami. "I'll let you out at the door, and I'll go find a place to park on the side-street and meet you inside," instructed Terri. I tripped on a raised place on the sidewalk and down I went! A nice, strong gentleman helped me up and into the church foyer, all the while asking me if I was all right. I said, "Thank you so much for helping me! I'll be all right; I'll wait here for my daughter, she's parking the car." By that time I realized that my hands and my right knee were burning, and I tasted blood. I found a tissue to dab my knee and held my hand over it, directing God's healing energy thru it, and of course my hands were also benefitting. Terri came in from parking the car and said, "What happened? Are you OK?" The choir was fantastic accompanied by a bass viol, piano, trumpet, organ and violins, which helped me forget about my burning knee. The Service began with a meditation session to help quiet the hustle and bustle of everyone. The Sermon was dynamic about "Living a Life of Service". I loved the candlelight time while singing "Silent Night".

I was so thankful that Terri suggested the church in Miami; the sermon was exactly what I needed to hear, and the music was so uplifting. I also was reminded that I must pay more attention to where my feet are going so as to avoid falling.

2005- My daughter Debbie's last dolphin swim, two weeks before she passed on. Her bright smile showed her delight!

2002- My grandson Eric Ehrler's Police Academy graduation with his proud mother, Debbie Ehrler (Miller).

2010- I'm having fun with a dolphin in Northern Florida on a trip with Terri.

2014- My daughter Terri in Ireland overlooking a castle.

1984- Bob's surprise retirement and 60th birthday party with family and friends at his favorite Pizza restaurant in East Detroit, MI.

1997- My ordination into United Metaphysical Churches by Dr. F. Reed Brown in Roanoke, VA. Even though I was highly qualified, I was humbled that he wanted to ordain me.

2001- My ordination into Divine Dimensions Church by Rev. Patricia Davis in Richmond, MI. With me are my daughters, Terri and Debbie, son, Robert and his wife Dana.

1995- At the Palmer Chiropractor College Centennial, I'm with Dr. Theresa Gray standing in front of Dr. Mabel Palmer's statue, the first lady of Chiropractic and wife of Dr. B.J. Palmer, the developer of Chiropractic.

THE

ATLAS ORTHOGONAL
HUMANITARIAN AWARD

Dr. Aileen Miller

October 21, 1995

*In Recognition Of Your
Commitment To The Development Of
Atlas Orthogonal Doctors. Your Dedication Has
Enriched The Lives And Careers Of These Doctors.*

*Your Efforts Have Served To Enhance
The Chiropractic Profession And Benefit
Those People Helped By Atlas Orthogonal Care.*

R.W. Sweat Foundation, Inc.

*1995- My Chiropractic Humanitarian Award presented in Atlanta, GA.
by Dr. Roy Sweat, developer of the Atlas Orthoginal Technique.*

2010-2017

THE VORTEX AND CRYSTAL ENERGY

During our Soul Progression sessions at the Vortex in Tavernier, Florida there have been two entities standing still in the middle of the street making others go around them on their way to the Vortex; across the street were three entities that just sat there leaning against the house week after week watching other Spirits ascend into the World of Spirit. I sent them mind-to-mind messages of encouragement each week. Kathleen said, "We've already planted crystals around the labyrinth (which is the outer edge of the Vortex) so that the entities can see their energies shining upward; how about if we plant some crystals over there across the street, on both sides of the street; maybe the crystal's energy will help raise those 'guy's' energies." The rest of us said, "Kathleen, that's a great idea!" I suggested, "Next week let's all bring some crystals, and we'll plant them along the street, and see what happens." Week after week, first one and then another entity came across the street to the Vortex and ascended to a higher Spiritual Plane! It's amazing how much energy crystals have! Oh, Happy Day! Kathleen and I have continued to open the Vortex once a week so that earthbound Spirits, and those who might have lost their way may have an opportunity to ascend to a higher spiritual plane of existence. Remembering to open the Vortex sometimes becomes tedious until I recall how many entities ascend each and every week; it's then that I realize that I, along with Kathleen, and others in previous years, have been presenting a great service to those who would otherwise roam the earth, and I am happy that I have this gift of discernment.

BLESSING THE WATER

After the oil spill in the Gulf of Mexico, the water became very polluted; MariEtta had an idea. "Let's go out on our boat and bless the water! We know that water responds to positive vibrations." Others in the group joined in saying, "That's a wonderful idea!" I said, "We've seen the pictures that Dr. Masaro Emoto took of a drop of water during a love sentence, and of a hate sentence, that showed that the structure of the water actually changed, and how beautiful the drop is when there is love. So Terri, MariEtta, five other friends, and I went out on the Gulf of Mexico (the Bay) in MariEtta's boat for prayer and meditation for healing the water. We offered Chod, various herbs, tobacco, and geranium as we blessed the water. "Look at the water on this side of the boat," I exclaimed, "see how it changes appearance almost immediately!" I had seen a video of Dr. Emoto's water droplets, but it had not occurred to me to bless the water as I turn on a faucet anywhere that I happen to be, or even when swimming. I learned a very valuable lesson that day on the boat, and I felt that it was a very magical, spiritual experience!

HEALINGS

One of my friends had fallen two days ago and her body was sore all over, and she asked me for a healing, so I gave her a special type of healing session. These are usually given in three sessions three weeks apart and are very gentle yet powerful. The vibrational energy knows precisely where it is needed the most. She felt so much better in every way that she was glad that she had asked for healing.

Another time, the woman on the phone urgently said, "My sister is in extreme pain, it's in her back and has been for days and she can't stand it any longer; can you see her this evening?" Well, I didn't expect to see a woman in a wheelchair being maneuvered through the door by two other women. No, she can't stand and she can't lie on her stomach so that I can adjust her spine. What do I do now? This is a new circumstance for me. Pray! I asked the two women to place their hands on the patient in certain strategic areas of her spine; I placed mine on the area of pain and on her head and we each said a prayer. I visualized her spine in perfect balance and then we were quiet. Suddenly there was a loud noise! One of the women exclaimed, "What was THAT?" The woman in the wheelchair suddenly opened her eyes wide and then exclaimed, "My pain is GONE!" and gently stood up. The other two women looked at her in amazement. The sister said, "I can't believe my eyes! Are you sure that your pain is gone?" All of us were so thankful that she could stand nearly pain-free, and thanked God for the miracle. I felt like dancing as I gave her a few instructions to follow for the next few days. The women left my office in wonderment.

A couple weeks later I called my dentist and said, "Let's have lunch at the Strawberry Restaurant." Strawberry Soup was on the menu. Strawberry Soup? You got to be kidding! Believe it or not, that Strawberry Soup was actually delicious! We talked about "energy healing" and I showed her how she can feel the energy between her hands, and then I gave her a Prema Agni healing. The Prema Agni Symbol can be given by anyone to anyone for the purpose of bringing in healing energy. There is a video demonstration on Youtube.com: www.DerekO'Neill.com, then type in Prema Agni for the demonstration. Before she left to return to her office I gave her a Prema Agni decal and said, "You can put this on your office door so that everyone who enters your office can feel that energy." She was delighted! I felt very happy that my dentist friend asked for a healing, and that she was interested in learning about it.

ARE CATS REALLY NECESSARY?

Now that I'm back home in Florida, it's time to feed and water the three cats at Summer Sea Condo where I live. Whenever I'm going away, I ask someone else to take that responsibility and Katy and Dana had volunteered. As I opened the back door of the building, I saw that the cat's dishes that were supposed to be within nine feet of the door are not there.

Let's back up a bit. When I moved into the Condo Complex there were two cats, which were being fed by a lovely lady volunteer. Not long after that there was only one cat. Not long after that the last cat had not been seen anywhere and had not eaten any of it's food. This volunteer told me that she thought that one of the residents, who didn't like cats had poisoned it, but she wasn't sure. At that time I didn't know much about cats and Condos; I thought the cats were there just because they were. Down by the pool one day, I over-heard someone say, "Have you seen any rats around your place? I saw one in the hallway this morning and it scared me!" Another lady said, "I saw two rats running around the Pool area, and one climbing up the side of the building the other day!" I heard another lady say, "What's going on around here? There have never been any rats around here as long as I've lived here, and that's over twenty years!" then she added, "Let's go report this to the Manager!" and off they went. After talking with a couple of the residents about what I heard at the pool, one lady said, "You are new here, we have no cats my dear, that's why there are rats around here; they keep the rat population under control." My eyes opened wide and I remarked, "Oh, since I've moved to the Keys I wondered why there were so many cats around the grocery store and every other store!" "Yes!" the lady said quite emphatically, "We must have some cats here again!" A Condo Board Meeting was held and soon there were three cages with four cats in them by the back door of the Condo. Since this former volunteer, Emma had been feeding the cats the members just presumed that she would take care of the new cats. However, she stood up and said, "I've taken care of our Condo cats for seventeen years and loved it; they were so sweet. My heart ached every time one of them died. No, I've put in my time, going through the wind and the rain to feed them over by the fence so they would stay around here; I don't want to do it anymore, some one else can take over that responsibility". There was much discussion and coaxing Emma, the former volunteer but to no avail. Finally the President of the Board asked of the members present, "Do we have any volunteers to feed the cats?" He asked a couple of times and finally I held up my hand; that's how I became the "Condo Cat Care Lady".

Now you are up-to-date, and I couldn't believe what I saw! The cat's dishes had been moved to where the garbage dumpster and an old door and tools are located. Not only that, the dishes were behind an extra dumpster that I had to move in order to get to the dishes. That very day it rained; the food in the dishes got wet, which meant that the cats and I also got wet. I was pretty angry by that time and I moved the dishes away from the noisy dumpster, to a place that I could get to easily, and to where the cats and their food would be dry in inclement weather. The next day when it was time to feed the cats, the dishes had been moved to behind the dumpster again, and because it was raining I got wet as I was moving their dishes to a drier location, and again the next day was a repeat. I called Emma and we talked about where she fed the cats for seventeen years. I said, "Well, I'm not going to feed them by the fence where they and I will get wet; I'm too old for that; I'm trying to feed them where they and I will be dry in inclement weather." She said, "Yes, I agree!" Then she said, "I was away for a while recently also, and when I returned there was a rat's nest with babies in my closet. That would never have happened if there had been cats here patrolling this property!"

I wrote a letter to the Board of Directors and the Manager read it to everyone present. I explained, "how important cats are to our property and that they should be treated with dignity and respect. They will have a desirable, protected dry place to eat, away from noise of the dumpster as long as I will be feeding them." There were new members present who were very surprised at what they heard. Emma then asked permission to speak and told her history with the cats, and that a rat had built its nest in her closet because there were no cats to protect our property! The letter and her testimony turned the tide, and the cat's dishes were never moved again from where I placed them. VICTORY! I learned a lot about the necessity of having cats in the Keys, and I was determined that our condo cats would be treated with respect from now on.

WATER WATSU

A week later my dear friend, Kathleen asked, "Aileen, would you like to go with me to give Jacki a special type of water massage, it's called Water Watsu?" Jacki is physically disabled and can not talk, but she smiles and waves her hands when she knows that she will get a water massage. A Lift lowers Jacki from her wheelchair into the water. Another friend and I went with Kathleen to assist with the massage. Kathleen held Jacki's head up out of the water, all the while massaging her neck and back and gently swaying her about in the water, while the friend massaged her hands and arms; I massaged her feet and legs and I felt the healing energy going into them.

During this process Jacki begins to relax, and really enjoys the session. This was another interesting experience for me; working with a disabled person in the water while using God's wonderful energy. I realized that there are many ways in which I can be of service.

MARINELAND, ST. AUGUSTINE & CHOCOLATE

Terri had decided to go to Marineland to inspect her jewelry display where it was being sold in their gift shop, so she asked me if I would like to travel with her. Well, you know how much I like to travel so I said, "I'd love to go with you!" When we walked into the gift shop the girls were eager to show us how beautifully they had displayed Terri's jewelry up on a pedestal that was covered in black velvet. Terri surprised me by pre-arranging an inter-active water playtime with two of the dolphins. "Look, Terri," I said excitedly, "she's smiling while I'm stroking her belly!" I felt the connection between the dolphin and me, and it was such a wonderful experience.

There were cheese and crackers, crab dip, fruit and a variety of beverages in the foyer as we entered the Bed and Breakfast in St. Augustine in mid-afternoon. Terri took a walk after dinner and when she returned she said, "Guess what!" It was no telling what she had up her sleeve. "I found two chocolate shops that are within walking distance!" "That's great!" I remarked. (I'm not a chocoholic, because most chocolate is processed with alkali. I learned by trial and error that it is the alkali processed chocolate that makes my stomach queezy.) After a breakfast of fruit, eggs and sweet rolls next morning I said, "Terri, I'm anxious to investigate these chocolate shops; how about you?" Down the street we went into the chocolate store and Glory Be! The chocolate is made without alkali! Then we went to our friend Susan's lovely house on a lake and later she showed us around the beautiful Historical St. Augustine. On Sunday we went with her to Church and heard a very good sermon about "Thankfulness and Gratitude". I certainly was! "Where are we going for lunch?" asked Terri. Susan said, "What would you like for lunch?" You won't believe this, especially from me; I said, "Let's go to the chocolate shop, if it's open, and see what they have." "Are you kidding me?" asked Terri. "Are you sure? I like that idea, they have delicious ice cream also," volunteered Susan. We went there for ice cream, but the chocolate lady at the store said that the machine was broken. She suggested, "We have hot chocolate with real whipped cream on top." We decided that would be very tasty, and with that we checked out their homemade cookies. The hot chocolate was so strong that I asked, "Do you have some milk to dilute this chocolate? It's just too strong for me." Susan and Terri had the same question. "Sorry, we have no milk today," was the reply. Oh no! The lady had a solution; "I can stir in some whipped cream!" Because she needed to add so much to make it palatable for us, we each had two cups of very delicious hot chocolate, which, of course required more cookies, hahaha. That was our lunch! If you know me, it's a "Believe it or Not" story. Reflecting upon the trip, I realized how well my daughter and I travel together, and I feel blessed that she arranged for me to have the opportunity to interact with the dolphins. I had fun surprising others by doing something out-of-character, such as suggesting that we have ice cream rather than a wholesome salad for lunch.

AMMA, THE HUGGING SAINT

After flying from Florida to Detroit I drove to my friend, Ellen's house; on the way I called her, "Ellen, the plane was late so I will be late, so don't worry." She answered, "I'm so glad that you called because I would have worried. I'll leave the light on." Ellen works for a Dental Lab and her arms were bothering her, so next day after church I gave her a Raindrop Therapy Session, which is a type of very gentle massage using pure essential oils, which helps her to relieve stress and discomfort. One day while I was still visiting her, she gave me a wonderful massage.

I had made reservations to attend the Annual Ashram Retreat in Dearborn, Michigan. My friend, Sarah had told me that she went to the Retreat a couple years ago and that it was a touching experience to be hugged by Amma! Ellen had heard about it and wanted to see Amma, but she didn't want to go alone, so this was my chance to drive her there and both of us could experience Amma's hug before the actual Ashram Retreat. There was much singing and meditation. There were many children dressed beautifully, sitting on the floor playing quiet games and whispering; other children were sitting close to Amma. There were tables full of pictures of Amma, books, shawls and other clothing, statues and jewelry for sale. Finally we were instructed to take a number at the door to the large hall, and get in line if we wanted a hug by Amma. As we drew closer there were flowers or fruit to give to Amma as we knelt for the hug. Our heads were to be lower than Amma's, who was sitting, which made it easier for her to be able to give hugs. As Amma hugged me she whispered, "My daughter" three times. I was so honored! Ellen and I drove back to her house that night, and the next morning I drove alone to the Ashram Retreat, which was to be held at a hotel. The rooms were lovely but the temperature was only 65 degrees and no way to increase the temperature. I had a sweater under my leather jacket but I was still cold, so I bought a beautiful handmade cream-colored wool and silk shawl to wrap over my leather jacket. Amma was on the stage with her interpreter. My favorite song was, "Om Nama Shivaya". One of her favorite sayings was, *"As the lash shades the eyes, the tree shades the earth, Mother (God) shades us from all worries."* We stood in line for our meals, which were vegetarian. There is a drink called Llassi, which is whipped yogurt with fruit; it tastes differently than ours does, but so delicious. The singing and speeches go on and on about living the right kind of life. I went to bed at 1:00 A.M; my roomy came in at 4:00A.M. when the classes ended. The next day we began with a delicious breakfast, meditation, a Q. & A. period, lead by a Swami who talked about living your life poetically. We stood in line again for that wonderful hug by Amma. I gave her a nutrition bar, which she put to her 3rd eye and laughed, then gave me an apple; apparently the apple is better. LOL. During some free time I bought some Holy Basil Leaves, several statues of the Buddha Ganesch, which I planned to give as gifts as well. Ganesch is a reminder that we have the energy within us to remove any obstacles that get in the way of our creations, our projects. I bought a blouse with the sign of "OM" on it, which says, *"OM is the essence of all you've been searching for, OM is your own true nature."* On day three my group received another teaching by Amma, *"Sadness is active anger..."* Day four was more of the same. *"Mistakes are lessons -- they are our best Guru..."* I'm glad that I had the opportunity to experience Amma's calm spiritual hugs, and that I was instrumental in Ellen's experiencing the same. This was the first time that I had attended an Ashram and concluded that this ethnic group's ideals are really no different than mine are.

BACK TO FLORIDA

It was only seven degrees outside when I got into the car to return to Florida from Michigan and I really didn't want to drive to the Detroit Airport in a heavy snowfall; it was that, or miss my plane. The heavy snowfall became a blizzard as I turned onto the expressway; I could hardly see where I was going, and it took me over twice as long to get to the airport; good thing I left earlier than usual. Even so, I was thinking, "Am I going to get there in time to turn in my rental car and get to the plane on time?" I just made it! My son, Bob picked me up from the airport in Florida and said, "I made chicken noodle soup for you, and I will pick up groceries for you while you rest". Where was his wife, Dana? She was on her way to Michigan! LOL! When Dana is out-of-town Bob and I go to a Chinese Restaurant for dinner; Dana doesn't like Chinese food, so I called Terri and said, "Bob and I are planning to eat at the usual Chinese Restaurant, would you like to join us at 6:00 tonight?" She replied, "Sure, Jay and I will be there." I told them all about the Ashram and added, "I am so glad that I had that opportunity to learn about their beliefs." A few weeks later Bob flew to Michigan to spend the Christmas holidays with his children and grandchildren. Terri and I watched the Andy Williams Christmas Special in Florida.

On Christmas Eve Terri and I went to the Candle Light Service at our local church; the church was already nearly filled so we had to sit up on the front row. Suddenly I felt something along side of Terri and I. I directed my attention, my awareness, to what or who it was; it was my daughter, Debbie's Spirit who had come to join us! I was elated as I looked at Terri and whispered, "Do you feel that?" Terri smiled and nodded her head. Debbie then sat on the step in front of the Alter looking over the congregation, and then, she went up and down the aisle singing. It was a joy to watch! After church Bob phoned from Michigan, "Hi Mom! MERRY CHRISTMAS! MERRY CHRISTMAS, TERRI!" Dana, Candace, Bobby's wife, Melissa and their two boys Nathan and Ryan were on the phone, as well as Kelly and Ted and their children, McKayla, Thad and Ethan; Dana ll and Ron and their son, Joshua, (Dana ll and Ron's daughter, Taylor and her son, Blake stayed in Florida.) wishing us a Merry Christmas! It's a joy to hear their voices on Christmas Eve every year, so that we feel like we are a part of their celebration also. I realize how much my son and daughter love me by always being there for me, and my Spirit daughter, Debbie is still a part of our family, and her son, (my grandson) Eric also called to wish me a very Merry Christmas. Even though we are not all together physically, I feel the happy, loving energy over the phone at Christmas time.

SPIRITUAL ANATOMY

The Rev. F. Reed Brown had given me a Spirit message in which he said, "I have a message for Aileen; something about Anatomy, not the usual Anatomy, but a different kind of Anatomy; do you understand? I see you teaching this to a group of people; it will be well attended." I was convinced that I should teach the class that I had taken in Seminary earlier. I began to doubt myself. "Where will I hold this workshop? All the Social Halls are so expensive here," I'm thinking to myself. Dr. Lu had finished remodeling her building for her Chiropractic Practice and had incorporated a Gathering Room into the design. "Dr. Lu," I asked, "Would you consider renting your new Gathering Room to me for a workshop? I will need it for a couple hours one evening." "Hmmm, what is this about?" she inquired. I told her all about the Spiritual Anatomy class that I had attended in Seminary, which explains how our Chakras and organs are connected, and decided to teach it here, if possible. "Well, I'll have to think about it and let you know," she said. A day later, "Terri," I said, "Guess what; Dr. Lu will rent her room for the Spiritual Anatomy workshop!!" I was excited, "I'll need some help." "Mom, I'll help with chairs and at the door," Terri volunteered. I said, "That will be a big help!" I volunteered Kathleen's help, "You can sit in at no charge if you will help pass out the notes, and help clean up afterward." Kathleen was thrilled and said, "Oh, I'll do anything that you need, just let me know what to do." Jay wanted to attend, so he took care of the water. With all that help I was eager for the class to begin. Well, it was so well received that it was well worth the time and effort that they and I put into it. "Thank you all for your help! Good job! Well done!" I was convinced that by following what Spirit had told me through a Spiritual Medium, I should teach others what I had learned.

ANOTHER GREAT GRANDSON

Bob's daughter, Candace was on "pins and needles" until her husband, Ray came home to Michigan from Iraq. Yes, he was as excited as Candace was when their baby boy, Joseph was born; a big healthy boy with lots of black hair. I don't know how long it will be before I'll get to see and hold him, since I'm in Florida.

Note: I was not intimately involved in Dana ll's children's birth's, who are Joshua and Taylor, and Taylor's son, Blake, or Kelly's children's births, who are McKayla, Thad and Ethan, however, I consider all of them as my great and great-great grandchildren as well.

A DIFFERENT HEALTH PERSPECTIVE

When I saw the blood pressure monitor on the end table in Bob's living room, just for fun I said, "Bob, do you mind if I take my blood pressure, since it has been a long time since it has been taken?" He smiled and said, "Sure, go ahead and take it." 176/ 91. I couldn't believe what I saw, so I took it again. "What? There must be some mistake! Bob, are you sure that this instrument is accurate?" I asked. "As far as I know it's accurate, according to my doctor," he replied. His wife, Dana had been a doctor's assistant, and she said, "You better go to a Cardiologist and find out if it's always high. Have you had any headaches or dizziness?" "No", I said, "I feel fine." So, I went to the doctor and was told that my blood pressure is too high. That night I had leg cramps and excess perspiration three times. "What's going on?" I'm thinking, "Is this all in my head, my imagination?" Blood pressure is still high during my next office visit, so I'm put on two blood pressure medications. Me! High blood pressure! That just doesn't make any sense in my mind. I have a positive attitude and eat healthfully most of the time, so why is my blood pressure too high? Perhaps I let too many things stress me out? I'm in my mid eighties and probably sit at the computer too long and don't get enough exercise. Terri helped me decide to go to the Gym three times a week to work out which has helped my strength and endurance and I feel even better than before; and my pressure has come down considerably. I came to the conclusion that even though I eat right most of the time and have a positive attitude, it also takes more oxygen and exercise to keep the blood circulating through the organs and tissues at optimal speed in order to maintain a normal blood pressure.

SMOKE

I was getting hungry, so I turned the electric stove on to 'warm' to heat up some leftover beef and gravy, and have a lettuce salad. It would take me only a couple of minutes to go down the three flights of stairs to check my mailbox to see if I have any mail. On the way back to my apartment I talked with a friend, completely forgetting about the beef and gravy on the stove. When I got off the elevator there were several people standing by my door, including my daughter-in-law and I could hear the smoke alarm going off in my apartment. "OH, NO!" I hollered, as I opened my door to turn off the stove, which set off the alarm in the entire building; smoke and people flooded into the hallway! One of the tenants followed me into the kitchen and put the pan into the sink before it would catch on fire. Someone had called the fire department and two men were into my apartment almost as soon as I got there; they were amazing! My studio apartment was totally filled with smoke! What a mess! I thought that my favorite pan was totally ruined, however, a neighbor cleaned it up beautifully. My daughter-in-law said, "You can't sleep in all this smoke, so come to our place for dinner and sleep there." I was very grateful when my son rented some kind of an oxygen unit that pulls the smoke out, and then had my area rug cleaned. My daughter, Terri said, "It will cost a fortune to wash and dry all of your clothes and things in the coin machines in your condo, I'll take them home and wash them while you're contacting your Insurance Company and washing the furniture." She washed about eighteen, or more loads, which I certainly appreciated. A friend took my comforter and pillow shams to the Laundromat. I didn't apply for Smoke Damage Insurance: the deductible was too high. I realized what a wonderful family I have, and wonderful friends who help as much as they can, without expecting anything in return. I AM blessed! Four days later, to help break the tension of the smoke damage and to relax for a few hours, I was invited to a thoughtful friend's house to listen to another friend play the Crystal Singing Bowls; I love the beautiful melody and feel its soothing vibration! What a treat!

EASTER DAY PLANS INTERRUPTED

Chocolate Easter Bunnies! I've been giving my children solid chocolate bunnies ever since they were old enough to eat chocolate. It's not all that easy to find them in the Keys that are more than three inches tall, and now that my son eats only white chocolate, it's even more difficult, but I did finally find four solid chocolate bunnies. Oh, it was so hot Easter day that it felt like 110 in the shade! It takes about thirty minutes to drive to Terri's house, so I packed the bunnies in ice so they wouldn't melt on the way there for Easter dinner. The last thing to do before leaving the condo is to feed the Condo Cats. My son said, "Dana and I will wait in my truck while you get the cat food." I was in a hurry because we were already late in leaving, so I began to run and caught my toe on an extra piece of carpeting at the door and slammed headlong into the heavy glass door, my right knee jammed onto the metal strip of the door jam, my left arm hitting the marble window sill, and dropped the cat food on the floor; fortunately it was in a closed container. The three cats were so happy to see me, and the food, as I poured it into their dishes. The beautiful gray cat hesitated long enough for me to pet him.

I got into Bob's red truck saying, "OK, I'm all set, let's go," as my knee was throbbing and swelling, and my head was throbbing. Bob looked at me and said, "Wait a minute! Your elbow is bleeding, what happened?" I told them what happened as Dana held some napkins on my elbow. Bob exclaimed, "I better get you to the hospital!" "No," I countered, "Let's get on to Terri's; I don't want to spoil her Easter dinner!" Reluctantly Bob drove on while Dana called Terri and said, "Mom hurt her knee and elbow; have some first aid stuff ready when we get there!" I said, "There's ice in that bag beside you, Dana, can you please hand some to me so I can put it on my knee?" The ice didn't really help the knee to feel much better as it was swelling more and more. As soon as we arrived at Terri's yellow house, with a young palm tree in front, she put a Band-Aid on my elbow and said, "I think you need stitches on that elbow!" and put Essential Oils on my knee under an ice pack. Terri and Jay had a delicious turkey dinner all ready for us to sit down to; everything was sooo good as I tried to keep my mind off my throbbing, swollen knee. As soon as I had given everyone their chocolate

Easter Bunnies, Bob said, "Now let's get you to the hospital, and get you stitched up!" I was more concerned about my knee than the elbow. In the emergency waiting room I asked Dana, "Would you go ask for an ice pack, please, maybe if the knee is frozen I won't feel the pain." She laughed as she went for the icepack. Finally we were invited into a room and as I sat up on the examining table the doctor came in and looked at my elbow and said, "How did this happen?" He wiped it clean, numbed it a bit and took three stitches to close the skin. In the meantime my knee is still pounding and I said, "What about my knee and my head?" He injected a painkiller in my knee, then looked at my swollen 'goose-egg' in the hairline above the left eye and said, "Your head is all right," then added, "be sure to follow up with your own doctor in a week. Thanks for stopping in. Goodbye." LOL. Bob and Dana took me home and made sure that I was comfortable with ice packs. I know better than to run, but I don't like to be late anywhere and the cats had to be fed before leaving; I realized later what a big mistake that was, to run! I noticed that Dana had the forethought to call Terri so that she would be ready to take care of my injuries; and Bob made sure that I got to the hospital for stitches before going home. I am so thankful that I have loving, caring children!

OFFICIATING A WEDDING

A former patient in Michigan called and said, "Hi Dr. Miller, I have a request to make. Remember my son, Kris?" "Yes, Debbie, I remember him and his spine very well," I laughed. "Well," Debbie went on, "he told me, "I like Dr. Miller more than any doctor, and now that she is also a Minister, Julie and I would like for her to marry us." I was surprised and excited as I answered, "What an honor! I would be happy to marry them!" I could hear and feel the happiness in her voice as she said, "I'm so excited that you will perform the ceremony!" I called my friend, Ellen, "May I stay with you in September? I've been asked to officiate a wedding." I asked her to be my guest at the Golf and Country Club wedding. When I saw that long brick curving walkway with little steps every so far apart, sloping down the green lawn to the Alter, I asked her to walk with me to help steady my balance. She was nervous and so was I. The day was so bright and sunny that my white robe and stole were a bit too warm. Julie's lovely bridesmaids wore simple short navy blue dresses with cowboy boots, carrying orange flowers. The lovely bride was very elegant in her flowing white strapless brocade gown trimmed with pearls at the waist, and pearls tucked amongst her braided hair. Thankfully her gown covered her brown cowboy boots.

"All rise!" I announced as the bride appeared on the walkway. After the bride and groom were standing in front of me, I forgot to tell the guests to "Please be seated"; thankfully the bride had asked for a very short ceremony, which initially I wasn't too happy about. One of the things that I told the couple was that "marriage is sacred, and even if you can give each other everything, if there is not Love, there is nothing in the sight of God. Abiding in Faith, Hope and Love, the greatest of these is Love". There were touching Readings by two others. The bride and groom were so happy that they kept looking at each other and almost laughing during the ceremony and could hardly repeat their vows. A nice touch was the "Sand Ceremony" where the bride, groom and their little boy took turns pouring different colors of sand in a glass vase, which signified them joining together as a family.

During the Reception the music was soft and soothing while we were served a sit-down delicious dinner. Ellen and I were seated at a table with my former Chiropractic Associate, Dr. Young and one of his daughters, and a former secretary, Theresa and her husband. Kris and Julie and his parents came by to chat a few minutes. Soon the Country Western music began and we could hear and see the stomping of western boots. Every one was having so much fun, but soon it was time to say "Goodbye" to my friends. Later, as I was reflecting on the wedding party, I realized how much of a positive impact I had had on my patients, and the faith that they had in me. I had seen the "Sand Ceremony" at other weddings, but only now did I realize how sacred and meaningful the blending of the sands is to a family unit. I was so honored to have married one of my former patients to his beautiful bride. I will always remember this wedding.

Soon after I returned home to Florida the phone rang, "Can you come clear this house and property of negative energies today?" came the urgent call from a friend, "My daughter has been crying ever since she came home today; she says, "I can't stand it here! It's so depressing!" and won't stay in the house." Sally continued to explain, "Betty has just come home from a weeklong fun school-trip." I know Betty and she is very sensitive to people's energies; whether they are happy, or if they are unhappy/sad. So when Betty walked into her home where the energies/vibration of the air were apparently very dense, she became overwhelmed. My daughter and I know how important it is to feel comfortable wherever we are, so I said, "Don't worry, Sally, take your daughter over to the park where she can calm down, and we will be right over." I could hear the relief in her voice as she said, "Oh, I'm so glad that you can come over now! I'll leave the key." Terri and I gathered together sage, incense and crystals for the "Negative Clearing". As soon as we walked into the house we could feel the negative energy, the dense atmosphere. I remarked to my daughter, "No wonder Betty was so uncomfortable here." My daughter replied, "We'll clear it and they both will feel better." I placed the crystals and lit the incense and Terri smudged the entire house, garage and property; we then performed a special ritual clearing away the dense, negative atmosphere and left the house. When Sally and her daughter re-entered the house, Sally called me right away. She told me how light the air felt and how her daughter re-acted when they came home. She said, "OH! This is better! I'm OK now." I had a very happy feeling knowing that my friend realized immediately that it was the negative, dense energy in her house that caused her daughter to react adversely. I know that she had faith in my daughter's and my ability, to clear away that negative, dense atmosphere.

TAKE STOCK IN CHILDREN

The United States Government, the Florida Department of Education, the Florida Lottery and local businesses fund the "Take Stock In Children" program. They pay for low-income children who want to go to college and could not otherwise attend. The students and Mentors are investigated and paired together. The students must have good attendance and keep up their grades; otherwise they are dropped from the program.

A friend suggested that I would be a good Mentor, so I have been mentoring a handsome boy through the eighth grade, Junior High and now I was looking forward to seeing my Mentee, Lazaro graduate from High School.

Fortunately Lazaro has a good father, which most of the low-income students are not privileged to have. After Lazaro told me that he and his Dad exercise and workout with boxing gloves and a bag every day after school, we talked more about eating more protein like fish and eggs, and drinking more water. Lazaro laughed and said, "I don't like the taste of water!" "Then ask your Dad to buy bottled water; pop/soda, will not take the place of water," I explained, "You need actual water to help clean the cells in your body and to flush the toxins out of your muscles after a big workout." It wasn't long before he was playing on the school basketball team, and I could see that his muscles were developing. "Lazaro," I began, "your muscles are really showing how much you workout; you're looking great!" He laughed and said, "I've been eating better too, and take water with me when I play basketball."

One day, Lazaro, with a big smile said, "I have something for you." I unwrapped a cute statue of two blue glass dolphins on a mirror; so very thoughtful of him, I nearly cried. Another year he gave me his picture in a silver frame that said, "When a man lay down his life for his friend, there is no greater love." I was very touched!

"You have made eight A's in ten different classes this past year, Lazaro! And you played basketball whenever you could. WOW! I am really proud of you!" Lazaro smiled his pearly white smile and said, "Yes, I really had to study a lot, but it has been worth it! I'm looking forward to studying Sport's Medicine in College." Lazaro is graduating from High School and he told me, "My Dad will be at the graduation and he will be up front to the left side of the stage in the gymnasium." "Oh good!" I said, "I will try to find him and sit with him." When I arrived all 160 students in their beautiful green robes and mortarboards were already lining up to march up the aisle to take their assigned seats. The bleachers were packed, but I managed to get to the fourth row, but I couldn't find Lazaro's Dad. After receiving his diploma, I did get a good picture of Lazaro as he stepped off the stage holding up his diploma, and looking toward his Dad as we applauded like crazy; I was so proud of him! "The High School in a different city will host the "Take Stock In Children" graduation," Ms. Vale informed me. "That is so thoughtful of them to acknowledge those children's endeavors, and to show their appreciation in a Special Graduation Ceremony," I remarked.

Lazaro and I text each other all the time while he's in College and he said, "I'm making mostly "A's"! and I have a job working with a Basketball Trainer." "Wow!" I exclaimed, "You are so lucky!" A year later he said, "I'm the Personal Training Director at a Fitness Club." I'm really proud of him! Reminiscing on the last five years of being a Mentor, I am thankful that my friend suggested that I participate in this volunteer program. I feel that it was quite a learning experience for me as well as being able to give advice and encouragement to a well deserving boy who wanted a college education more than anything else in this world.

WHAT YOU HOPE NEVER HAPPENS, DID

I like to go Grocery shopping, especially when I can pick out a few special items, like snack bars that have walnuts, cranberries and raisins, yummm! Usually a stock boy will offer to take my groceries out to my car; well, it was a very busy day, so no one was available, and my cart was packed full! I began unloading the groceries in the back of my Pontiac Van, and opened the side door to put in a few more items. As I pushed the cart up to the curb I didn't see my purse but I usually put it into my Van first, so I got into my Van and didn't see my purse; then it hit me! My purse has been stolen! I reported the incident to the manager of the store and went home. I was a bit shaken! There were ninety-two dollars left, even after the shopping, plus ninety-five dollars of my own money in that purse, (I was planning to finish shopping at another grocery store.) AND my cell phone! Of course pictures of some of the family and friends were in the purse. I was very upset! But, there is a good part; my driver's license and my credit cards were NOT in that purse! For some reason I had removed a handful of items from my purse before going shopping. My dear daughter, Terri knew how to lock the cell phone so no one could get any information from it, and ordered a new one. She made many phone calls and e-Mails for me. She said, "Now, you must get a purse that will hang around your body, so it will never be in the grocery cart." The sheriff came the next day to get all the information. Nothing was ever found. I certainly learned the hard way to be more alert to my surroundings, even when it seems that there is no one around. I realized again, that my daughter is so special, knowing what to do and ready to help.

QUANTUM ILIFEINFINITY

When I was in my Colleagues office for a spinal checkup she said, "You can use our Massage Room when it's not being used and you won't need to drive so far to take care of some of your clients." (That's perfect, now I have two places where I can treat my clients.) Then she said, "I want you to give every professional person who works here a healing treatment." Then she said, "I want you to receive a treatment from each one of them." Hmmm, that's a new idea! One of the healing treatments that I didn't know anything about was the Quantum iLifeiNfinity Biofeedback System. After I had had two sessions with the Biofeedback System, I was impressed and very interested in purchasing the APP for myself. It offers yet another way in which I could help people, as well as myself to regain and/or maintain health. Quantum iLifeiNfinity Biofeedback System is Energetic Healing, a balancing of energies thru the entire body; some clients like to see what's going on during treatment, as opposed to the Laying-on-of-Hands where you cannot see just what is happening in the body. Since moving to Florida I am not a Practicing Chiropractor, however, I still like to help people to be healthier. After witnessing the positive response that some of my clients received, I've concluded that because there are so many different health conditions and attitudes that people have, it's good to have many different kinds of modalities available. Quantum iLifeiNfinity Biofeedback System seems to be another answer to a healthier lifestyle, as well as other Aura Healing methods that I use.

NORTH CAROLINA VISIT

I've known Connie Ann since she was around three years old, and have visited her and her husband, Jim many times in the past. Our families have traveled together. Connie Ann and Jim had invited me to their new home in North Carolina. Their son, James and his baby, Sophia and James's Dad, Jim met me at the airport, then I met Bethany and Connie Ann at James's house; from there I enjoyed a delicious dinner with the family at the Steak House. Connie Ann and Jim's house is on a hill overlooking a golf course; WOW! What a beautiful two-story Georgian Style brick house, surrounded with low-cut shrubs and tall trees! The inside was just as beautiful with a huge crystal chandelier greeting me in the entry foyer. As I looked up I saw the open hallway from which three bedrooms and a sitting room emerged. Connie Ann said, "I finally have the house of my dreams!"

James drove his family and me through a "Drive-thru" Animal Reserve where there were different kinds of cattle, goats, sheep, giraffe, deer and an emu; the ostrich and the giraffe ate out of our grain buckets as we held them out of the car windows. There were also rhino, buffalo, zebra, and fish in a stream. In another section were chickens and many different kinds of ducks, a huge brown turtle, beautiful yellow canaries, yellow and a couple of aqua colored parakeets, two gorgeous white cockatoos, black geese with red bills, a peacock showing off his beautiful blue and white feathers, ring-tailed black and white lemurs, and ancient farm machinery. Another day James took his family and me to a well-known attraction to see The Queen's Wishing Well where it is thought that two lovers died there when the Queen's Ship landed; it is thought that their spirits roam that area and grant wishes to those who wish at the Wishing Well. Another day James took his parents and me to a famous mansion that houses an art gallery; the pictures that took my eye were made of rolled colored paper, especially the one of a pinkish, white lighthouse with a white light on top, on a hill of greenery and a brown log cabin in the foreground; it was amazing! There were other unique pictures of flowers and animals made of rolled paper! A Water Lily of rolled paper had a price tag of $750.00. In the mansion were rows and rows of shelves of dolls of all kinds and sizes, hand-painted masks, Indian Lore and more. Nearby is a Hiddenite Mine; the only place in the U.S. that Hiddenite is to be found. I would like to have mined the Hiddenite, but the people who came out of the mine were quite muddy. Hiddenite is green and has a strong energy that is good for the heart chakra and helps an individual recover from addictions, and keeping one "on track". I splurged and brought a tiny one home. I am so thankful that James took me to see all of those interesting attractions; otherwise I would never have known about that area of North Carolina.

Connie Ann, Jim and I celebrated Connie Ann's birthday with dessert of watermelon, vanilla ice-cream with peaches and chocolate cake; what a combination! Connie Ann and Jim have five children plus grandchildren, have been married fifty-one years and are as happy as ever! I feel very blessed to have been invited to their home and treated so royally. I shall always remember that wonderful visit!

MY 90TH BIRTHDAY PARTY

My daughter, Terri said, "90 years is quite a milestone!" She invited all of my friends, near and far, for a delicious luncheon, held in the Summer Sea Condo Social Room; the condo where I lived before moving in with her. (Remember, I was the "Condo Cat Lady"?) Dana and her visiting granddaughter, Taylor along with Kathleen and a couple of other friends helped Terri decorate the room beautifully with blue and white streamers, red balloons and colorful flowers. Beautiful colorful flower arrangements adorned the long tables draped with white tablecloths. I was really impressed! Terri took pictures of all 50 guests as each arrived and then put the pictures in an album with their signatures. My General Practitioner was there, who said, "She's the healthiest of all of my patients!" Terri also presented me with a beautiful "This Is Your Life" Album in which she wrote a beautiful, very touching introductory letter; I was in awe! MariEtta read a touching poem that she had written; Bonny had sent a very touching letter; all of this left me quite emotional. I felt the love of all of those hugs, letters and cards for months afterward. As I recounted that wonderful day I know that I'm loved not only by my family, but also by the community in which I live. What a humbling yet joyous feeling I have!

A ROAD TRIP WITH MY FRIEND, SUSAN

My Michigan friend, Susan text me, "Let's go on a road trip!" So off we went to Warm Mineral Springs, Florida. I love that energizing water, and since Susan had never been there we went nearly every day for a week after doing the Transcendental Meditation exercises that she taught me. It had been several years since I had been to those springs, and was disappointed that the larger than life statue of Ponce De Leon had been removed, and the beautifully decorated hallway walls leading to the water, were painted grey. We met a Doctor of Chiropractic from New York who specializes in working with Sports Teams, keeping their spines in alignment. I met a lady from Canada who rents out half of her Duplex, and kept the information for future reference.

Then off to Pompano Beach, Florida after attending a Deep Trance Class and receiving a personal message. Susan and I enjoyed the swimming pool right outside of our condo there more than the Atlantic Ocean. In a church nearby I received a message from spirit that advised me to pass on what I have learned, as well as in my Autobiography.

Susan and I have traveled together many times, and regardless of 30 years age difference, it's the mutual likes and dislikes, flexibility and positive attitudes that make for fun trips.

THE SENIOR CENTER IN TAVERNIER, FLORIDA

Upon returning home I began attending the "Computer Class for Seniors", in Tavernier, Florida so that I wouldn't have to ask my daughter, Terri so many questions about what to do. As I talked to a group of ladies who were playing cards there, it seemed that they didn't get much exercise and didn't know much about proper nutrition. I asked the Program Director, "Has anyone ever given a talk on nutrition or exercise?" She looked rather surprised and said, "Why, no, why?" "I think that these women need something more to do than playing cards, to exercise their brains. How about if I give a talk on both subjects, since they are here every day?" She laughed and said, "I think that is a perfect idea!" Soon I gave a talk on Proper Nutrition, which was also within their grocery budget, and they "ate it up", so to speak. The next week I had the "girls" interact in a workshop on Chair Exercises; everyone was laughing so much that they could hardly follow directions. I was following a suggestion that I had received from Spirit in West Palm Beach, ie: "Pass on what you have learned", and we all had fun in the process.

MOVING TO VENICE, FLORIDA

I had called my daughter about the duplex that Susan and I had looked at while on vacation with Susan; she was thrilled and she decided to rent it for the whole summer. Terri had been talking about visiting some of the gift shops where her Dolphin Tails Jewelry is being sold, and to visit Warm Mineral Springs again, so she rented the duplex and said, "Mom, let's you and I spend a few days at the Springs, and I'll show you around some of the nearby towns." She didn't have to twist my arm. We had a lot of fun exploring the area, especially Venice, and visiting her gift shops where her Dolphin Tails Jewelry is selling. After a few days we came home; she repacked her bag and she and her friend went back for another week. While there, Terri called me and said, "Mom, how would you like to move to Venice?" I said, "Do you like it that much?" She said, "I found just the house for us; it has more rooms and overlooks a lake. You won't be so crowded with your computer, and I'll finally have all of my business in one place. Oh, and I found a Unity Church; I really like the minister." I became a little excited because I like Venice also and said, "If you like Venice that much, then let's do it!" Terri put her house up for sale; houses were not selling very fast in the Keys, but we began giving away things and getting other items ready to sell. Only a few weeks went by and Terri said, "Mom, those people who just looked at our house, bought it! And we have to move out in twenty eight days!" "What?" I exclaimed, "They want us to be out of our house in twenty eight days? How are we going to do that?" I could hardly believe it! What a rush that was; to make arrangements for everything concerning moving! Oh My! Before we moved away, some of Terri's and my friends gave us a farewell luncheon at our favorite restaurant on a canal. We had a great time reminiscing about the fun times and the serious times that we've had together at the Keys To Peace Organization, Meditation and Prayer Group, the Vortex Group, when the Monk's designed the beautiful Mandala, the Awareness Group, Healing the Water Group, and other fun times. We asked all of them to come visit us in Venice. I stayed in the same condo complex as my son and his wife for a month, while Terri and Jay unpacked and painted my room in our new home, which I moved into in October of 2015. Terri loves it here because she has more space for her Custom Tails Jewelry business; the stores are close by, as well as the church. The beaches stretch for miles, and bike paths are endless; yes, Terri bought a bike. I eat my breakfast on the patio overlooking the lake, watching the ducks swim by, and the Anhinga dry its feathers. Connie, a woman who I met in church invited me to her home to play the game Rummikub. "Rummikub? I've never heard of it," I said. "Well, it's a very old game; it's good for our brain cells, and we play it every Saturday," she explained. Yes, I've enjoyed playing Rummikub nearly every Saturday ever since then.

Until we were actually going to move, I had not realized how many friends we both had who wished us well in our new location. I realized that even though the preparation and actual moving to another location is stressful, it's a good stress because it's a happy stress. I'm happy that we moved to a larger house where everything fits in better; I love the peacefulness of the lake. It's important for me to be close to a Metaphysical Church also. I notice that my daughter is happier since we have moved. I love it here!

MY SON, BOB'S DAD AND YELLOWSTONE NATIONAL PARK

Bob and Dana visited us on their way to Washington State. Bob had been asked to drive a friend's car from the Keys to his home in Washington, so they left the next morning. This was to be a trip of a lifetime for them. Bob had wanted to go to Yellowstone to see the place where his father had played with Indians or fought them, as a little boy, and shoot bears with a slingshot to keep them away from the food storage, while his Dad helped build the first hotel in Yellowstone National Park, and Bob's grandmother baked pies for all of the crew. While at Yellowstone, my son asked to see ledgers of when his grandfather and grandmother worked there. Amazingly, he read in the ledger the actual dates that his grandfather had worked there and how small his paycheck was. They had the opportunity to visit a couple other places on the way to Washington, such as the popular Wall Drugs, Mt. Rushmore and Crazy Horse Mtn. I was so pleased that my son was so interested in checking out where his father and grandfather had lived and worked in Yellowstone National Park so many years ago!

MY BIRTHDAY VISIT TO THE KEYS

It's been a year since I moved away from the Keys and I wanted to visit my friends there. Since my son does not have space for me to stay in his condo he asked a friend of his when his condo would be available to rent;

he said, "It will be available in October." My dear daughter, Terri put out a notice to our mutual friends to meet us on October 3, 2016 at our favorite restaurant for lunch; sixteen of them helped to celebrate my 92nd birthday! We had so much fun just talking and sharing stories. I am so grateful to have so many loving friends, including the ones who were unable to attend. I had my hair done by my favorite hairdresser, Marcia who has been taking care of my hair ever since I had hip surgery in 2004. She said, "When I got to the restaurant and sat down, I looked up and down the table and back again and I thought, "Oh my! I'm sitting at a table of Angels! Aileen has some really nice friends here in the Keys!" When my hairdresser told me that, I said, "It takes an Angel to know one!" Then on October 4th (my birthdate), my son, Bob and his wife, Dana and my daughter, Terri treated me to the most delicious Seafood birthday dinner at another favorite restaurant overlooking the ocean. Terri's friend, Dana's granddaughter, Taylor, Jordan and their one year-old baby boy, Blake (who is also my great, great grandson), also joined us for a lovely get-to-gather. It was fun bringing each other up-to-date on our lives' happenings. "Happy Birthday" was sung as I blew out a candle on key lime pie and shared it with everyone at the table. A joyous time was had by all of us! I am so thankful to have such a wonderful loving family here in Florida as well as in Michigan. I am so proud of my families and I love them very much.

The very next day Hurricane Matthew was expected to hit the Tavernier, Florida area so all hurricane shutters had to be closed. Fortunately the eye of Hurricane Matthew passed us with strong winds and very heavy, blinding rain. I enjoyed many happy hours with Bob and Dana, and had fun with friends at lunches, and exchanging healing services. Thank you so much Terri, for arranging the Friends Gathering. I realize how fortunate I am, and I am very grateful for them and you. I am so lucky!

LIVING IN VENICE

I was so happy that Bob and Dana visited us in Venice during Thanksgiving weekend; he even roasted the turkey and it was delicious! Bob and Dana always spend all but one of the holidays and many of our birthdays with Terri and me; we have so much fun! (Ever since we all moved to Florida,

Bob and Dana go to Michigan to be with their children and grandchildren at Christmas-time.) This time while they visited us, Bob bought me a new office chair that fit me better, since I spend so much time at the computer.

Terri and her friend, Ron had received an invitation to an "Art of Living Retreat" in North Carolina, which was to be held during the Christmas holidays; I was perplexed as to why it was to be held at that particular time, and I was a bit sad. After considering the honor that had been bestowed upon them by this invitation, and the education that they would receive, I felt that I was being selfish by expecting my daughter to stay home with me. So I said, "Terri, when will you have another opportunity to attend an important Retreat at no charge, plus to see what the surrounding area is like? You go; I'll be all right." Terri responded, "Are you sure? You won't mind spending Christmas by yourself?" I reassured her that I would be Ok. At that particular time Becky, a friend from Michigan text me and said, "I'll be in your area around Christmas time; I would like to visit you for a few days." "That sounds great!" I replied, "Come on down!" She then said, "I have to dog-sit for another friend on Christmas Day, so I won't be with you then." I was happy that she could visit anytime and said, "That's Ok, we'll have a few days together anyway." A few days later, while talking to Susan, my friend in St. Augustine, she said, "I don't like for you to be alone on Christmas Day, so I will spend Christmas morning with my sister and then come down and have Christmas dinner with you and stay a few days." I was so happy that she thought of being with me, and after a bit of discussion I said, "That's a great idea!" During both visits I gave my friends Biofeedback treatments, and we drove around looking at beautiful Christmas lights displayed in the neighborhoods. Becky who is a Structural Integrationist, worked on my shoulder, and then we watched a rider on a horse farm in Venice. (I didn't even know that there was a horse farm in Venice!) I enjoyed Warm Mineral Springs, the Historical Museum, watching a Christmas Special on TV and playing Rummikub with Susan. My son called from Michigan on Christmas Eve, and it was fun talking to the rest of the family and wishing everyone there a "Very Merry Christmas!" Terri called from the Retreat wishing me a "Very Merry Christmas!" also. WOW! I think God is so awesome the way He maneuvers circumstances around for the best for all concerned.

I think that my long trip traveling days are over, however, one never knows what is in the future; nevertheless, I enjoy short jaunts with my daughter and with the many friends who come to visit us here in Venice.

In February Terri treated me to the Shun Yen Show, which was fabulous; unusual, colorful dancing, acrobatics with amazing choreography. The Botanical Gardens that we visited were so pretty; there was much walking so she pushed me in my little basic wheelchair most of the time. We sat along the water under the beautiful Oak trees and watched the fishing boats glide past us. It was so relaxing!

We were so excited that the sky was clear enough in August to view the Solar Eclipse behind one of my X-Rays so we could watch it come to its fullness. Back in 1979 was another Solar Eclipse that my colleagues and I and some of our patients watched from behind their X-Rays; the patients thought this was a very clever idea! This brings to mind the time a few years ago that my friend, Susan and I met a man on the Ft. Myers Beach looking through a huge telescope. When he became aware of our interest he asked us if we would like to see what he was looking at. What a thrill to see how red Mars actually is, and I think it was Jupiter and Saturn all lined up in a row with Mars, which is quite unusual; we could actually see the colors of Saturn's rings; amazing! With a powerful telescope like his I can see how easy it would be to become an Astronomer.

We began watching the weather report very closely in September 2017 when we saw Hurricane Irma coming toward the Keys and gathering up force to a category 5. Bob and Dana evacuated the Keys and lived with us till it had passed. After hitting the Keys the weather report said that it turned and was headed in the direction of Venice. We were not prepared, so my son helped us secure our windows. The force dropped down to a category 2 (thank the Lord), and hit us at around 2:00 A.M. The wind and rain sounded pretty fierce, however Venice had minimal damage; mostly downed trees and temporary fences. We, and many others had no electricity for 10 days.

There was extreme devastation in most of the Keys. The condo building in which my son lives had minimal damage, but the condo that he manages was hit pretty hard. Our friend, Ron went to Tavernier in the upper Keys to help another friend clear out the debris from her two homes that were devastated. He's the man who walked barefoot across America, THE LONG WALK HOME.ORG, to make our people more aware of our Veteran's PTSD, so that they can receive Government Care; too many commit suicide.

Last year I spent my birthday month, October in the Keys, but this year Hurricane Irma put a roadblock in that idea. Instead, Bob and Dana came to celebrate my 93rd birthday a couple of weeks later, and of course Bob visited the German Market. I was just getting up from my nap when there was a knock on the door. Who could that be? As I rounded the corner of the hall, whom do I see but my great grandson, Bobby (Bob's son)! I nearly fell over because he lives in Michigan! He said, "Hi Grandma, Surprise! Happy Birthday!" Then he went on to say that he was working in Orlando for a few days and could come here for an overnight, to celebrate my 93rd birthday with me. How thoughtful of him; I know how much he loves me.

Silver Sneakers Classes at the YMCA are fun. Half of the hour we do standing exercises and half of the time we sit while exercising, which is more helpful for me than working out on the various machines. People of all disabilities and/or capabilities are in this class and we do what we're capable of doing.

Well, here I go again! I guess I'm not really retired, LOL, because Terri and I cleared a beautiful three-story house of negative energies, and I did a remote clearing of another house. I'm also called upon for consultations and doing remote healings from time to time; and some of our guests ask for healings, or we're happy to exchange Services.

We've enjoyed our many guests; they love the Warm Mineral Springs, as well as the beaches, the Unity church and the lovely city of Venice. I've even taught some of them the game of Rummikub!

Terri, Ron and I enjoyed the Christmas Eve Church Service at Unity, especially the Candlelight time when all you see are the lights from all of the candles, which remind me that each one of us IS a LIGHT, to be an example of Faith, Hope and Love to everyone with whom we come into contact every day of our lives.

My grandson, Eric had text me a "Very Merry Christmas!" while we were in church. After we came home we opened our gifts, one of which had been there for a couple of weeks from Bob and Dana; I was anxious to see what it could be. Just as I opened the package the phone rang and it was Bob on Face-time just in time to watch my surprised expression when I said, "An I-Phone?! An I-Phone 7?!!" I couldn't believe my eyes! (My iPhone 4 had not been working correctly.) Then I talked to Dana and her children, Dana ll and Ron and their son, Joshua, (their daughter, Taylor was in Florida with her son, Blake). Kelly and Ted talked, then their children, McKayla, Ethan and Thad. Bob's children, Bobby and Melissa were on the phone, then their children Nathan and Ryan. Finally Candace with her son, Joey and her husband, Ray had a chance to talk. (I had to put them in order on paper, but they were all mixed up, first one and another talked on the phone.) Everyone was so excited! Terri said, "Now you need a protective cover for your new phone; what color would you prefer?" So she ordered a new blue cover; I love it! My children are very supportive and make sure that I have whatever I need along the remainder of my journey. What a wonderful family I have! I AM so blessed!

MY DESTINY CONTINUES

I continue to support people on their paths to wellness. When we realize that we all can heal one another we become more in tune with the God Source, and become more positive in our life's calling. I love this pathway. My Destiny of helping humanity reach the fullness of their potential in life, my being of Service in many ways, is being fulfilled every day of my life.

One More Thing; For those of you who have read about some of my life's experiences, my fervent desire is that you have gained some knowledge about the many purposes of life, one of them being: Evolution through self-effort; even when you're not aware of it, you gather assistance along the way, but it's up to you, and you alone, as to what you do with it. By relating to some of my experiences, I hope that you have found a deeper and profound sense of purpose and direction in your life, and perhaps found a deeper insight into your own Self.

Namaste'

Life is a fun adventure!
Infinite Love and Gratitude to All!

REFERENCES

Chapters:

1934-1944:
Palmer College of Chiropractic and 1980-1990
"A Little Bit Of Heaven", Dr. Aumann

1955-1964:
Edgar Cayce and 1969-1974, 1979, 2001-2009
Napoleon Hill, Norman Vincent Peale, W. Clement Stone
Thomas Sugrue-"There Is A River"

1969-1974:
International Lion's Club, Association For Research And Enlightenment and 1980-1990

1980-1990:
Akhenaton, Queen Hatshepsut, Nefertiti, The Reverend F. Reed Brown and 1980-1990-1995,
Dr. John Grostic, The Reverend Dr. B. H. Crewe, Tutankhamen

1991-2000:
Hannah Kroeger, Sister Kenny, Mt. Qingcheng, Hope Lodge

2001-2009:
Dolphin Research Center, Queen Nefertiti, Akhenaton, Dolphin Cove, Island Dolphin Care, Derek O'Neill

2010-2018:
Masara Emoto, "Winter"- the Dolphin

24136186R00138

Made in the USA
Columbia, SC
18 August 2018